Lundy & Irish Sea Pilot

Land's End to Portpatrick

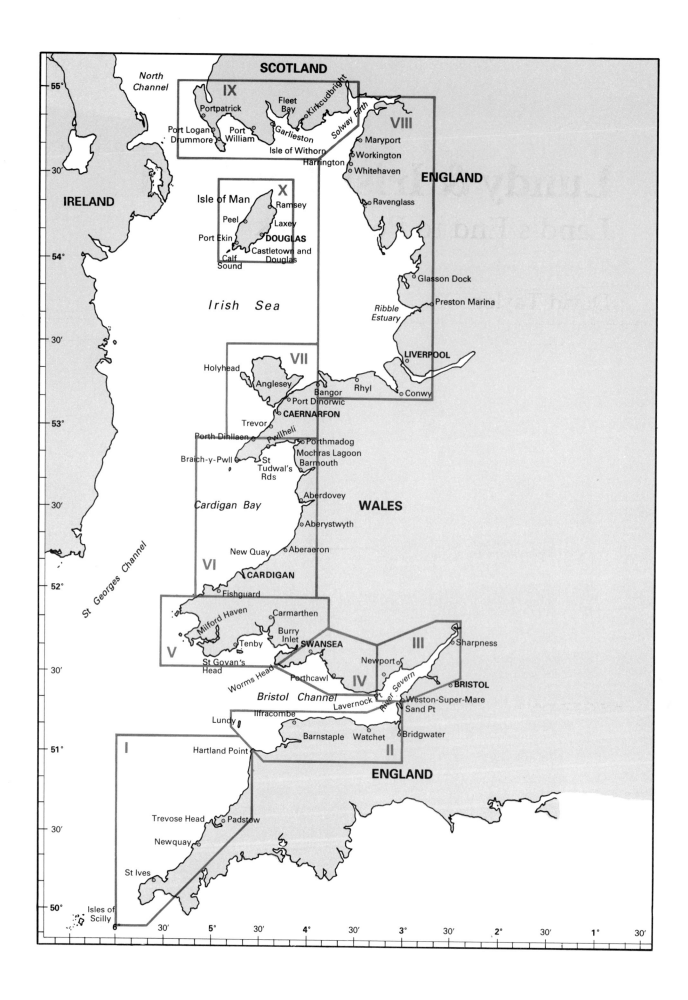

Lundy & Irish Sea Pilot

Land's End to Portpatrick

David Taylor

Imray Laurie Norie & Wilson Ltd
St Ives Cambridgeshire England

Published by
Imray, Laurie, Norie & Wilson Ltd
Wych House, St Ives, Huntingdon,
Cambridgeshire, PE17 4BT, England.
☎ (0480) 462114 *Fax* (0480) 496109
1994

British Library Cataloguing in Publication Data.
A catalogue record for this book is available from
the British Library.

ISBN 0 85288 249 1

CAUTION
Whilst every care has been taken to ensure accuracy,
neither the Publishers nor the Author will hold
themselves responsible for errors, omissions or alter-
ations in this publication. They will at all times be
grateful to receive information which tends to the
improvement of the work.

PLANS
The plans in this guide are not to be used for navigation. They are designed to support the text and
should always be used with navigational charts.

The last input of technical information was May
1994.

Printed in Great Britain by The Bath Press, Avon

Contents

Preface

Most of my cruising years have been spent experiencing the delights and tribulations of the Irish Sea, St George's Channel and the Celtic Sea, and I have long been aware of the lack of a good yachtsman's cruising guide to the area.

The current volume incorporates an updated version of the guide to the Bristol Channel first published in 1988. My original idea was to produce a guide covering Lundy, Fastnet and the Irish Sea, and it was initially decided to subdivide the area into three manageable volumes.

I have always believed that an author of cruising guides should be prepared to visit by sea at least once, and more often if possible, every harbour and anchorage covered by the volume. The logistics of carrying this out, since my cruising is limited by the weather and by other demands on my time, have meant that the planned second volume has taken longer to prepare than anticipated. During this time Imray, Laurie, Norie & Wilson have taken over the publishing of the Irish Cruising Club sailing directions, so it seemed a good time to reconsider the original proposal. The publishers suggested that as the Bristol Channel cruising guide was now five years old, it would make good sense to incorporate an updated version of it into a single volume covering the coast from Land's End to Portpatrick.

I trust that the end result will be useful in highlighting the delights and lessening the tribulations of sailing this gratifying cruising area.

Acknowledgements

My thanks go to all who have helped me with this publication. To my sailing friends who have lent documents and added their own useful comments, to those who have sailed the region with me, and to the local yachtsmen, harbourmasters and fishermen who have made useful comments. To Willie Wilson and the staff at Imray, Laurie, Norie & Wilson for their amiability and tolerance. My thanks to you all.

David Taylor
Madoc Yacht Club
Porthmadog, Gwynedd. 1994.

Introduction

This volume has been prepared as a cruising guide for yachtsmen, and is intended to be read in conjunction with the relevant Admiralty and/or Imray charts.

General description

This cruising guide covers a diversity of sailing grounds. For the most part the coast is subject to prevailing winds, and the harbours and anchorages are often isolated and limited in their times of access. Harbour approaches can be difficult, and many are impossible in heavy weather. There are few marina facilities, although these are increasing. The result is a challenging cruising area with the added factor of strong tidal streams which demand careful passage planning.

The Bristol Channel is a formidable cruising area, with its strong tidal streams and ocean swells, and yet it is rich in nautical history and in its variety of scenery, from the rugged Cornish cliffs to the gentle wooded slopes of the River Cleddau.

The Welsh coast for the most part has less strong tidal streams than the Bristol Channel, but it includes Jack and Ramsey Sounds, Bardsey Sound and the Swellies, where notoriously strong currents demand the greatest care from the yachtsman. The delightful scenery extends from the gentle resorts of the Gower and Cardigan Bay to the sheltered cruising grounds of the Menai Straits, with their Snowdonian backdrop.

The harbours of the northwest coast of England have declined along with the old industrial base of the region, as alternative forms of transport have been established and the fishing trade has diminished. The introduction of new marinas along this coast and the improvement of harbours to provide amenities for yachtsmen are indicative of the increasing demand for such facilities.

The Isle of Man not only provides an excellent cruising ground in its own right but is also, by virtue of its position, a useful resting point for yachtsmen crossing the Irish Sea.

The harbours of the southern coast of Scotland which are covered by this guide are for the most part small and limited in their times of access, but offer the reward of the gentle scenic beauty that is characteristic of this part of the country.

Equipment for yachts

The physical characteristics and nature of the area make a good reliable engine a prerequisite for successful cruising. Good fuel and water capacity will facilitate passage planning. To explore the area fully it will be an advantage to have a yacht that can take the ground; the harbours and anchorages where a yacht may stay afloat are in the minority. Good ground tackle is essential for cruising the area, and a reliable depth sounder will prove its worth.

Plans and sketch maps

These have been prepared by the author, some based on available charts, others based on his personal survey. Some of the harbours, anchorages and facilities will be subject to man-made or natural change, and the plans should be used with prudence.

Waypoints

Waypoints have been included in this volume for most harbours. They have been given close to harbour entrances so as to be of the greatest possible benefit, but it is essential that the navigator check the waypoint position in relation to his line of approach in order to avoid any possible dangers.

Meteorological

The weather of the region is very variable, and it is difficult to summarise because of the frequent day-to-day changes.

Winds Predominantly from the southwest and west throughout the summer months; more variable in spring, when winds from the northeast and east are fairly frequent. Gales are infrequent in the summer months, but when they occur they are more likely to be severe in the exposed areas such as the approaches to the Bristol Channel. In the more sheltered areas gales are likely to be less severe and of shorter duration. The most frequent directions for gales are from the southwest and west.

Fog On the whole, fog and poor visibility are not common in the area. Sea fog occurs on an average of 2 to 3 days a month in the southern part of the area, decreasing to 1 to 2 days a month further north, and being more frequent in the earlier months. The fog may persist for as long as 2 to 3 days, although the average duration is only from 6 to 10 hours.

Precipitation and temperature May and June are usually the driest months, although September can be relatively dry for the time of year. July and August are generally the warmest months, with a mean air temperature of 16°C.

Weather forecasts

Forecasts for the region are readily available from a variety of sources.

BBC Radio shipping forecasts Broadcast on BBC Radio 4 on 200kHz (1500m) daily at 0033, 0555, 1355 and 1750. The BBC inshore waters forecast follows the 0033 shipping forecast at about 0038.

Coast radio stations weather bulletins Broadcast on VHF after an initial announcement on Ch 16 at 0733 and 1933 GMT from Ilfracombe Radio on Ch 05 and from Celtic Radio on Ch 24, and at 0703 and 1903 GMT from Cardigan Bay Radio on Ch 03, from Anglesey Radio on Ch 26, from Morecambe Bay Radio on Ch 04 and from Portpatrick Radio on Ch 27. Gale warnings are broadcast on receipt.

HM Coastguard Broadcast on VHF Ch 67 after an announcement on Ch 16, normally every four hours, but every two hours if a strong wind or gale warning is in force. Strong wind or gale warnings for their local area are broadcast on receipt. Area forecasts are every four (or two) hours from Swansea 0005, Clyde 0020, Falmouth 0140, Liverpool 0210, Holyhead 0235, Belfast 0305 and Milford Haven 0335.

Marinecall Automatic telephone weather service with recorded forecasts updated twice daily. For the southwest (Lyme Regis to Hartland Point) ☎ 0891 500 458, for the Bristol Channel (Hartland Point to St David's Head) ☎ 0891 500 459, for Wales (St David's Head to Great Ormes Head) ☎ 0891 500 460 and for the north Irish Sea ☎ 0891 500 461.

Navtex Transmissions on a common frequency of 518kHz can be received by radio teleprinter or purpose-built receiver. Weather messages for the area re-broadcast at 0818 and 2018 UT from Niton, and at 0930 and 2130 UT from Portpatrick. Gale warnings are broadcast on receipt and are repeated at scheduled times.

Radiobeacons

Nash Point *NP* (−·/−−·) 299·5kHz 50M
  51°24'·03N 3°33'·06W
Point Lynas *PS* (·−−/··) 304kHz 50M
  53°24'·97N 4°17'·3W
Walney Island *FN* (···/−·) 306kHz 50M
  54°02'·92N 3°10'·55W
South Bishop *SB* (···/−···) 290·5kHz 70M
  51°51'·15N 5°24'·65W
Mizen Head *MZ* (−−/−··) 300kHz 100M
  51°27'·05N 9°48'·80W
Old Head of Kinsale *OH* (−−−/····) 288kHz 50M
  51°36'·27N 8°31'·97W
Tuskar Rock *TR* (−/·−·) 286kHz 50M
  52°12'·15N 6°12'·38W
South Rock LtV *SU* (···/··−) 291·5kHz 50M
  54°24'·47N 5°21'·92W
Bailey Lt *BY* (−···/−·−−) 289kHz 50M
  53°21'·68N 6°03·09W
Round I Lt, Isles of Scilly *RR* (·−·/·−·) 298·5kHz 150M 49°58'·7N 6°19'·33W

Aero radiobeacons

Penzance Heliport *PH* 333kHz 15M
  50°07'·67N 5°31'·00W
Cardiff *CDF* 388·5kHz 20M
  51°23'·57N 3°20'·23W
Swansea *SWN* 320·5kHz 15M 51°36'·10N 4°03'·88W
Ronaldsway, Isle of Man *RWY* 359kHz 20M
  54°05'·15N 4°36'·45W
St Mawgan *SM* 356kHz 20M 50°26'·51N 4°59'·36W
Blackpool *BPL* 420kHz 15M
  53°46'·17N 2°59'·3W
Strumble Head *STU* 400kHz 40M
  52°00'·50N 5°01'·01W
St Mary's, Isles of Scilly *STM* 321kHz 15M
  49°54'·82N 6°17'·43W
Aberporth *AP* 370·5kHz 20M
  52°06'·92N 4°33'·57W
Killiney *KLY* 378kHz 50M
  53°16'·17N 6°06'·33W
Dublin Rush *RSH* 326kHz 30M
  53°30'·73N 6°06'·60W

List of major lights

Bishop Rock Fl(2)15s44m24M Horn Mo(N)90s Partially obscured 204°-211°, obscured 211°-233°, 236°-259°. Racon
Peninnis Head Fl.20s36m17M 231°-vis-117°, partially obscured 048°-083° within 5M. F.R lights on radio masts 1·6 and 1·66M N and 0·7M NE. 2F.R(hor) on wind generator 1·4M NE
Round Island Fl.10s55m24M Horn(4)60s 021°-vis-288° RC
Seven Stones LtF Fl(3)30s12m25M Horn(3)60s Racon
Longships Iso.WR.10s35m19/15M Horn 10s 189°-R-208°-R(unintens)-307°-R-327°-W-189° F.R on radio mast 4·9M NE
Pendeen Fl(4)15s59m27M Siren 20s 042°-vis-240°
Godrevy Island Fl.WR.10s37m12/9M 022°-W-101°-R-145°-W-272° 4F.R(vert) shown on radio mast 6·5M ESE
Trevose Head Fl.R.5s62m25M Horn(2)30s Storm signals. R Lt on radio mast 180m ESE. F.R on mast 4·7M SSE
Hartland Point Fl(6)15s37m25M Horn 60s
Instow Ldg Lts 118° *Front* Oc.6s22m15M 104·5°-vis-131·5° F.R on radio masts 4M NNW *Rear* 427m from front Oc.10s38m15M 103°-vis-133°
Lundy I Near N Point Fl.15s48m17M 009°-vis-285°
Southeast Point Fl.5s53m24M Horn 25s 170°-vis-073°
Bull Point Fl(3)10s54m25M Obscd by high gound from shore-056° F.R.48m12M 058°-vis-096°
Lynmouth Foreland Fl(4)15s67m18M 083°-vis-275°
Watchet W breakwater head F.G.9m9M F.R 206m on each of 2 radio masts 1·6M SSW

Burnham-on-Sea entrance Fl.7·5s28m17M
074°-vis-164°

Dir Lt 076° DirF.WRG.24m12-10M 071°-G-075°-
W-077°-R-081°

East Usk Fl(2)WRG.10s11m15-11M 284°-W-
290°-R-017°-W-037°-G-115°-W-120°
Oc.WRG.10s10m11-9M 081°-G-022°-W-024°-
R-028°

Portishead Point Q(3)10s9m16M Horn 20s 060°-
vis-262°

Black Nore Point Fl(2)10s11m15M 044°-vis-243°
Obscured by Sand Point when bearing less than
049°

Cardiff Ldg Lts 349° *Front* F.4m17M
Rear 520m from front F.24m17M F marks raft
350m E

Flat Holm LtHo SE Point
Fl(3)WR.10s50m16/13M Horn 30s 106°-R-140°-
W-151°-R-203°-W-106°

Monkstone Rock Fl.5s13m12M

Barry W breakwater head Fl.2·5s12m10M

Wenvoe Aero Q.365m12M

Breaksea LtF Fl.15s11m12M Horn(2)30s Fixed
riding light. Racon. Replaced by LFl.10s7M light
buoy with whis (T) 1994.

Nash Point Fl(2)WR.10s56m21/17M 280°-R-
290°-W-097°-R-100°-R(intens)-104°-R-120°-W-
128° RC. 150m west Siren(2)45s

Mumbles Head Fl(4)10s35m17M Horn(3)60s
Fog Det Lt Fl. 5mins 28m 331·5°-vis-336·5°

Whiteford Fl.5s7m7M

Caldey Island Fl(3)WR.20s65m14/12M 173°-R-
212°-W-088°-R-102°

St Anne's Head Fl.WR.5s48m18-14M
Horn(2)60s 233°-W-247°-R-285°-R(intens)-
314°-R-332°-W-124° 129°-W-131°

Skokholm Island Fl.R.10s54m17M Horn 15s
Partially obscured 226°-258°

The Smalls Fl(3)15s36m25M+F.R.33m13M
Horn(2)60s Racon 253°-vis-285° over Hats and
Barrels Rock

South Bishop Fl.5s44m24M Horn(3)45s RC

Strumble Head Fl(4)15s45m26M 038°-vis-257°

Fishguard N breakwater Fl.G.4·5s18m13M
Bell(1)8s

New Quay Fl.WRG.3s12m8/5M 135°-W-252°-G-
295°-R-shore

Aberaeron Fl(3)G.10s6M 125°-vis-200°

Aberystwyth S breakwater head Fl(2)WG.10s
12m10M 030°-G-053°-W-210° 4F.R(vert) on
radio tower 2·8M S

St Tudwal's West Island Fl.WR.20s46m15/13M
349°-W-169°-R-221°-W-243°-R-259°-W-293°-R-
349° Obscured by East Island 211°-231°

Bardsey Island Fl(5)15s39m26M Horn Mo(N)
45s Obscured by Bardsey Island 198°-250° and in
Tremadoc Bay when bearing less than 260°

Llanddwyn Island Fl.WR.2·5s12m7/4M 280°-R-
015°-W-120°

South Stack Fl.10s60m23M Horn 30s Obscured
to northward by North Stack and may also be obscured in Penrhos Bay by the high land of Pen-

rhyn Mawr, but is visible over the land from the
southward when in line with Rhoscolyn Beacon.
Fog Det Lt Fl(4)-(7)W at 6s intervals every 4
mins. 145°-vis-325°

Holyhead harbour breakwater head Fl(3)15s
21m14M Siren 20s F.R on chimney 2M SSE

Skerries Fl(2)10s36m22M + F.R.26m16M
Horn(2)20s Racon 231°-vis-254°

Lynas Point Oc.10s39m20M Horn 45s 109°-vis-
315° Fog Det Lt F.25m16M 211·8°-vis-214·3°
RC

Trwyn Du Fl.5·5s19m15M Bell(1)30s 101°-vis-
023° F.R on radio mast 2M SW, R Lt on radio
mast 3·3M W

Bar LtF Fl.5s10m12M Horn(2)20s Racon

Formby LtF Iso.4s11m6M

Crosby LtF Oc.5s11m8M

Walney Island Fl.15s21m23M RC Obscured
122°-127° when within 3M of shore

St Bees Head Fl(2)20s102m21M Obscured shore-
340° F.R lights on tower 14·6M SSE

Whitehaven west pier head Fl.G.5s16m13M

Workington S pier Fl.5s11m8M Siren 20s

Silloth, East Cote F.G.15m12M 046°-vis-058°,
intens 052°

Hestan Island E end Fl(2)10s7M

Little Ross LtHo Fl(5)50m12M Obscured in
Wigton bay when bearing more than 103°

Mull of Galloway SE end Fl.20s99m28M 182°-
vis-105° 3F.R on radio mast 16M ENE

Crammag Head Fl.10s35m18M

Killantringan Black head Fl(2)15s49m25M F.R
lights on radio masts 3·6M N

Corsewall Pt Fl(5)30s34m22M 027°-vis-257° R
Lts on tower 1·9M E

Ireland

East Maiden LtHo Fl(3)20s29m23M and Aux-
iliary Fl.R.5s15m8M 142°-vis-182° over Russel
and Highland rocks

Black Head Fl.3s45m27M

Mew Island Fl(4)30s37m24M Racon

Donaghadee Iso.WR.4s17m18/14M Siren 12s
shore-W-326°-R-shore R Lt on radio mast 2·5M
NW

South Rock LtF Fl(3)R.30s12m20M Horn(3)45s
RC Racon

Haulbowline Fl(3)10s32m19M+F.R Horn 30s
196°-vis-208°

St John's Point Q(2)7·5s37m23M+Fl.WR.3s14m
14/11M Horn(2)60s 064°-W-078°-R-shore

Dundalk N training wall head Fl.WR.15s10m
21/18M Horn(3)60s 124°-W-151°-R-284°-W-
313°-R-124° Oc.G.5s8m 331°-vis-334°

Drogheda Lts in line 248° *Front* Oc.12s8m15M
203°-vis-293°
Rear 85m from front Oc.12s12m17M 246°-vis-
252°

North Light Fl.R.4s7m15M 282°-vis-288°

Rockabill Fl.WR.12s45m23/19M Horn(4)60s
178°-W-329°-R-178°

Baily Fl.20s41m27M Dia 60s RC

Howth harbour E pier head
  Fl(2)WR.7·5s13m17/13M 256°-W-295°-R-256°
Dublin Poolbeg Oc(2)R.20s20m15M Horn(2)60s
Dublin North Bull Fl(3)G.10s15m15M
Dublin North Bank Oc.G.8s10m16M
Dun Laoghaire E breakwater head
  Fl(2)15s16m22M Dia 30s
Kish Bank Fl(2)30s29m22M Horn(2)30s Racon
Codling Lanby Fl.4s12m15M Horn 20s
Wicklow Head Fl(3)15s37m26M
Arklow Lanby Fl(2)12s12m15M Horn Mo(A)30s
Tuskar Rk Oc(2)7·5s33m27M Horn(4)45s RC
  Racon
Coningbeg LtF Fl(3)30s12m24M Horn(3)60s
  Racon
Dunmore East Pier LFl.WR.8s13m16/12M 225°-
  W-310°-R-004°
Hook Head Fl.3s46m23M Horn(2)45s Racon

Isle of Man

Calf of Man Fl.15s93m28M Horn 45s 274°-vis-
  190°
Chicken Rk Fl.5s38m13M Horn 60s
Port St Mary, Alfred Pier head Oc.R.10s8m6M
  Bell(3)12s
Langness. Dreswick Point Fl(2)30s23m21M
Douglas Head Fl.10s32m24M Reduced range
  shore-220° Obscured when bearing more than
  037° F.R lights on radio masts 1 and 3M W
Maughold Head Fl(3)30s65m21M
Point of Ayre Fl(4)20s32m19M Horn(3)60s
  Racon Det Lt UQ Vis 148°
Peel Oc.R.7s8m5M 156°-vis-249°

VHF direction-finding service

This service is for emergency use only. Each VHF
direction-finding station is remotely controlled by
an HM Coastguard Maritime Rescue Coordination
Centre (MRCC) or Maritime Rescue Sub-Centre
(MRSC). Watch is kept on Ch 16. Ship transmits
on Ch 16 (distress only) or Ch 67 so that the station
can determine its bearing. Ship's bearing from the
station is transmitted on Ch 16 (distress only) or Ch
67.

St Ann's Head RG Controlled by MRSC Milford
  Haven
Mynydd Rhiw RG Controlled by MRSC Holyhead
Great Ormes Head RG Controlled by MRSC
  Holyhead
Walney Island RG Controlled by MRSC Liver-
  pool
Snaefell RG Controlled by MRSC Liverpool
Hartland RG Controlled by MRCC Swansea
Pendeen RG Controlled by MRCC Falmouth
St Mary's, Isles of Scilly RG Controlled by
  MRCC Falmouth
Trevose Head RG Controlled by MRCC Fal-
  mouth

Coast radio stations

VHF calls to all coast radio stations should be made
on a working channel (bold).

Cardigan Bay VHF transmits and receives Ch **03**,
  16 24hrs. Traffic lists on Ch 03 at 0203, 0303,
  0603, 0703, 0903, 1003, 1403, 1503, 1803, 1903,
  2103, 2203
Anglesey VHF transmits and receives Ch 16, **26**,
  28[1], **61**[2] 24hrs. Traffic lists on Ch 26 at 0203,
  0303, 0603, 0703, 0903, 1003, 1403, 1503, 1803,
  1903, 2103, 2203
  1. For vessels in the Mersey and for Autolink or manual calls.
  2. For vessels in the Morecambe Bay Gas Field and for
    Autolink or manual calls.
Morecambe Bay VHF transmits and receives Ch
  04, 16, **82**[1]. Traffic lists on Ch 04 at 0203, 0303,
  0603, 0703, 0903, 1003, 1403, 1503, 1803, 1903,
  2103, 2203
  1. For Autolink or manual.
Portpatrick VHF transmits and receives Ch 16,
  27[1] 24hrs. Traffic lists on Ch 27 at 0203, 0303,
  0603, 0703, 0903, 1003, 1403, 1503, 1803, 1903,
  2103, 2203
  1. For Autolink or manual.
Dublin VHF transmits and receives Ch 16, **67**[1], **83**.
  Ch 16 24hrs. Traffic lists on Ch 83 at 0103, 0503
  and every odd H+03 (0903–2303)
  1. For safety messages only
Ilfracombe VHF transmits and receives Ch **05**,
  07[1], 16 24hrs. Traffic lists on Ch 05 at 0233,
  0303, 0633, 0733, 0903, 1033, 1433, 1503, 1833,
  1933 2103, 2233
  1. For vessels in the Severn Area and Autolink or manual calls.
Land's End VHF transmits and receives Ch 16,
  27, **64**[1], **85**[2], **88**[2] 24hrs. Traffic lists on Ch 27, 64
  at 0233, 0303, 0633, 0733, 0903, 1033, 1433,
  1503, 1833, 1933, 2103, 2233
  1. For vessels in the Scilly Isles area
  2. For Autolink or manual calls

Weather services

Cardigan Bay Storm warnings: Ch 03 at the end
  of the first silence period after receipt 0303, 0903,
  1503, 2103. Gale warnings for Irish Sea. Weather
  messages: Ch 03 at 0703, 1903 and on request.
  Navigational warnings: Ch 03 at 0203, 0603,
  1003, 1403, 1803, 2203 for Area Echo.
Anglesey Storm warnings: Ch 26 at the end of the
  first silence period after receipt 0303, 0903, 1503,
  2103. Gale warnings for Irish Sea. Weather messages: Ch 26 at 0703, 1903 and on request. Navigational warnings: Ch 26 at 0203, 0603, 1003,
  1403, 1803, 2203 for Area Echo.
Morecambe Bay Storm warnings: Ch 04 at the
  end of the first silence period after receipt 0303,
  0903, 1503, 2103. Gale warnings for Irish Sea.
  Weather messages: Ch 04 at 0703, 1903 and on
  request. Navigational warnings: Ch 04 at 0203,
  0603, 1003, 1403, 1803, 2203 for Area Echo.
Portpatrick Storm warnings: Ch 27 at the end of
  the first silence period after receipt 0303, 0903,
  1503, 2103. (Gale warnings for Lundy, Irish Sea,
  Malin). Weather messages: Ch 27 at 0703, 1903
  and on request. Navigational warnings: Ch 27 at
  0203, 0603, 1003, 1403, 1803, 2203 for Areas
  Alpha, Bravo, Charlie and Echo.

Dublin Storm warnings: Ch 83 on receipt. Weather messages: Ch 83 at 0103, 0403, 0703, 1003, 1303, 1603, 1903, 2203. Navigational warnings: Ch 83 at 0033, 0433, 0833, 1233, 1633, 2033 for E and SE coasts of Ireland and approaches.

Ilfracombe Storm warnings: Ch 05 at the end of the first silence period after receipt 0303, 0903, 1503, 2103. (Gale warnings for Lundy, Fastnet.) Weather messages: Ch 05 at 0733, 1933 on request. (Gale warnings, synopsis, 24hr forecast, for Lundy, Fastnet.) Navigational warnings on Ch 05 at 0233, 0633, 1033, 1433, 1833, 2233 for area Foxtrot.

Land's End Storm warnings: Ch 27, 64[1] at the end of the first silence period after receipt and 0303, 0903, 1503, 2103. Weather messages: Ch 27, 64[1] on request. Gale warnings for Shannon, Fastnet, Lundy, Sole, Plymouth, Portland, Wight, Dover, Thames, Humber, Tyne, Dogger, German Bight, Biscay, Finisterre. Navigational warnings: at 0233, 0633, 1033, 1433, 1833, 2233 for areas Delta, Foxtrot, Golf, Hotel.

1. For vessels in the Scilly Isles area

Key to symbols used on the plans

Post office	✉
Toilets	wc
Harbourmaster	⊕
Water tap	⊥
Public car park	P
Parking for boats/trailers	⊥
Fuel	▮
Yacht or sailing club	▶
Slip for small craft	▬
Church	⊹
Lifeboat	✦
Castle	⊓

Table of navigable distances (in nautical miles)

	Longships LtHo	Padstow	Ilfracombe	Cardiff	Swansea	Dale	Fishguard	Pwllheli	Holyhead	Conwy	Fleetwood	Port St Mary	Ramsey	Maryport	Isle of Withorn
Padstow	47														
Ilfracombe	90	53													
Cardiff	133	97	42												
Swansea	113	77	26	44											
Dale	107	69	52	89	57										
Fishguard	136	86	82	116	87	35									
Pwllheli	187	149	133	167	138	86	57								
Holyhead	210	172	156	190	161	109	83	56							
Conwy	222	184	168	202	173	121	97	70	36						
Fleetwood	283	245	229	263	234	182	155	128	73	53					
Port St Mary	251	213	197	231	202	150	125	98	46	58	62				
Ramsey	272	234	218	252	223	171	144	117	64	67	55	28			
Maryport	305	267	251	285	256	204	179	152	94	89	59	63	40		
Isle of Whithorn	295	257	241	275	246	194	166	139	86	87	69	46	23	30	
Portpatrick	295	257	241	275	246	194	166	139	94	105	97	52	44	65	36

Pilotage

I. Land's End to Hartland Point

Land's End

Land's End peninsula is a 100-metre-high plateau with low rolling hills and 60-metre-high granite cliffs facing the sea. There are traffic separation zones to the west of the peninsula. In unsettled weather Land's End should be rounded to the west of the Longships Reef. In fair weather Longships Passage can be used. Tidal streams can run strongly in the area (maximum 2½ knots at springs, 1¼ knots at neaps); the north stream begins at HW Dover, the south stream at HW Dover −0510.

Longships Passage

A ½-mile-wide passage between Land's End and Kettle's Bottom which may be used in settled weather. Kettle's Bottom, a rock which is only just covered at MHWS and can always be identified by broken water, and Shark's Fin rock (dries 3·4 metres ½ mile NNW of Kettle's Bottom) are left to seaward. The Brisons, two rocky islets ½ mile southwest of Cape Cornwall, lead the passage, with the highest part of the north (high) Brison bearing 001° and open to the west of the south (low) Brison.

Sennen Cove

An attractive drying fishing harbour lying at the south end of Whitesand Bay. A stone breakwater gives limited protection to the harbour; the approach is fully exposed to the Atlantic and there are offlying dangers. Anchorage is available 100 metres north of the harbour in 5 metres sand only in the most settled conditions or offshore winds.

Whitesand Bay

Anchorage can be obtained off the centre of the bay in offshore winds. Rocks extend from the shore at the north and south ends of the bay, which is exposed to the Atlantic swells.

The Brisons

Two steep-sided rocky islets (27 and 22 metres) ½ mile southwest of Cape Cornwall; connected to the mainland by a rocky shallow reef, parts of which dry to 1·8m.

Cape Cornwall

A steep cliffed point (85 metres high) with a coastguard lookout hut and a disused chimney marking the site of the abandoned Cape Cornwall tin mine on its summit. There is a radio mast (red lights) 2½ miles to the ESE and a TV mast 2 miles to the ENE.

St Ives

Waypoint 50°13'·4N 5°27'·9W ½M NE of St Ives Head
Population 10,052 (1981)
Local High Water is Dover −0605
Charts Admiralty 1149, 1168; Imray C7

General

A picturesque drying harbour busy with fishing vessels and pleasure craft. The narrow streets and granite-paved lanes of the town provide a haven for artists, and visitors flood to the resort in the holiday season. The harbour was formed by the building of a stone pier in 1770, becoming Cornwall's biggest pilchard port over the following century. Facilities are fair and the town offers a good range of shops.

Approaching St Ives, with green buoy marking former jetty in the foreground

ST IVES BAY

Depths in Metres

6°30'W

50°15'N

Stones
Q
Bell Whis
BY

The
Stones

Godrevy
Island
Fl.WR.10s37m
12/9M

ST IVES

Carracks

Knills Mont
166

HAYLE

0   1   2

Nautical Miles

Entrance to St Ives harbour

Warning

The harbour can be entered for 2½ hours either side of HW, although the visitors' moorings can only be reached within 2 hours of HW. The harbour dries to firm sand and has approximately 4·5 metres at MHWS at the harbour entrance. The harbour entrance is wide and does not prevent the swell from entering with strong onshore winds. If such winds are forecast, shelter can be found in nearby Hayle.

Approach

By day Enter St Ives Bay between St Ives Head and Godrevy Island with its offlying rocks. To clear the rocks off St Ives Head, Knills Monument (166 metres) should be kept open of the Tregenna Castle Hotel (conspicuous, to the south of the town) on a course of approximately 195°. A green buoy marks the end of a ruined stone jetty, which is submerged at HW and must be left to starboard.

ST IVES

St Ives Head

Depths in Metres

WC

Sand

2F.G(vert)
8m 5M

2F.R(vert)
5m 3M

WC

ST IVES

Station

Carracks
(dr.0·6m)

0   5

Cables

By night The harbour can be reached using the following lights:

Pendeen Fl(4)15s59m27M Siren 20s
Godrevy Island Fl.WR.10s37m12/9M
St Ives east pier 2F.G.8m5M
St Ives west pier 2F.R.5m3M

St Ives harbour at low water. Visitors' moorings are in front of Woolworth's four-storey light-coloured building, to right of centre in photograph

Anchorage in the approach

Anchor in 5 metres sand 2 cables ESE of harbour entrance in settled weather.

Entrance

Between the two stone piers forming the harbour.

Moorings

Six visitors' moorings are provided, marked by white buoys. These are on the west side of the harbour in front of Woolworth's (four-storey beige building fronting the harbour).

Berths

It is possible to berth along the north side of the west pier, but this is untenable if any swell enters the harbour.

Harbourmaster

At north end of east pier.

Charges

There are harbour charges.

Facilities

Fuel From tankers (only occasionally).
Water Three taps on west pier.
Slip Northwest corner of harbour.
Provisions Good range of shops in the town.
Showers At limited times at the sailing club; see harbourmaster.

Post office Main post office on High Street.
Gas Calor Gas and *Camping Gaz* from P. N. Harvey, High Street. Only *Calor Gas* from Bennet's, behind former lifeboat house.
Chandlery Limited chandlery available from United Cooperative Fishermen's Association, on the harbour.
Refuse disposal Litter bins around the harbour.

Hayle

Waypoint 50°12'·3N 5°26'·0W ½M N of harbour entrance
Population 6,179 (1981)
Local High Water is Dover −0605
Charts Admiralty *1149, 1168*; Imray *C7*

General

Formerly a busy port exporting copper and tin. The closure of a large foundry in the town in 1904 started its decline. The drying harbour is now used by a small fishing fleet. Although strong onshore winds make entrance impossible, the harbour itself is well protected and is the place to head for if bad weather is forecast.

Warning

The harbour should not be approached in strong onshore winds. In more settled conditions, approach should ideally be made one hour before HW, although the harbour can be entered for 2 hours either side of HW. There is approximately 5 metres at the harbour entrance at MHWS.

Approach

By day Enter St Ives Bay between St Ives Head and Godrevy Island with its offlying rocks.
By night A night approach and entrance are not advised.

Anchorage in the approach

Anchorage here in 5 metres sand is only possible in the most settled weather. A more suitable anchorage in which to wait for the tide can be found in Carbis Bay 1 mile southeast of St Ives, avoiding the Carracks to the north of Carbis Bay.

Entrance

The green conical buoy to the north of the line of posts marking the training wall must be identified and all should be left approximately 30 metres to starboard. The church on the hillside is conspicuous and an approach on a bearing of 180° will lead to the channel.

When alongside the training wall make for the timber-boarded house and the larger white house above and behind. Turn to port alongside the houses, keeping all red buoys and the posts marking the central island to port. Enter the channel with the warehouse building on the east side.

Depths in Metres

N

Ldg Lts 180°

5°25'·5W

50°12'N

Sand

Dunes

Posts

Dunes

House
White building

F

F

Posts

HAYLE

Mud

HAYLE

0   5

Cables

Hayle, looking NW back towards the harbour entrance, showing central island with marker poles

Hayle, looking SE towards town centre. Moor alongside quay or another boat on the right-hand quay of this channel

Berthing
Along west side of channel at vacant place on quay or alongside fishing boat.

Harbourmaster
At entrance to berthing channel.

Charges
There are harbour charges.

Facilities
Fuel From filling station just out of town centre on the road to Redruth.
Water Tap near harbourmaster's office.
Provisions Adequate shops for everyday requirements in the town centre.
Post office In Foundry Square.
Camping Gaz and paraffin Biggleston's, on road facing the quay.

Godrevy Island, looking NE

Godrevy Point
The Stones are three groups of dangerous drying rocks lying between ¾ mile and 1½ miles northwest of Godrevy Point. A north cardinal whistle and bell buoy marks their seaward extremity. The area abounds with overfalls and should be passed to the northwest of the buoy in all but the most settled conditions. There is an inshore passage between Godrevy Island and Godrevy Point which can be used in calm conditions, care being taken to avoid Bessack Rock 1 mile SSW of Godrevy Island.

Portreath
Waypoint 50°16'·2N 5°18'·1W ½M NW of harbour entrance
Local High Water is Dover −0600
Charts Admiralty *1149*; Imray *C7*

General
In 1760 the building of the pier at Portreath formed a harbour to serve the local copper and tin mines. Coasters continued to visit the harbour until the 1960s, when a housing estate was built on the land surrounding the harbour. Portreath is now a small holiday resort with limited facilities for yachtsmen.

Warning
The harbour can only be entered for 2 hours either side of HW and should not be attempted in strong onshore winds. In these conditions the swell can find its way into the harbour. The harbour dries to a firm bottom of sand and small stones.

PORTREATH

Depths in Metres

N

50°15'·9N

5°17'·7W

8

7

5

Horse Rock
(23)

3

3₄

1₈

1

White Daymark

Small
concrete
tower

2

Sand

3₃

Outer
Basin

Inner
Basin

WC

0   100
Metres

Approach

By day The monument on Carn Brea (221 metres), 3 miles to the southeast of Portreath, is conspicuous. A mast (red lights 401 metres) is ¾ mile southeast of the monument. These indicate the approach to Portreath from seaward when they are in alignment. Approaching from the south, Gull Rock should be passed to seaward. The white 8-metre-high daymark on the headland at an elevation of 37 metres to the north of the harbour entrance is also conspicuous.

By night A night approach and entrance should not be attempted.

Entrance

A small concrete tower marks the end of the stone pier. Approach should be made with the northeast face of the pier just open, leaving Horse Rock to the northeast. Keep close to the pier until into the turning basin, then pass through the central opening into the outer harbour.

Entrance to Portreath

13

Berthing

Alongside the wall in the outer harbour. There is a shortage of fixed ladders, and the harbour bottom is some 4 metres below the top of the harbour wall.

Harbourmaster

An officer of the Portreath Harbour Association will visit the boat. Charges are levied.

Facilities

Slip In southeast corner of inner harbour.
Fuel From filling station on the road to Redruth just beyond the post office.
Provisions Small shopping centre close to the harbour.
Post office By the shopping centre.

Trevaunance Cove

The location of three former harbours, the last destroyed in 1934. Temporary anchorage may be had in 5 metres sand, although the bay is open from the west through north to northeast and subject to the Atlantic swells.

Bawden Rocks

Two islets 1 mile north of St Agnes Head.

Ligger or Perran Bay

Anchoring or fishing is prohibited in an area extending for 3 miles seaward of the bay, owing to the presence of scientific instruments and cables. Two orange buoys are moored in the bay.

The Gannel

A narrow picturesque creek, drying almost completely to firm sand. Entrance is through Crantock Bay, leaving The Goose, a rock to the west of Pentire Point East, to the north. Approach should not be made in strong onshore winds, although good shelter is to be found further up the creek. Enter up to 1½ hours either side of HW, keeping ½ cable from the south shore of Pentire Point East until the entrance to the creek opens. There is a wooden footbridge over the main channel ¾ mile from the entrance to the creek, which is exposed at LW and only passable by shallow-draught boats at HW.

Newquay

Waypoint 50°25'·8N 5°05'·2W ½M NE of Towan Head
Population 15,280 (1981)
Local High Water is Dover −0604
Charts Admiralty *1168, 1149;* Imray *C7*

NEWQUAY

Depths in Metres

Towan Head

Newquay
Bay

Old Dane Rock
(dr.6·2m)

Listrey
Rk

Hotel

Hotel

2F.G
2F.R

50°25'N

Sand

NEWQUAY

0   500

Metres

5°05'W

Newquay harbour

General

Cornwall's biggest holiday resort boasts a number of expansive, exposed beaches which make it the foremost surfing centre in the country. The harbour is a sufficient distance from the town centre to miss most of the holidaymakers' noisier activities, whilst still being close enough for provisioning. The drying harbour is shared between a small fishing fleet and a number of pleasure craft.

Warning

There is water in the harbour entrance for 3 hours either side of HW, and alongside the quay within 2½ hours of HW. Swell in Newquay Bay can produce strong surges in the harbour; otherwise it is reasonably well protected. The swell decreases at the harbour entrance closer to HW.

15

Approach

By day Newquay Bay is entered between Towan Head and Trevelgue Head, 1¼ miles to the east. There are two conspicuous hotels between Towan Head and Newquay. Old Dane Rock (dries 6·2 metres) lies 3 cables offshore ½ mile southeast of Towan Head. Listrey Rock, with a depth of 0·5 metre, lies 1 cable east of Old Dane Rock.

By night Approach by night is not recommended because of the lack of major lights. The harbour is lit with 2F.G.5m2M on the north pier and 2F.R.4m2M on the south pier.

Anchorage in the approach

Anchor in 5 metres sand 2½ cables to the northeast of the harbour in settled conditions.

Entrance

Narrow entrance between north and south piers, turning south immediately on entering to pass east of central pier.

Berthing

Along west side of south pier. There are ladders, but these are in poor condition.

Harbourmaster

On south pier.

VHF radio telephone

Call *Newquay Harbour* on Ch 16, work Ch 12 or 14.

Charges

There are harbour charges.

Facilities

Fuel From tanker which visits frequently.
Water From tap on south pier; key for tap with harbourmaster.
Provisions Good range of shops in town.
Post office In town centre.
Refuse disposal Litter bins on quay.

Trevose Head

The headland has an elevation of 51 metres, although its hinterland is much lower. The white tower of the lighthouse (Fl.5s62m25M) stands on its northwest corner. The Bull is an above-water rock 3 cables to the southwest of Trevose Head. The Quies are a group of above-water rocks 5 to 8 cables west of The Bull. In settled conditions it is possible to pass between The Bull and The Quies.

Polventon Bay

Anchorage is available in 4 metres sand off the lifeboat slip, although the bay is exposed to the northwest through north to east.

River Camel estuary

The River Camel flows into Padstow Bay and tidal waters make their way many miles inland.

Approach

By day From the west Gulland Rock can be passed on either side. From the northeast it is possible to pass between Newland (with its offlying rocks) and Roscarrock shoals in settled weather, but it is advisable in any other conditions to pass to seaward of Newland.

Padstow Bay is entered between Stepper Point (with its conspicuous 12-metre-high stone tower daymark) and Pentire Point.

By night The estuary can be reached using the following lights:
Trevose Head Fl.5s62m25M Horn(2)30s
Stepper Point LFl.10s12m4M

Anchorage in the approach

It is possible to find a sheltered anchorage in the lee of Stepper Point in all conditions (except with the wind between north and west) while waiting for water at the Doom Bar.

Entrance

There is always water over the Doom Bar at the entrance to the estuary; however, it is impassable at MLWS. The same applies at MLWN except in very calm conditions. Extra care should be taken at half-ebb and below when any swell is running. The bar also becomes impassable in strong northwest winds. The channel lies to the east of the estuary, the first red buoy (Fl(2)R.10s) marking the limit of the rocks off Trebetherick Point. Leave the green Bar buoy (Fl.G.5s) to starboard and head for the red Channel buoy (Fl.R.5s).

Padstow

Waypoint 50°34'·6N 4°56'·7W ½M N of Stepper Point
Population 2,806 (1981)
Local High Water is Dover −0550
Charts Admiralty *1168, 1156*; Imray *C58*

General

An attractive fishing port and holiday resort, with a network of narrow streets leading down to the harbour. The trading nature of the harbour declined with the advent of larger vessels and the silting of the estuary. The outer harbour is now busy with fishing vessels; the inner harbour (in which, thanks to the new lock gates, vessels now lie afloat in 3.5m) is mostly used by pleasure craft. The inner harbour is well protected from all winds.

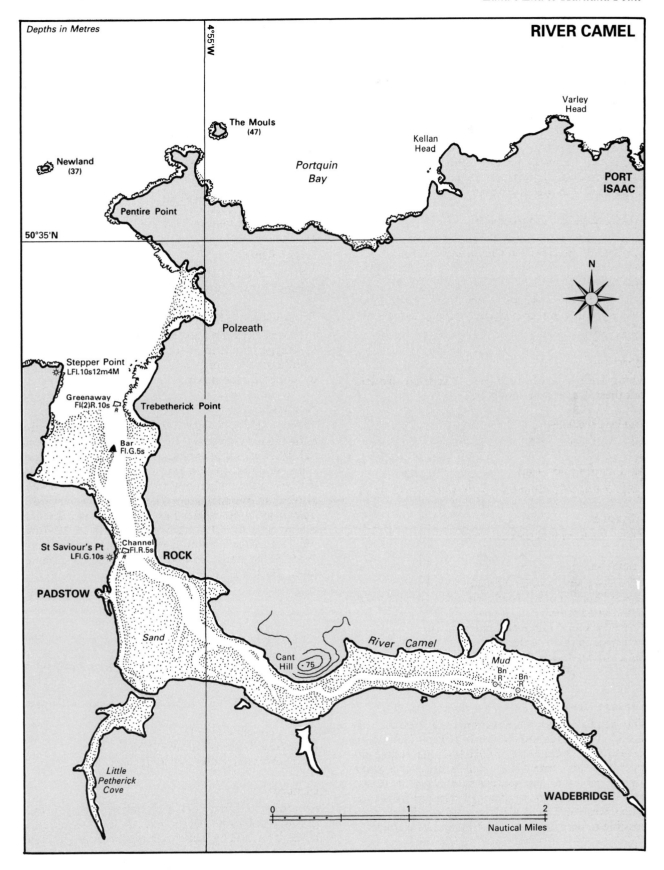

Depths in Metres

RIVER CAMEL

4°55'W

Varley
Head

The Mouls
(47)

Kellan
Head

Portquin
Bay

**PORT
ISAAC**

Newland
(37)

Pentire Point

50°35'N

N

Polzeath

Stepper Point
LFl.10s12m4M

Greenaway
Fl(2)R.10s

Trebetherick Point

Bar
Fl.G.5s

Channel
Fl.R.5s

St Saviour's Pt
LFl.G.10s

ROCK

PADSTOW

Sand

River Camel

Cant
Hill

·75

Mud
'Bn'
R

Bn
R

*Little
Petherick
Cove*

WADEBRIDGE

0   1   2

Nautical Miles

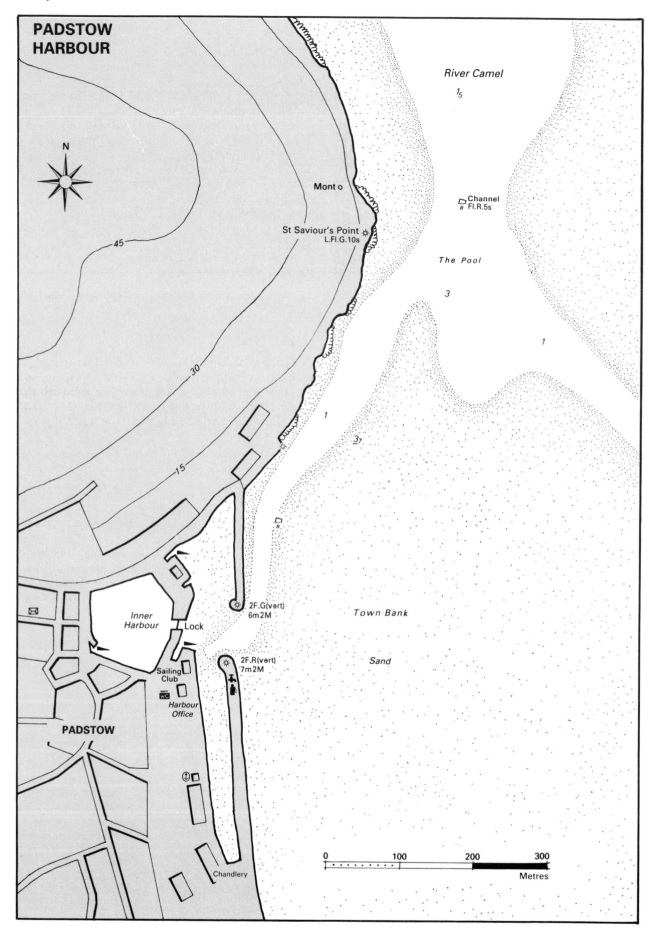

PADSTOW
HARBOUR

N

River Camel

1₅

Mont o

Channel
Fl.R.5s
R

St Saviour's Point
L.Fl.G.10s

The Pool

45

3

30

1

15

3₇

R

2F.G(vert)
6m 2M

Town Bank

Inner
Harbour   Lock

2F.R(vert)
7m 2M

Sand

Sailing
Club

WC

Harbour
Office

PADSTOW

Chandlery

0   100   200   300

Metres

Padstow inner harbour, looking back at harbour entrance

Approach

By day From the Channel red buoy, keep close to the west shore after St Saviour's Point. Red and green buoys mark the channel between the north quay and the Town Bank, a large sand spit that has built up between the harbour and the main channel of the River Camel.

By night The harbour can be reached using the following lights:

Stepper Point LFl.10s12m4M
Greenaway buoy Fl(2)R.10s
Bar buoy Fl.G.5s
Channel buoy Fl.R.5s
St Saviour's Point LFl.G.10s
North quay 2F.G(vert)6m2M
South quay 2F.R(vert)7m2M

Anchorage in the approach

In the pool to the south of the Channel buoy for vessels waiting to enter the inner harbour or wishing to stay afloat. The anchorage becomes uncomfortable with strong SE winds against the flood.

Entrance

Between the north and south quays, and through the lock gate, which is open for 2 hours either side of HW; then pass through into the inner harbour.

Berthing

Alongside in the inner harbour as directed by the harbourmaster.

Harbourmaster

Office by the harbour.

VHF radio telephone

Padstow Harbour Ch 16, 14 (0900–1700).

Charges

There are harbour charges.

Facilities

Fuel Diesel on south quay. Petrol from filling station close to south side of inner harbour.
Water On south quay, and tap at harbour office.
Toilets, showers and laundry In new red brick building to N of lock gate.
Slip Three slips as indicated on harbour plan.
Provisions Good range of shops in town centre.
Post office Duke Street.
Yacht club Padstow Sailing Club.
Chandlery Rig Marine, at south end of inner harbour.
Boat repairs At south end of inner harbour.
Refuse disposal Bins on quay.

Rock

There are moorings available off the small town of Rock on the opposite side of the Camel estuary to Padstow. The moorings dry onto firm sand. Rock Sailing Club operates from a converted warehouse on the foreshore and there is a chandlery nearby.

Wadebridge

The channel of the River Camel is constantly changing, but is navigable up to Wadebridge, which should ideally be reached just before the last of the flood. Quayside moorings are available, although the southwest quay has silted and is only suitable for fin-keelers to lie to. There are moorings in the main channel to the northwest of the town centre. There is a sailing club and a boat repair yard.

Port Isaac

Waypoint 50°36'·3N 4°50'·1W ½M N of harbour
 entrance
Local High Water is Dover −0555
Charts Admiralty *1156*; Imray *C58*

General

A small fishing harbour within a cove made attractive by the small cottages and narrow streets that make up the town. There is limited space in the part of the harbour that dries to firm sand, due to the large outcrop of rock to the west of the harbour and the moorings of the resident fishing craft.

Warning

The harbour can only be entered for 2 hours either side of HW. Strong onshore winds make the entrance impassable and produce a strong surge in the harbour itself.

Entrance to Port Isaac. Keep white oriel window open of cliff face to avoid offlying rocks to west of harbour entrance

Port Isaac. Moor fore and aft as close to fishing boats as possible

Port Isaac and Port Gaverne

Approach

By day St Endellion Church with its square tower is conspicuous 1¼ miles south of Port Isaac; approaching the church on a bearing of 171° will lead to Port Isaac.

By night A night approach and entrance should not be attempted.

Entrance

There are drying rocks to the east of the harbour entrance. A building with distinctive oriel windows fronting the shingle beach should be kept open of the east cliff face to avoid the rocks until Lobber Point is abeam. Make directly for and enter between the two stone breakwaters.

Moorings

Anchor fore and aft as close as possible to the fishing-boat moorings and check that you will be drying on sand by asking the harbourmaster or local fishermen. Alternatively, test physically with a long pole as the water shallows; on a calm day the sea bed is often visible.

Harbourmaster

Office by the shingle beach.

Charges

There are harbour charges.

Facilities

Provisions Adequate shops for everyday requirements.

Post office On the road to the east of the harbour.

Port Gaverne

A narrow creek ½ mile east of Port Isaac. The houses at the head of the creek are prominent as the entrance opens. There is no protection from onshore winds. The creek dries to a stone and pebble bottom.

Port Gaverne

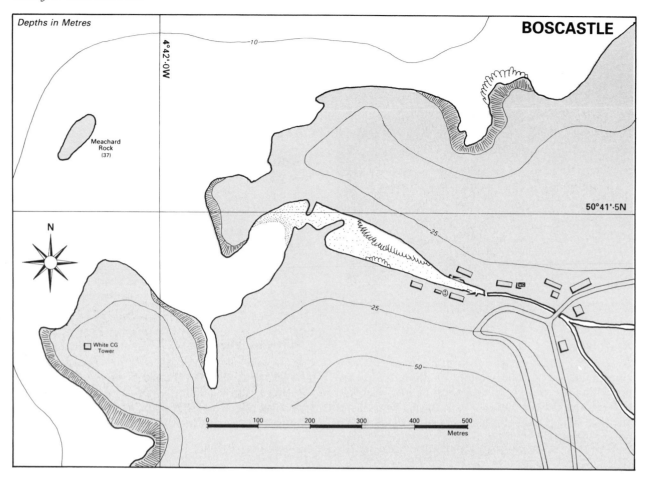

Boscastle

Waypoint 50°41'·45N 4°43'·0W ½M W of harbour
  entrance
Local High Water is Dover −0543
Charts Admiralty *1156*; Imray *C58*

General

An intricate entrance between the cliffs leads to the harbour, beyond which is a picturesque village restored and preserved by the National Trust. The small drying harbour is home to a small number of fishing boats and pleasure craft.

Warning

Entrance should only be made in settled weather; onshore winds or ground swell can make the harbour inaccessible and produce surges in the harbour itself. Enter up to 2 hours either side of HW. The harbour dries to a firm bottom of sand and small stones near the entrance, with rock outcrops along the north side and further up the harbour.

Approach

By day Tintagel Head with its prominent hotel is conspicuous to the south. Meachard Rock must be identified at the harbour entrance and can be passed on either side, although leaving it to the north would make for an easier first-time entrance.

The white former coastguard lookout tower on the headland to the south of the harbour is conspicuous, resembling a keep with its turreted corners.

By night A night approach and entrance should not be attempted.

Approaching Boscastle looking east

Boscastle harbour, looking back at entrance

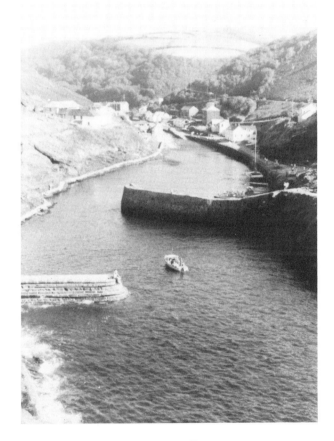

Boscastle harbour, looking towards village

Entrance

Make for the centre of the bay until the channel opens up to the north. Keep to the centre of the channel and head for the small stone breakwater. Leave the outer breakwater to port, and keep close to the end of the inner mole when turning into the harbour.

Berthing

Alongside the south quay.

Harbourmaster

Office on the south side of the quay.

Charges

There are nominal harbour charges.

Facilities

Slip Two slips at the head of the harbour.
Provisions Small range of shops in the village.
Post office Up the old road into the village.

Pencarrow Point, looking east

Bude Haven

Waypoint 50°50'·0N 4°34'·1W ½M W of harbour entrance
Population 2,789 (1981)
Local High Water is Dover −0540
Charts Admiralty *1156*; Imray *C58*

General

A holiday resort famous for its surfers' beaches. Bude Canal, which opened in 1823 to carry sea sand inland for use as an agricultural fertiliser, now provides sheltered accommodation for visiting yachtsmen, although facilities are limited.

Warning

Entrance to the harbour can only be made up to 2 hours either side of HW, and as close to HW as possible is advisable, as the breaking surf moves further up the beaches away from the harbour entrance. The entrance is impassable in strong onshore winds or with a large ground swell running.

Approach

By day The radio dish aerials 3½ miles to the north of the harbour are conspicuous. Approaching from the southwest, the harbour lies at the north end of a 2-mile-long line of low cliffs with a stone tower at the north end.
By night A night approach and entrance should not be attempted.

BUDE

Entrance

Identify and align the leading marks on the hillside to the north of the harbour: a white post with a yellow diamond topmark and a white flagstaff above and beyond it. The leading marks give a course of 75·5° passing close to Barrel Rock, marked with a post topped with a barrel. Immediately on passing Barrel Rock turn to starboard, picking up the leading marks close to the lock gates (two white posts with yellow triangular topmarks) on a bearing of 131·5°. A sand spit has started to build up off Chapel Rock. This should be given a little more clearance than the leading marks indicate.

Moorings

It may be possible to find a vacant drying mooring in the outer harbour, but there is little room to anchor.

Berthing

The lock requires a water level of approximately 5 metres over chart datum to operate. Yachts can then pass through into the shelter of the canal basin.

Approaching Bude

Bude inner harbour

Bude outer harbour, with inner leading marks

Hartland Point

A 100-metre tableland slopes steeply to the sea at the headland, with adjoining perpendicular rocks. The white round tower and white buildings of the lighthouse (Fl(6)15s37m25M) are halfway down the cliff face. Tense Rocks are drying rocks extending 2 cables northwest from the foot of the cliffs. A tidal race extends 2 miles to the northwest of the point, and is to be avoided during the strength of the tidal streams.

The tidal stream can reach 3 knots at springs; it begins in a northeast direction at HW Dover +0120 and in a southwest direction at HW Dover −0440.

Hartland Point at low water, looking NE, with the appropriately named Tense Rocks exposed

Harbourmaster
Office by canal basin.

VHF radio telephone
Call Bude Haven on Ch 16, work Ch 12.

Charges
There are harbour charges and lock fees.

Facilities
Provisions A good range of shops in the town.

II. Hartland Point to Sand Point

Lundy Island

Position 51°10'·0N 4°40'·0W
Population 52 (1981)
Local High Water is Dover −0530
Charts Admiralty *1164*; Imray *C58*

General

A small island, 2½ miles long and ¾ mile wide, with steep granite cliffs rising to more than 120 metres in places. It is owned by the National Trust and is administered as a bird sanctuary by the Landmark Trust.

Warning

Lundy Island is surrounded by tidal races and overfalls, and should only be approached near slack water. The east-going stream begins at HW Dover −0030 and the west-going stream at HW Dover −0530. The streams run at 4 knots at springs, 2½ knots at neaps.

A race known as The White Horses forms over the Stanley Bank 3 miles northeast of the island, being particularly turbulent during the east-going stream.

Similar races extend 1 mile north of the island and 1½ miles east of Rat Island. During the west-going stream tidal races exist, although they are of less ferocity, with the race off the south of the island extending 1 mile southwest of Shutter Point.

Approach

The island lies 10 miles NNW of Hartland Point and 16 miles west of Morte Point. North West Point, the north extremity of the island, has a white round light tower (Fl.15s48m17M). A similar light tower (Fl.5s53m24M) is on a peninsula at the southeast end of the island.

The church tower 1½ cables northwest of the southeast lighthouse is conspicuous from the south or east. The stone tower of a disused lighthouse is conspicuous on the west side, ½ mile north of the south end of the island.

Anchorage

The only recognised anchorage is in the bay immediately to the north of the southeast lighthouse, in 6 metres shingle. Ample anchor scope is necessary, with a tidal range of up to 7 metres at springs and 3 metres at neaps. The anchorage is exposed to winds from the north through east to the southeast. Landing is made on the shingle beach of the cove.

In east winds shelter can be found in Jenny's Cove, on the west side of the island, although swell can make this uncomfortable.

Facilities

Provisions Limited provisions are available from the Marisco Tavern.

The anchorage at Lundy Island

Clovelly

Position 50°59'·9N 4°23'·7W
Population 419 (1981)
Local High Water is Dover −0524
Charts Admiralty *1179*; Imray *C58*

General

Picture-postcard village with whitewashed cottages flanking the narrow cobbled main street that winds down the wooded hillside to the harbour. The small drying harbour provides limited shelter for a few small fishing and pleasure craft.

Warning

The harbour should only be entered close to HW. It should be avoided if there is any swell running, as this can cause surges in the harbour.

Depths in Metres

N

Hen and
Chickens
(2)

Fl.15s48m17M

4°40'W

Stanley Bank

North
West
Bank

30

20

30

LUNDY
ISLAND

20

Jenny's Cove

East Bank

10

20

30

51°10'N

Derelict
light house

Rat Island

Fl.5s53m24M
Horn 25s

20

50

Black
Rock
(5)

0   1   2

Nautical Miles

LUNDY ISLAND

Clovelly Harbour

Approach

By day Easily visible as a built-up break in the wooded hillside when approached from the northeast; less so from the west. There are no offlying dangers.

By night The anchorage should only be approached with care; the light (Fl.G.5s5m5M) at the harbour entrance must be identified.

Anchorage in the approach

Anchor off the harbour in 5 metres mud. Shelter from offshore winds is good.

Entrance

The harbour is small. It should be entered keeping close to the end of the quay to avoid a shingle bank that has built up close by.

Berthing

There is limited space alongside the quay for use in settled weather. The harbour dries to a firm bottom of sand and small stones.

Harbourmaster

The harbourmaster lives close to the harbour, behind the lifeboat house.

Approaching Clovelly

Facilities

Water From the lifeboat house.
Provisions Limited provisions in the village.
Post office On the main street.

Depths in Metres

Nautical Miles

2   1   0

TAW AND TORRIDGE

FREMINGTON

Quay

Power

Bn

Bn

Bn

Line of disused railway

River Taw

Power Station
(red lights)
2 Chys (36)

Red

Oc.6s22m15M

Oc.10s38m15M

Tower

INSTOW

Fl.R.5s

Sand

Moorings

Ferry

Red

Sand

Sand

Power

Bn

Bn

2₁

3₆

5₄

3₃

Skearn
Point

APPLEDORE

River Torridge

BIDEFORD

0₁

0₁

0₁

Outer
Pulley Q.G.

Pulley G

Middle
Ridge 2₄

1

1₂

0₆ 1

0₈

2

1₆

0₂

0₈

Bar
By

118°

Bideford Fairway
L.Fl.10s
Bell

4°15'W

N

11

8

51°05'N

River Taw and River Torridge estuary

Local High Water at Appledore is Dover −0520
Charts Admiralty *1179, 1160*; Imray *C58*

General
The rivers flow into Barnstaple Bay and tidal waters extend several miles inland to a number of harbours and anchorages.

Warning
Entrance should not be attempted until 2½ hours before HW; strong onshore winds can produce a large, dangerous swell, any swell also making the buoys difficult to identify.

Approach
By day Barnstaple Bay is entered between Hartland Point and Baggy Point. The red and white Bideford Fairway buoy (LFl.10s) must be identified.

By night The estuary can be approached using the following lights:

Hartland Point Fl(6)15s37m25M Horn 60s
Bull Point Fl(3)10s54m25M + F.R.48m12M
Bideford Fairway buoy LFl.10s
Instow leading lights 118°
Front Oc.6s22m15M
Rear Oc.10s38m15M

Anchorage in the approach
Anchor in 5 metres sand only in the most settled conditions. Alternative anchorages in which to await the tide are Clovelly to the southwest and Morte Bay to the north, depending on the prevailing wind direction.

Entrance
Leading lights indicate the channel between the Bideford Fairway buoy and the drying Old Wall Rocks. In line the two white light towers bear 118°. This course is followed, passing three buoys to starboard: the Bar, Middle Ridge, and Outer Pulley buoys. Passing the Outer Pulley, change course to 160° to leave the Pulley green conical buoy to starboard, heading close to the southeast tip of Greys Hill before turning to the pool to the north of Skern Point.

Appledore
A small shipbuilding and fishing town, said to have been granted 'free port' status by Elizabeth the First in return for the part played by local ships and sailors in the defeat of the Spanish Armada. Yachts wishing to remain afloat can anchor in the pool to the north of Skern Point. It is possible to lie alongside the drying quay, but this gets busy in summer, and the mud and stone bottom can contain obstructions which could damage a yacht. There are

Appledore

Looking across the river Torridge towards Instow at low water

virtually no ladders. Toilets and a post office are on the quay and there is a limited chandlery on Market Street.

Bideford
The 2-mile channel up the River Torridge to Bideford is navigable after 2 hours before HW. An attractive town lies behind the long tree-lined quay. The quay along the west bank below Bideford Bridge is used by coasters, although it is possible for yachts to lie alongside and dry onto soft mud. There are no ladders. Toilets and the post office are on the quay.

Instow
The home of the North Devon Yacht Club, on the east bank of the River Torridge, with a large expanse of moorings drying onto firm sand. The moorings are exposed to northwest winds. Water

Approaching the quay at Bideford

has to be carried from the yacht club, where there are showers.

Fremington Quay

Passage up the River Taw should not be made until 2 hours before HW. Dangerous rocks on either side of the channel are marked with pole beacons. The river is navigable with care up to the former railway quay at Fremington. Now deserted, the drying quay is exposed to northwest winds; there are no facilities.

Barnstaple

The channel up the River Taw to Barnstaple is tortuous and liable to change. Navigation is possible with care for shallow-draught boats arriving in Barnstaple with the last of the flood. There is a quay along the north bank of the River Taw close to the town centre. Local boats lie alongside the quay of

Alongside the quay at Bideford

Entrance to river Yeo at Barnstaple

Fremington Quay

Alongside the quay to river Yeo at low water

the River Yeo, where the shelving bank makes investigation prior to mooring necessary.

Baggy Point

Headland 3½ miles north of Bideford Fairway buoy. The Baggy Leap green conical buoy marks the end of the rock shoal 6 cables WNW of Baggy Point.

Morte Point

Low cliffed sloping headland 2½ miles north of Baggy Point. The Morte Stone green conical buoy marks the west extremity of the rock ledge extending from the headland. A dangerous race can be experienced off Morte Point during strong tides and contrary winds.

Bull Point

The white round tower of the lighthouse stands on the point 3½ miles west of Ilfracombe. At the strength of the tide, overfalls extend 2¾ miles north

Barnstaple quay to river Taw, looking downstream

from Bull Point to Horseshoe Rocks. A north cardinal buoy marks the extremity of these rocks and overfalls. The tidal stream at springs can reach 3 knots. The east-going tide begins at HW Dover +0040, the west-going at HW Dover −0525.

Ilfracombe

Waypoint 51°13'·15N 4°06'·6W ½M N of pierhead
Population 10,479 (1981)
Local High Water is Dover −0525
Charts Admiralty *1160, 1179, 1165*; Imray *C58, C59*

General

North Devon's largest holiday resort has terraces of elegant Victorian houses rising above a safe harbour. There are good facilities for yachts in this lively resort. The harbour is very busy during the summer, and the drying inner harbour can be full of resident boats. There is usually space available in the outer harbour, part of which dries to firm sand. There is water at the entrance to the harbour at all stages of the tide.

Approach

By day The approach is straightforward and there are no offlying dangers.

By night The harbour can be reached using the following lights:

Bull Point Fl(3)10s54m25M + F.R.48m12M
Lantern Hill F.R.39m6M
Ilfracombe Pier 2F.G(vert)

Approaching Ilfracombe

Ilfracombe inner harbour, looking back towards entrance from lifeboat slip

Ilfracombe outer harbour

Entrance

Entrance is made between Lantern Hill and Hillsborough, the headland to the east of the harbour, keeping close to the pier to avoid the rocks to the south of the harbour. The whole of the outer harbour is accessible at half-tide. The inner harbour is available for 2 hours either side of HW.

Moorings

Visitors' moorings are available in the outer harbour. Anchorage is also possible, keeping clear of the pier to allow passenger boats to manoeuvre.

Berthing

There is limited space available alongside the quays in the inner harbour.

Harbourmaster

Office on the quay to the northeast of the inner harbour.

Charges

There are harbour charges.

Facilities

Fuel Diesel by can from the chandlery in the southwest corner of the harbour. Petrol from filling stations on both main roads out of the town centre, each a 20-minute walk from the harbour.

Water By hose from quay (by arrangement with harbourmaster) or from tap by car park on main pier.

Slip At west end of inner harbour, although this must be kept clear for the lifeboat.

Provisions Occasional shop selling provisions amongst the plethora of gift shops, fast food outlets and restaurants.

Post office St James Place.

Yacht club Ilfracombe Yacht Club, in attractive premises over the harbourmaster's office on the quay. Bar, showers and washing facilities.

Chandlery Harbour Chandlery and Marine, on the quay in the southwest corner of the harbour.

Calor Gas Harbour Chandlery and Marine.

Refuse disposal Bins on the quay.

WATERMOUTH COVE

Depths in Metres

Approaching Watermouth Cove

Watermouth Cove, looking back towards entrance

Watermouth Cove

Waypoint 51°13'·4N 4°04'·5W ½M N of harbour entrance
Local High Water is Dover −0525
Charts Admiralty *1164, 1165, 1179*; Imray *C58, C59*

General

A narrow haven, drying to sand and fine shingle, 4 cables east of Rillage Point. There is a small holiday camp at the head of the cove, close to Watermouth Castle.

Warning

There is always water at the entrance to the cove, but the moorings within the cove are only available for 2½ hours either side of HW. The harbour is sheltered to all but the strongest northwest winds. The tide runs strongly across the entrance to the harbour, and conditions with contrary winds can produce rough water.

Approach

By day There are conspicuous cottages on Rillage Point (4 cables west of the harbour) and an observation post on Widmouth Head, immediately to the west of the entrance. The circular stone pill box on Burrow Nose, immediately to the east of the entrance, is conspicuous when approaching from the east.

By night A night approach and entrance should not be attempted.

Anchorage in the approach

Anchorage is possible within the harbour entrance at all states of the tide.

Entrance

Entrance to the harbour is made between Widmouth Head to the west and the lower Burrow Nose to the east.

Moorings

Visitors' moorings within the harbour are indicated by the red buoys with yellow handles.

Harbourmaster

The harbourmaster can be contacted at the chandlery at the head of the cove, and should be reported to on arrival.

Charges

There are harbour charges.

Facilities

Water Tap on wall of chandlery.
Slip There are two slips at the head of the cove.
Yacht club Watermouth Yacht Club, at the head of the cove.
Chandlery Watermouth Marine Services, adjacent to the yacht club.

Combe Martin Bay

Temporary anchorage is available in 6 metres off the village of Combe Martin.

Lynmouth

Waypoint 51°14'·6N 3°49'·6W ½M N of harbour entrance
Population 2,075 (1981)
Local High Water is Dover −0515
Charts Admiralty *1165, 1179*; Imray *C59*

General

One of Devon's most picturesque resorts, Lynmouth has a small drying harbour which should only be visited in the most settled conditions.

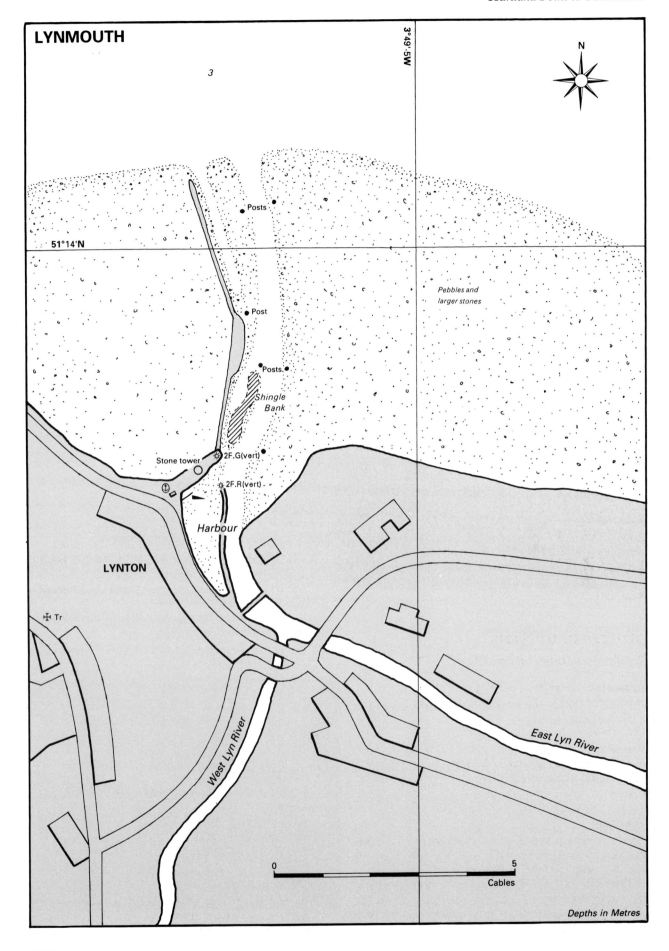

LYNMOUTH

3°49'·5W

3

51°14'N

Posts

Post

Posts·

Pebbles and larger stones

Shingle Bank

Stone tower ⚹ 2F.G(vert)

⚓ ⚹ 2F.R(vert)

Harbour

LYNTON

☦ Tr

West Lyn River

East Lyn River

0   5

Cables

Depths in Metres

Lynmouth harbour, looking back towards entrance at low water

Warning

Entrance should only be made within one hour of HW. The east quay formed by the river training wall is covered at HW springs. The harbour is only available to shallow-draught craft at neaps and becomes uncomfortable if there is any north in the wind. Strong winds create a surge, making the harbour untenable.

Approach

By day From the green conical Sand Ridge buoy, 1½ miles west of Foreland Point, head directly for the poles marking the entrance to the harbour.

By night A night approach and entrance should not be attempted.

Anchorage in the approach

Anchorage may be had in 6 metres in Lynmouth Bay only in settled conditions.

Entrance

The line of the river is marked by timber posts as far as the harbour entrance.

Berthing

Visitors should tie alongside the east quay, although this is covered at HW springs.

Harbourmaster

Office on the quay above the slip.

Charges

There are harbour charges.

Facilities

Slip In northwest corner of harbour.

Foreland Point

The most prominent headland on this stretch of coastline has a lighthouse with a white round tower (Fl(4)15s67m18M). Foreland Ledge lies parallel to the coast ¾ mile north of Foreland Point. In strong tidal conditions with contrary winds there are dangerous overfalls extending over a mile to the northwest and northeast of the point.

Porlock Weir

Waypoint 51°13'·6N 3°37'·6W ½M N of harbour entrance
Local High Water is Dover −0455
Charts Admiralty *1160, 1165, 1179*; Imray *C59*

General

A small, well sheltered drying harbour, surrounded by an attractive grouping of buildings, lying 1½ miles from the village of Porlock.

Warning

The harbour can only be entered for 2 hours either side of HW.

Approach

By day Porlock Bay can be approached from any direction. There are no offlying dangers.

By night A night approach and entrance should not be attempted.

Anchorage in the approach

Anchorage may be had in 5 metres shingle in Porlock Bay in settled conditions.

Approaching Porlock Weir

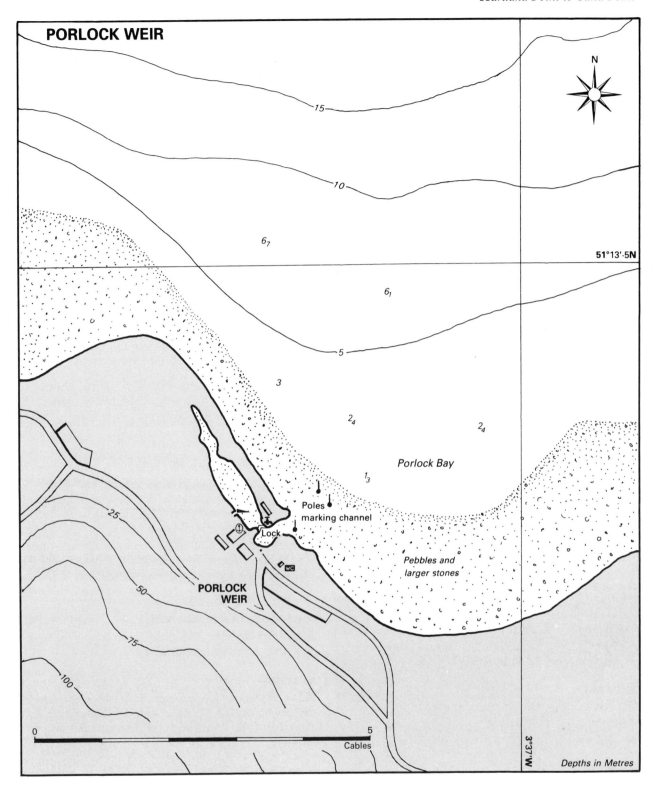

PORLOCK WEIR

51°13′·5N

Porlock Bay

Poles
marking channel

Lock

Pebbles and
larger stones

PORLOCK
WEIR

3°37′·W

Depths in Metres

0   5
Cables

Entrance

The harbour entrance and channel are marked with poles, painted red and white, and green and white. They have been painted and positioned in such a way that the red and white posts must be left to port and the green and white posts to starboard both when entering and when leaving the harbour. There is a steep pebble bank to either side of the narrow entrance.

Moorings

There is limited mooring space in the outer pool.

Berthing

Keel boats may lie alongside the southwest quay in the inner harbour, although the space available is again limited.

Harbourmaster

Office at southwest corner of inner harbour.

Charges

There are harbour charges.

Facilities

Water From tap by lock gates to inner harbour.
Slip On west side of inner harbour.

Entrance to Porlock Weir at low water, showing channel marker poles

Porlock Weir: the pool at low water

Provisions Limited provisions in Porlock Weir. Full range of shops in Porlock, 1½ miles away. Restaurant and bar snacks are available at the hotel overlooking the harbour.
Post office In Porlock.

Minehead

Waypoint 51°13'·1N 3°28'·1W 3 cables NNE of pierhead
Population 11,211 (1981)
Local High Water is Dover −0450
Charts Admiralty *1160, 1165, 1179*; Imray *C59*

General

A popular holiday resort, dominated by a large holiday camp at its eastern end. The drying harbour is set apart from the bustle of the town and provides good shelter in all except east winds, although seas have been known to break over the pier at MHWS during inshore gales. The harbour is busy in the summer months.

Warning

The harbour can only be entered for 2 hours either side of HW.

Approach

By day The harbour is best approached from the north or northwest to avoid the drying shingle bank ½ mile ENE of the pier. The holiday camp to the east of the harbour is conspicuous.
By night Approach at night can be made with care. The lights of the holiday camp are conspicuous; the Fl(2)G.5s4M light at the end of the pier must be identified.

Anchorage in the approach

Anchorage may be had (in 4 metres, north of the pier) only in settled conditions.

Entrance

Leave the green-topped beacon marking the end of the sewer outfall to starboard, and keep 200 feet away from the pierhead until able to turn into the harbour.

Moorings

There are no visitors' moorings, although it is possible to anchor away from the moorings belonging to resident boats.

Berthing

Visitors can lie alongside the pier wall. There are good ladders; the harbour dries to a firm bottom of sand, mud and small stones. Visitors planning an

Minehead harbour at low water

extended stop and capable of taking the bottom will be moved up closer to the slip to dry out onto firm sand.

Harbourmaster

Office on north side of harbour.

Charges

There are harbour charges.

Facilities

Fuel Only from filling station about 1 mile from harbour.
Water From tap by harbourmaster's office.
Slip On west side of harbour.
Provisions Full range of shops in town centre, ½ mile from harbour.
Post office The Avenue, in the town centre.
Refuse disposal Litter bins on quay.

Watchet

Waypoint 51°11'·5N 3°19'·7W ½M N of harbour entrance
Population 3,357 (1981)
Local High Water is Dover −0450
Charts Admiralty *1160, 1152, 1179*; Imray *C59*

General

An old-established commercial port with a well sheltered drying harbour which can take vessels of up to 2,500 tons.

Warning

Entrance to the harbour can only be made up to 2½ hours either side of HW.

Approach

By day The two radio masts to the southwest are very conspicuous. When approaching from the north, Culver Sand must be avoided.

To clear the offlying rocks it is advisable to keep ½ mile offshore until the entrance between the piers is well open. The harbour should then be approached directly.

By night The harbour can be approached using the following lights:
Lynmouth Foreland Fl(4)15s67m18M
West pierhead F.G.9m9M
East pierhead 2F.R(vert)3M

Entrance

The harbour is entered between the two stone piers. The F.G light at the end of the west pier is displayed from a red tower. Allowance should be made for the strong currents that can be experienced close to the west pier, especially on the ebb.

Anchorage in the approach

Anchorage is available in Blue Anchor Roads (1 mile to the west of the harbour) in settled conditions.

Berthing

Visitors should lie alongside the west quay, where there are good ladders. The harbour dries to soft mud and is well sheltered.

Harbourmaster

Office on the quay in the southeast corner of the harbour.

Charges

There are harbour charges.

Watchet harbour

Facilities

Fuel There is no filling station in Watchet; the nearest is over 2 miles from the harbour.

Water Water tap in gents' toilet at south end of west quay.

Slip On south side of harbour.

Provisions There is a good range of shops in the town.

Post office In town centre.

Yacht club Watchet Boat Owners' Association, at south end of west quay.

Chandlery Limited chandlery available from Swantel's, at the south end of the west quay.

Calor Gas and Camping Gaz Available from Swantel's.

Refuse disposal Refuse bin by toilets at south end of west quay.

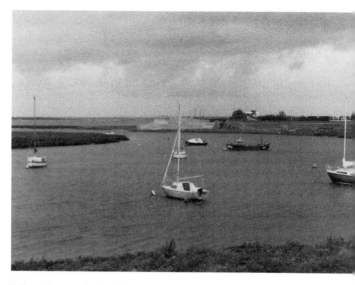

Safe anchorages in the river Brue, Burnham-on-Sea

Burnham-on-Sea

Position 51°15'·0N 3°00'·0W
Population 17,341 (1981)
Local High Water is Dover −0430
Charts Admiralty *1152, 1179*; Imray *C59*

General

A holiday resort offering sheltered moorings as a reward for negotiating the shoals of Bridgwater Bay.

Warning

Approach should only be made within 3 hours of HW. Entry should not be attempted in strong on-shore winds.

Approach

By day Bridgwater Bay is entered between Stoke Bluff and Brean Down, a bold promontory 10 miles to the northeast. It is necessary to locate the Gore bell buoy. Hinkley Point power station to the south is very conspicuous.

By night Entry is possible at night, as the buoys and leading marks are lit; however, it is not advisable without local knowledge.

Anchorage in the approach

Yachts can lie afloat in 3 metres approximately 3 cables east of No. 2 buoy.

Entrance

From the Gore bell buoy, a course of 80° is made towards Brent Knoll (133 metres; 2 miles ENE of Burnham) along the buoyed channel before picking up the leading marks: the old light tower with the main lighthouse beyond. The lighthouse should be

kept just open to the south of the old tower until the church tower (5 cables south of the lighthouse) and the white mark on the sea wall are in line on a bearing of 112°.

Moorings

The anchorage off the town is protected by Stert Island, but the best shelter is to be found in the River Brue. The river is best entered 2½ hours before HW, and dries to soft mud. There are moorings near the yacht club slipway for deep-keel boats.

Facilities

Water There are water taps in the public toilets by the yacht club.

Slip In the River Brue, by the yacht club.

Provisions There is a good range of shops in the town.

Post office In the town centre.

Yacht club Burnham-on-Sea Yacht Club, at the entrance to the River Brue.

Depths in Metres

3°0'W

10

5

≤7

2F.G(vert)

Birnbeck
Island

25

50

75

Anchor Head

WC

Bn

WESTON
-SUPER-
MARE

51°21'N

6₁

Mud

2F.G(vert)

4₉

N

7₃

0   1000

Metres

WESTON-SUPER-MARE

Weston-super-Mare

Position 51°20'·8N 2°59'·3W
Population 62,261 (1981)
Local High Water is Dover −0435
Charts Admiralty *1152, 1176, 1179*; Imray *C59*

General

A popular holiday resort that expanded rapidly in Victorian times. Knightstone Harbour, at the north end of Weston Bay, dries to a bottom of small stones and firm mud, and is sheltered from all directions except south.

Warning

The harbour should only be entered up to 2 hours either side of HW.

Approach

By day Weston Bay is entered between Brean Down and Anchor Head. The whole of the bay dries to mud in a line from the centre of Brean Down to the west extremity of Birnbeck Island.

By night The harbour can be reached using the following light:

Grand Pier 2F.G(vert)

Entrance

Direct entrance, leaving the Grand Pier to starboard, and the causeway at the entrance to the harbour (marked with a beacon) to port.

Moorings

The yacht club should be contacted to ascertain which of the vacant moorings in the harbour are available. Sheltered moorings can be found in the River Axe, at the south end of Weston Bay. Entrance to the river, which dries to soft mud, is possible for 2 hours either side of HW, leaving Black Rock to port.

Berthing

Raft alongside the yacht club dolphin, leaving room alongside the slip for local boatmen.

Facilities

Slip In north corner of harbour.
Provisions Full range of shops in town.
Post office In town centre.
Yacht club Weston Bay Yacht Club.

The quay at Weston-super-Mare

III. Upper reaches of the Bristol Channel and the River Severn

Clevedon Pill

Position 51°25'·8N 2°52'·8W
Population 18,099 (1981)
Local High Water is Dover −0420
Charts Admiralty *1176, 1179*; Imray *C59*

General

Clevedon Pill lies ¾ mile southwest of the holiday resort of Clevedon, and offers a limited number of drying moorings on the banks of the pill by arrangement with the Clevedon Sailing Club.

Warning

The pill should only be entered between 2½ hours either side of HW. The moorings at the entrance to the pill are exposed to the west, although the moorings further up the pill offer good shelter. The damaged pier 1 mile northeast of Clevedon Pill must be given a wide berth. The tide runs at 3½ knots at springs.

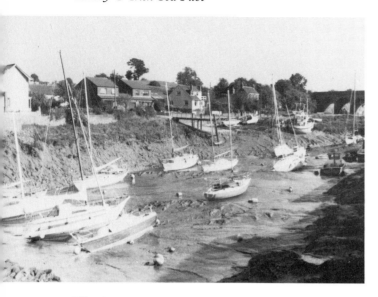

Pill at low water

Approach

By day From Sand Point to Clevedon, shoals with drying patches extend up to 3 miles offshore. There is a conspicuous radio mast 6½ cables southeast of Wain's Hill.

By night A night approach and entrance should not be attempted.

Entrance

Entrance is made between Wain's Hill and Blackstone Rocks, the channel being marked with withies.

Moorings

Moorings are available on the banks of the pill by arrangement with Clevedon Sailing Club. The banks are steep and dry to soft mud.

Facilities

Slip The slip at the head of the pill can be used at HW springs.
Provisions From town centre, ¾ mile from the pill.
Yacht club Clevedon Sailing Club, on the promenade in Clevedon Bay.

Walton Bay

Anchorage is prohibited off the conspicuous fuel storage tanks 6 cables northeast of Walton Bay.

Black Nore Point

Black Nore Point lies 1·2 miles WSW of Portishead Point, with a light (Fl(2)10s15M) shown from a white tower on a framework base.

Portishead

Position 51°29'·7N 2°45'·1W
Population 13,867 (1981)
Local High Water is Dover −0405
Charts Admiralty *1176, 1179*; Imray *C59*

General

Except in an emergency, yachts are not allowed to enter Portishead, Avonmouth or Royal Portbury Docks. Shelter from southwest winds can be had temporarily off Portishead Dock, at the direction of the dockmaster.

Warning

The approaches to the dock dry 2 hours either side of HW to soft mud. The approach is exposed to north to northeast winds, which will create choppy conditions and make taking the ground inadvisable. The dock is used for commercial shipping, and yachts should not be left unattended in the approach.

Approach

By day The chimneys of Portishead power station are very conspicuous. The Firefly Rocks, with a least depth of 0·9 metre, lie 2 cables NNW of Portishead Pier head. A green conical bell buoy marks their north extremity and should be rounded before approaching the pier.

By night The dock may be approached at night using the following lights:
Portishead Point Q(3)10s9m16M Horn 20s
Firefly buoy Fl(2)G.5s
Portishead Pier Iso.G.2s5m3M Horn 15s

Anchorage

Anchor at the direction of the dockmaster to the east of the outer pier. Do not moor close to the permanent yacht moorings in the 'Hole', where there are some drastic changes in level.

Anchorage off Portishead at low water. The boats shown in the photograph above have 'vanished' into the hole, leaving just their masts showing

PORTISHEAD

N

2°45'W

51°30'N

Depths in Metres

Outer
I.Q.G.12s
G

2₁

10

4

Firefly
Fl(2)G.5s
G
Bell

Iso.G.2s3M
Horn 15s

The 'Hole'
7₉

8₉

3₁
Anchorage
Prohibited

Lock

Chimney's

Chimneys
(119)

Portishead
Dock

5

15

15

20

King Road

Newcome
Fl(3)R.10s
R

Q(3)10s16M
Horn 20s

Portishead
Point

Woodhall
Bay

10

5

51

Anchorage off Portishead at high water

VHF radio telephone

Call *Avonmouth Radio* on Ch 16, work Ch 12 or 14.
Call *Portishead Dock* on Ch 16, work Ch 12 or 14
(HW−2½ to HW+1½).

Turning into the basin leading to the city centre at Bristol.
Visitors' moorings on right-hand quay

Bristol

Position 51°27'·0N 2°37'·0W
Population 420,234 (1981)
Local High Water (Avonmouth) is Dover −0405
Charts Admiralty *1859, 1176*; Imray *C59*

General

Bristol City Docks provide floating moorings along-side the quay in the heart of Bristol, after navigating the River Avon for 5½ miles from Avonmouth Docks.

Approach

On approaching Avonmouth Docks, contact Avonmouth Radio for instructions to enter the River Avon. Alternatively, Avonmouth signal station should be signalled with international flag 'R' or letter 'R' by Morse. Reply will be by light or loud-hailer.

The tidal stream off the entrance to the River Avon runs at up to 5 knots at springs (being stronger on the flood) and 3 knots at neaps.

Do not enter the river until 2 hours before HW. Enter the river leaving the commercial dock to port, keeping close to the south pier until the leading marks (white posts) are in line on 127°. These should be kept in line until approaching the next bend, from where yachts should keep to the centre of the channel.

There is limited mooring space available at Pill, the creek drying to soft mud, but mooring is only advisable with prior local knowledge.

City centre moorings in floating harbour at Bristol

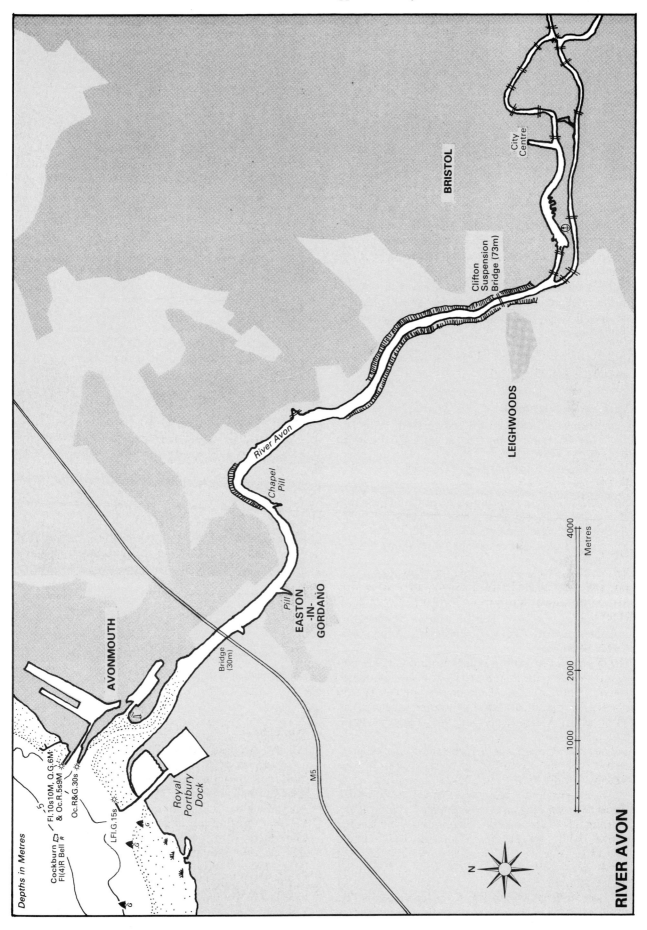

Depths in Metres

Cockburn ⌑ Fl.10s10M, Q.G.6M
Fl(4)R Bell R & Oc.R.5s9M
Oc.R&G.30s
LFl.G.15s

AVONMOUTH

Royal Portbury Dock

Bridge (30m)

M5

EASTON
-IN-
GORDANO

Pill

Chapel Pill

River Avon

LEIGHWOODS

Clifton Suspension Bridge (73m)

BRISTOL

City Centre

N

Metres

4000

2000

1000

RIVER AVON

Traffic signals are exhibited at two positions on the east bank of the river, 1½ and 2½ cables above Clifton Suspension Bridge. A fixed green light signifies 'come ahead with caution'; a fixed red light signifies 'stop and await orders'. Yachts should arrive at the Cumberland Basin entrance to the City Dock by HW. There are usually 3 lockings either way as from HW −2 hours 50 minutes. Yachts can lie alongside the pontoons before the docking signal at the Cumberland Basin entrance.

When proceeding inwards there will be less turbulence at the seaward end of the lock.

Moorings

Quayside moorings, as instructed by the dockmaster.

Dockmaster and office

Duty dockmaster's office is on south quay of entrance lock to Cumberland Basin. Dock office at Underfall Yard, on south side of City Docks by Junction Lock.

Charges

There are harbour charges.

VHF radio telephone

Call *Avonmouth Radio* on Ch 16, work Ch 12 or 14.
Call *City Docks Radio* on Ch 16, work Ch 12 or 14 (HW−3 to HW+1).

Facilities

Fuel Bristol Marina, on south side of City Docks.
Water At various points around City Docks.
Electricity At various points around City Docks.
Provisions Full range of shops, restaurants etc. in town centre.
Showers At the dock office and at Bristol Marina.
Chandlery Bristol Marine Engineering Centre and Bristol Yacht Centre.
Boat repairs, engineers Bristol Marine Engineering Centre; David Abel's, boatbuilders; Albion Marine Services.
Refuse disposal At various points around City Docks.

Leading marks north of the shoots in the river Severn, above Avonmouth

River Severn above Avonmouth

The Shoots

A narrow passage, only 1½ cables wide at its narrowest part, 4 miles north of Avonmouth Dock. An extensive area of rock, the English Stones, lies to the east of The Shoots; its southwest end is marked by a pole with a green topmark and its northwest end by a pole with a west cardinal topmark. Leading marks for The Shoots are the white stone beacon on Charston Rock and the Redcliffe beacon, a white lantern on a black metal framework tower, 9 cables NNE of Charston Rock.

Oldbury Pill

A pill drying to soft mud ½ mile south of the conspicuous Oldbury Power Station. Thornbury Sailing Club occupies conspicuous premises on the north bank of the pill. Entrance should only be made between 2 hours either side of HW. Visiting yachts requiring moorings should contact the club in advance.

Oldbury Pill at low water

Sharpness

Yachts can pass through the locked entrance to the commercial docks and into the marina at the entrance to the Gloucester and Berkeley Canal. The lock normally operates HW−2½ to HW+½. Yachts should arrive off Sharpness at about HW−1.

Tidal streams run at up to 6 knots at springs off Sharpness, with the flood beginning 2 hours before HW at Avonmouth and the ebb beginning 1 hour after HW at Avonmouth.

For VHF radio telephone, call Sharpness Control on Ch 16, work Ch 14.

Diesel fuel, water, *Calor Gas* and chandlery are available from Sharpness Marine, at the marina.

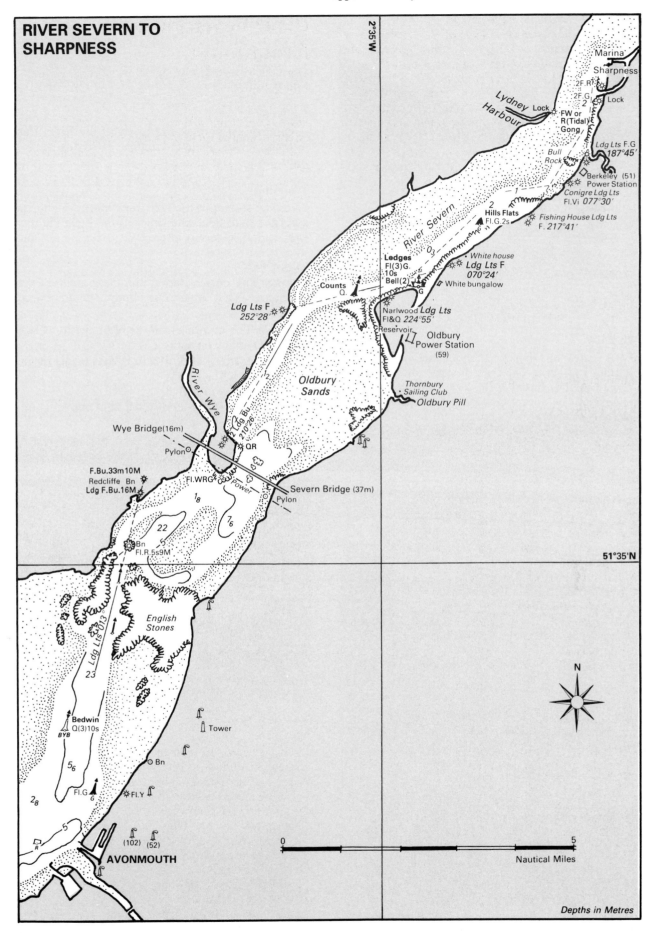

RIVER SEVERN TO SHARPNESS

2°35'W

Marina
Sharpness
2F.R
2F.G
Lydney Harbour
Lock
Lock
FW or R(Tidal) Gong
Ldg Lts F.G 187°45'
Bull Rock
Berkeley (51) Power Station
River Severn
Conigre Ldg Lts Fl.Vi 077°30'
Hills Flats Fl.G.2s
Fishing House Ldg Lts F. 217°41'
0 3
White house
Ledges Fl(3)G. 10s Bell(2)
Ldg Lts F 070°24'
Counts Q.
G
White bungalow
Ldg Lts F 252°28'
Narlwood *Ldg Lts* Fl&Q 224°55'
Reservoir
Oldbury Power Station (59)
Oldbury Sands
Thornbury Sailing Club
Oldbury Pill
River Wye
Ldg Bn 210°26'
Wye Bridge(16m)
Pylon
QR
F.Bu.33m10M
Redcliffe Bn
Ldg F.Bu.16M
Fl.WRG
Power
Severn Bridge (37m)
Pylon
1 8
7 6
22
Bn Fl.R.5s9M
5
Ldg Lts 013°
English Stones
23
Bedwin Q(3)10s
BYB
Tower
5 6
Bn
Fl.G G
Fl.Y
2 8
5
(102) (52)
R
AVONMOUTH

51°35'N

N

0 ——————————— 5
Nautical Miles

Depths in Metres

55

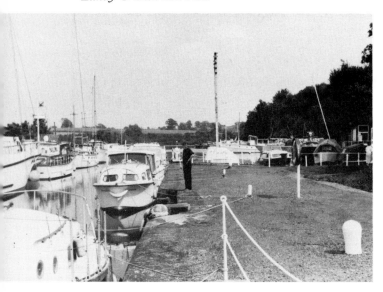

Sharpness marina

Lydney

Lock gates opening for 1 hour before HW give entrance to about one mile of canal offering secure moorings. The future of the lock is uncertain, and it should not be approached prior to checking locally as to its availability. Anchoring off the lock entrance is not possible, due to the strength of the tidal stream.

Entrance to Lydney harbour

Newport

Waypoint 51°31'·3N 2°58'·4W start of entrance channel
Local High Water is Dover −0420
Charts Admiralty *1176, 1152, 1179*; Imray *C59*

General

A commercial port on the banks of the River Usk, offering yachts sheltered moorings drying to soft mud.

Warning

The tidal stream in the river runs at 4 to 5 knots at springs at half-tide. Moorings off the yacht club dry to soft mud 3½ hours after HW.

Approach

By day The power station chimneys are very conspicuous. The West Usk buoy should be approached directly.

By night The moorings can be approached at night using the following lights:

East Usk lighthouse Fl(2)WRG.10s11m15/11M +
Oc.WRG.10s10m11/9M
West Usk buoy Q.R Bell
English & Welsh Grounds pillar light buoy
LFl.10s Bell + Whis Racon(0)
No. 1 buoy Q.G
No. 2 and No. 4 buoys Fl.R.3s
No. 3 and No. 5 buoys Fl.G.3s
Alexandra Dock South Lock
West pierhead 2F.R(vert)9m6M Horn 60s
East pierhead 2F.G(vert)9m6M
Julian's Pill leading lights 057° F.G.4M

Entrance to Newport

Yacht moorings in river Usk, Newport, at low water

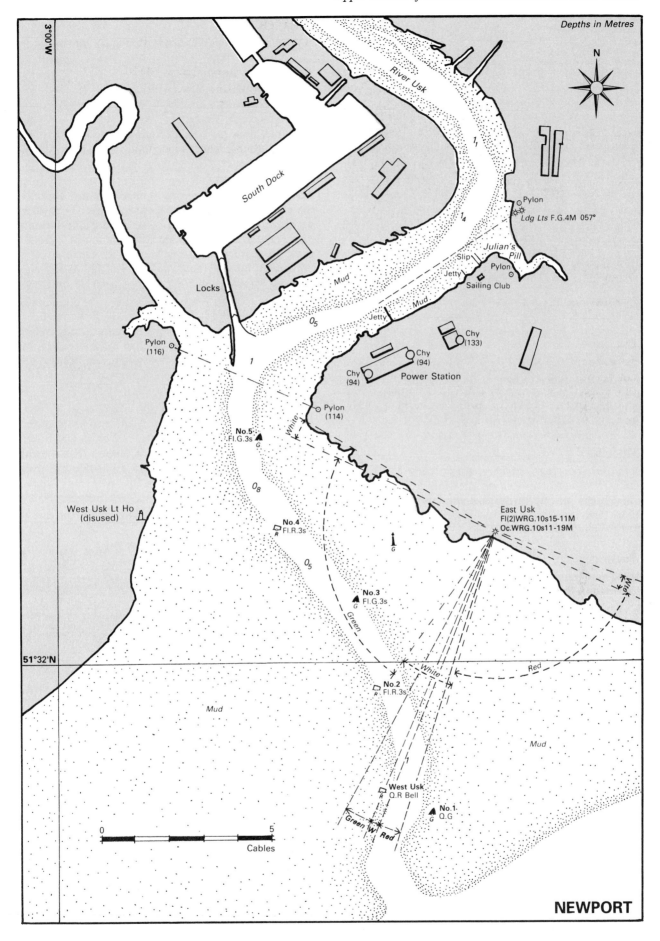

3°00'W

Depths in Metres

N

River Usk

1₁

South Dock

1₄

Pylon

Ldg Lts F.G.4M 057°

Julian's Pill

Slip

Jetty

Pylon

Sailing Club

Mud

Locks

0₅

Jetty

Mud

Chy (133)

Chy (94)

1

Pylon (116)

Chy (94)

Power Station

Pylon (114)

White

No.5
Fl.G.3s G

East Usk
Fl(2)WRG.10s15-11M
Oc.WRG.10s11-19M

0₈

West Usk Lt Ho
(disused)

No.4
R Fl.R.3s

0₅

White

Green

No.3
Fl.G.3s G

G

1

51°32'N

White

Red

No.2
R Fl.R.3s

Mud

Mud

0   5

Cables

West Usk
R Q.R Bell

No.1
G Q.G

Green W Red

NEWPORT

Cardiff, looking towards clock tower

Entrance

Follow the buoyed channel to the South Lock entrance, then follow the river to the northeast. The moorings lie on the south side of the river, beyond the power station pier.

Moorings

Visitors' moorings, drying to soft mud 3½ hours after HW, are available on the sloping river bank. Keel boats can lie in the soft mud of Julian's Pill. Only temporary mooring for watering etc. is permitted alongside the pontoon.

Anchorage

It is possible to anchor immediately outside the moorings. An anchor light is essential at night.

Facilities

Water From the end of the sailing club pontoon.
Slip The slip by the sailing club is accessible at most states of the tide.
Yacht club Newport and Uskmouth Sailing Club.

Cardiff

Waypoint 51°26'·0N 3°08'·7W start of entrance channel
Population 273,537 (1981)
Local High Water is Dover −0425
Charts Admiralty *1182, 1152, 1179*; Imray *C59*

General

The capital city of Wales is a commercial port where yachts may find good shelter. Cardiff was formerly one of the largest ports in the world; its early prosperity was based on coal. The docks are approximately 2 miles from the town centre. The yacht moorings dry to soft mud. The Cardiff Bay Barrage plans recently approved by Parliament will radically alter the nature of the subsequently enclosed harbours and ensure the future of the bay as a major yachting venue.

Warning

There is a dredged channel to beyond the entrance to Queen's Dock; however, the moorings beyond dry to soft mud, with the pontoon at the head of the bay accessible for 3 hours either side of HW.

Approach

By day The Ranie buoy marks the extremity of the rocks and sand spit off Lavernock Point. The South Cardiff cardinal bell buoy marks the south extremity of the Cardiff Grounds. From a position between the two buoys make directly for the Outer Wrach west cardinal buoy.

By night The harbour can be reached making use of the following lights:
Monkstone lighthouse Fl.5s13m12M
Ranie buoy Fl(2)R.5s
Cardiff Docks leading lights 349°
Front F.4m17M
Rear F.24m17M
South Cardiff buoy Q(6)+LFl.15s Bell
Mid Cardiff buoy Fl(3)G.10s
Penarth Pier 2F.R(vert)8m3M
Outer Wrach buoy Q(9)15s
Penarth Head buoy Q.R

Yacht harbour at Cardiff at low water, looking from the clock tower with the floating pontoon on the left

Depths in Metres

3°10'W

Clock
Tower

Pontoon

F.17M

River Taff

Mud

Queen's Dock

0₆

R

R

2F.R

G

2F.G

51°27'N

R

G

Mud

Cambrian Marine
Services boatyard

Pontoon

1₂

4₃

G

Inner Wrach
Fl.G

G

Penarth Marina

Lock

0₉

Penarth
Head

R Q.R

PENARTH

Outer Wrach
Q(9)15s
YBY

0₉

2F.R(vert)

0 5
Cables

Slip

Outfall

2₁

CARDIFF AND PENARTH

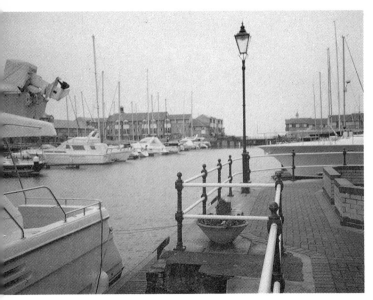

Penarth Marina

Inner Wrach buoy Fl.G
Queen's Dock
South pierhead 2F.G(vert) Dia 60s
North pierhead 2F.R(vert)

Entrance

The channel is buoyed to the yacht moorings with painted oil drums beyond the entrance to Queen's Dock.

Moorings

Visitors' moorings by prior arrangement with the yacht club. All moorings dry to soft mud.

Berthing

There is a limited amount of space at the end of the pontoon for temporary berthing.

Facilities

Fuel Diesel fuel may be obtained from Castletown Oils, Collingwood Road. First right out of dock gates, approximately ½ mile from yacht club pontoon.
Water Tap at side of yacht club.
Electricity At the head of the slip.
Slip By yacht club.
Provisions Some shops near dock entrance. Town centre approximately 2 miles from docks.
Yacht club Cardiff Yacht Club.
Boat engineers The docks have numerous mechanical and electrical engineers.

Penarth

There are numerous moorings in the River Ely, and visitors may tie to the floating pontoon by the Penarth Motor Boat and Sailing Club. The pontoon dries to soft mud.

PENARTH MARINA

A well sheltered marina, offering 420 fully serviced berths, within the former Penarth Dock.

Approach

The marina is approached by following the pilotage information for Cardiff until midway between the small port-hand buoy and the Inner Wrack buoy, when a course is shaped to the marina's port-hand round pink entrance buoy. There is a dolphin pier to the N of the entrance channel.

Drying moorings on the River Ely

Entrance

The lock gates have traffic signals to control boat movements. The lock is not opened until there is 1.5m over the entrance sill. Entrance is restricted to within 3½ to 4 hours either side of HW. When the pink entrance buoy is afloat, there is 1.5m over the sill.

Anchorage in the approach

In unsettled conditions it is possible to wait inside the entrance to Queen's Dock, as long as the lock gates are not obstructed.

Berthing

As directed by the berthing master. There are always visitors' berths available.

Charges
There are marina charges.

VHF radio telephone
Call *Camper Base* on Ch 80.

Facilities
Fuel Fuelling pontoons in inner basin.
Water On all pontoons.
Toilets and showers In Marina Services Building for Outer Basin and Inner Basin Services Building.
Provisions Full provisions available in Penarth, about 10 minutes' walk from the marina.
Brokerage Penarth Boat Sales, by Marina Services Building.
Boat repairs and engineers Wigmore Wright Marine Services, The Boatyard, Marina Inner Basin. Cambrian Marine Services, River Ely.
Marine electronics RGB Electronics, Penarth.

IV. Lavernock Point to Worms Head

Barry

Waypoint 51°23'·0N 3°15'·5W ½M S of harbour
  entrance
Population 46,520 (1981)
Local High Water is Dover −0430
Charts Admiralty *1182, 1152, 1179*; Imray *C59*

General

A holiday resort, with a large holiday camp close to
the commercial docks. The outer harbour to the
commercial docks is popular with yachtsmen, and
there is sufficient water to enter at all states of the
tide.

Warning

The outer harbour provides good shelter except in
strong east or southeast winds, when yachts are
advised to enter the docks (by prior arrangement).
Although it is possible to enter the harbour at all
times, the bays to the east and west of the outer
harbour dry to soft mud at LW.

Approach

By day Sully Island and Bendrick Rock, to the east
of the harbour, must both be passed to seaward;
otherwise the approach is straightforward. The
white round tower of the lighthouse is conspicuous
at the head of the west breakwater.

By night The harbour can be approached and en-
tered using the following lights:
West breakwater Fl.2·5s12m10M
East breakwater Q.G.7m8M

Entrance

Straightforward entrance between the two breakwaters. Keep clear of commercial traffic at all times.
The dock can only be entered for 3 hours either side
of HW.

Moorings

There are no moorings for visitors, but many owners will allow visiting yachts alongside, although
they may not be left there unattended or overnight.
Yachts wishing to stay for any length of time should
contact the yacht club.

Berthing

Anchorage is possible in the east bay of the outer
harbour, which dries to soft mud.

Barry harbour, looking back towards entrance

Charges

There are no harbour charges in the outer harbour.

VHF radio telephone

Call Barry Radio on Ch 16, work Ch 10, 11 or 22
(HW−4 to HW+4).

Facilities

Fuel Diesel fuel from Ray Harris Marine.
Water Tap by slip with hose extension out to side of
  lifeboat slipway.
Slip On west side of outer harbour.
Provisions Good range of local shops.
Yacht club Barry Yacht Club, with lounges, bar,
  toilets and showers.
Chandlery and repairs Ray Harris Marine, by the
  slipway.
Sailmakers and riggers Breaksea, No. 1 Dock, Barry.

Barry Old Harbour

The old harbour lies 1 mile west of the main harbour and is rapidly silting. It is exposed to south
winds and dries to firm sand.

Breaksea Point

A low headland 5½ miles west of Barry main harbour, with three very conspicuous power station
chimneys. A low concrete tower with a domed top
stands ½ mile SSW of the point, with a red buoy to
its south side.

51°24'N

Dock

Dock

Swing
bridge

Lock

Dock

Lock

N

Bendrick
Rock (2)

Mud

Lifeboat

Mud

Q.G.8M

BARRY ISLAND

Lt Ho
Fl.2·5s10M

Barry Roads

Whitemore
Bay

CGFS

Nell's Point

3°15'W

0 — 5
Cables

BARRY

Depths in Metres

Tower and chimneys at Breaksea Point

Nash Point

A prominent headland 5½ miles WNW of Breaksea Point. The white round tower of Nash lighthouse (Fl(2)WR.10s56m21/17M) stands 4 cables ESE of the point, with the white round tower of a disused lighthouse standing on the cliffs of the headland.

Nash Passage

A narrow passage (1 cable wide) running between the east end of Nash Sand and the rocky ledge at the foot of Nash Point. There is a least depth of 6 metres in the fairway. The east-going stream causes heavy overfalls off Nash Point. The east-going stream begins at HW Dover +0130 and the west-going stream begins at HW Dover −0445. The tidal stream runs at up to 5 knots at springs.

Porthcawl

Waypoint 51°28'·0N 3°41'·9W 3 cables S of harbour entrance
Population 15,625 (1981)
Local High Water is Dover −0500
Charts Admiralty *1169, 1165, 1179*; Imray *C59*

General

A former commercial port; now a holiday resort. The commercial trade was ruined by the expansion of Barry harbour. The old dock was filled in to be used as a car park, although the outer harbour remains, with limited space for the use of pleasure craft.

Entrance to Porthcawl

Warning

The harbour should only be entered between 2 hours either side of HW; it dries to soft mud at half-tide.

Approach

By day From the east the approach is through the Nash Passage, between Nash Sand and the rock ledge off Nash Point. Leave the red buoy marking the Tusker Rock (dries to 4·2 metres) to starboard and (heading no more than 312° to avoid Fairy Rock) make for a position 5 cables due south of the lighthouse and then directly for the harbour. Porthcawl lighthouse, at the end of the breakwater, has a white hexagonal tower with a black base .

From the west the ideal approach leaves Scarweather Sands to the north, passing south of the West Scar and South Scar cardinal light buoys. There is a passage to the north between the sands and the Hugo Bank, but this should only be used in settled weather. In such conditions passage may also be made between the Kenfig east cardinal buoy and Sker Point.

In conditions with strong tidal streams and contrary winds, overfalls can build up to the west of Porthcawl Point. Again the approach is to a position 5 cables south, erring west of south, of the lighthouse, and then directly to the harbour.

By night Numerous lights make approach and entrance possible, but the number of offshore hazards, coupled with strong tidal streams, makes this inadvisable without prior local knowledge.

Anchorage in the approach

This is possible off the harbour entrance only in the most settled conditions.

Entrance

Keep close to the end of the breakwater and then close to its north side until near to the slip, before turning north to avoid an old collapsed breakwater, marked with a pole (with a 'keep left' sign) at its south end.

Berthing

There is limited space for visitors to tie alongside the east quay of the harbour.

Harbourmaster

On south side of inner harbour.

Charges

There are harbour charges.

Porthcawl harbour, looking back towards entrance, with warning pole marking end of ruined breakwater clearly visible

Yachts moored in the River Afan, Port Talbot

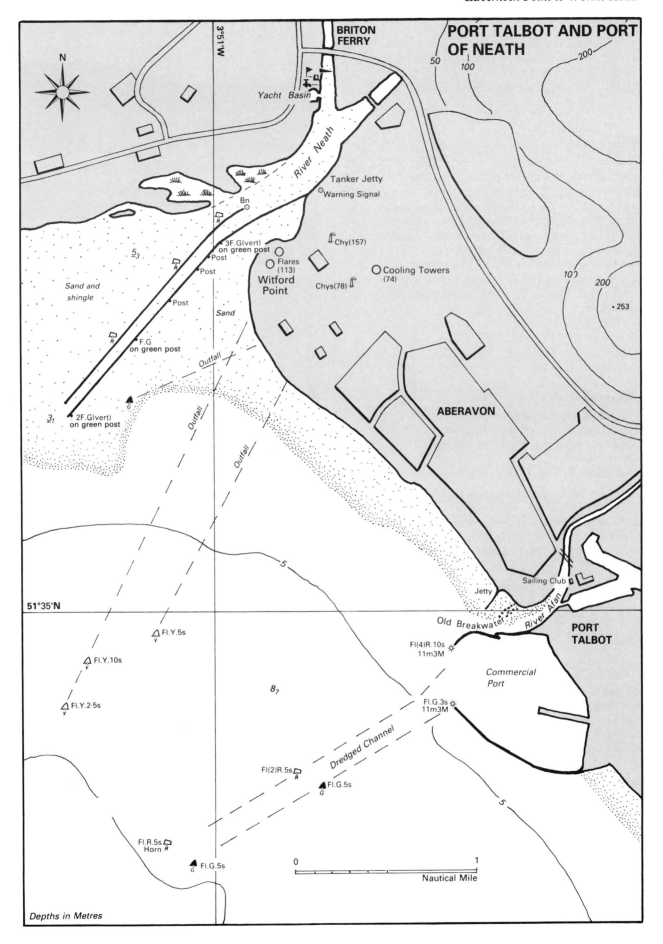

PORT TALBOT AND PORT OF NEATH

BRITON FERRY

Yacht Basin

River Neath

N

3°51'W

50

100

200

Tanker Jetty
Warning Signal

Chy(157)

Cooling Towers
(74)

Chys(78)

Flares
(113)

**Witford
Point**

3F.G(vert)
on green post
Post

Post

Post

F.G
on green post

2F.G(vert)
on green post

Bn
R

R

R

R

G

5₃

*Sand and
shingle*

Sand

Outfall

Outfall

Outfall

3₁

100

200

· 253

ABERAVON

Sailing Club

Jetty

Old Breakwater

River Afan

**PORT
TALBOT**

5

51°35'N

Fl.Y.5s
Y

Fl.Y.10s
Y

Fl.Y.2·5s
Y

8₇

Fl(4)R.10s
11m3M

Fl.G.3s
11m3M

*Commercial
Port*

Fl(2)R.5s
R

Fl.G.5s
G

Dredged Channel

Fl.R.5s
Horn *R*

Fl.G.5s
G

5

5

0

1

Nautical Mile

Depths in Metres

67

Facilities

Slip Alongside the breakwater at its west end.
Provisions Good range of shops in the town centre.
Post office On the main street in the town centre.
Calor Gas and Camping Gaz Protheroe's DIY, in town centre.

Port Talbot

A large commercial port, used principally for the importation of iron ore. The port is prohibited to pleasure craft. There are a number of industrial outfalls in the bay, marked with yellow buoys. The River Afan flows into Swansea Bay on the north side of the north breakwater. The ruins of an old breakwater project from the shore along the north side of the river channel. The Port Talbot Small Boat Club has premises on the east bank of the river ½ mile from the entrance; there are moorings alongside the clubhouse.

Monkstone Cruising and Sailing Club Marina, Port of Neath

Briton Ferry

Position 51°36'·0N 3°52'·0W
Local High Water is Dover −0500
Charts Admiralty *1161, 1179*; Imray *C59*

General

A declining commercial port that offers sheltered accommodation for yachtsmen. The local sailing club have excavated a basin and laid out pontoons for yachts to complement their river moorings, although there is limited space for visitors.

Warning

The River Neath dries out at LW, and entry should only be made between 2½ hours either side of HW. Entrance should not be attempted in strong onshore winds.

Approach

By day Approach is direct across Swansea Bay, and the green post carrying the 2F.G(vert) lights at the head of the training wall must be identified. There is a group of chimneys, cooling towers and flares to the east of the harbour; these are conspicuous.

By night The harbour can be approached and entered by night, using the lights along the training wall. However, this is not recommended without prior local knowledge.

Entrance

A training wall extends 1·8 miles southwest from the harbour, marked with green posts. It should be left close to starboard. The northwest side of the entrance channel is formed by a training bank marked by red buoys. There is a warning signal exhibited from high above the tanker jetty which

Drying moorings outside the Monkstone Cruising and Sailing Club Marina, River Neath

flashes red when a large vessel is manoeuvring; entrance is prohibited until the signal turns green. The sailing club is on the west bank of the river, with the new mooring basin to the south of the clubhouse.

Moorings

There are drying moorings on either side of the slip in front of the clubhouse.

Berthing

There are approximately 70 berths in the new basin, but these are allocated to club members.

Facilities

Water From tap by the clubhouse.
Slip Slip into the river in front of the clubhouse; another at the entrance to the new basin.
Yacht club Monkstone Cruising and Sailing Club.

SWANSEA MARINA

N

River
Tawe

Lock

Marina
Office

Lock

2F.G
(vert)

2F.R
(vert)

Kings
Dock

Traffic
Signals

F.G.6M

West
Pier

Oc.G.4s
5m2M

Shingle

Ldg Lts 020°

Fl(2)R.10s
11m9M

Sand

2F.G(vert)
Siren (30s)

Dredged Channel

Fl.G.2·5s
Bell

G

0   5

Cables

3°56'W

51°36'N

Depths in Metres

69

Swansea

Waypoint 51°35'·5N 3°56'·06W starboard-hand
  buoy 9 cables SSW of East Breakwater head
Population 186,907 (1981)
Local High Water is Dover −0515
Charts Admiralty *1161, 1179*; Imray *C59*

General

A large commercial port which houses the Swansea
Yacht Haven, offering excellent facilities and marina
berthing in former commercial docks. The comple-
tion of the Tawe Barrage has improved access to the
marina and increased the number of berths to 360,
with space available for visitors.

Approach

By day There is a conspicuous radio mast (245
metres) 1·5 miles to the north of the harbour. The
dredged entrance channel should be approached
directly once in Swansea Bay and clear of Mumbles
Head. The tidal stream runs anticlockwise around

Entrance lock, Swansea marina

Swansea marina

Approaching Swansea marina

Swansea Bay for 9½ hours from HW Swansea
−0330 to +0600. During this time a race may form
off Mumbles Head. At the start of the flood tide the
flow reverses, running N round Mumbles Head and
setting towards Swansea from HW Swansea −0620
to −0325.

By night The harbour can be approached and entered using the following lights (note that the marina is only open between 0700 and 2200):

Fairway buoy Q.G Bell
Inner fairway buoy Fl.G.2·5s
East Breakwater head 2F.G(vert)10m6M
Jetty leading lights 020°
Front Oc.G.4s5m2M
Rear F.G.6M
West Pier head Fl(2)R.10s11m9M

Entrance

Entrance to the docks and marina is controlled by
traffic signals, displayed at the west side of the entrance to Kings Dock. There are three rows of red
and green lights in three columns. The middle row
light of the left-hand column controls the movement
of yachts. When a red light is shown yachts are
prohibited from entering the port or the approach
channel. When a green light is shown yachts may
proceed to the Barrage Sea Lock. Entrance should
be made close to the West Pier. Two holding buoys
are situated downstream of the barrage lock, although these should not be used at LWS because of
the danger of drying out. Access to the Yacht Haven
is via the Barrage Sea Lock, usually on demand.
The lock can hold some 25 yachts, and is controlled
by traffic signals. It will close when the tide reaches

1.0m above chart datum – usually only during LW spring tides. The lock operates from 0700–1900 (0700–2200 at weekends) during the winter months, and from 0700–2200 during the summer. The last lock out is 30 minutes before the close of the business day. The marina lock operates the same hours as the barrage lock, the water level in the marina being one metre higher than the impounded level above the barrage.

Berthing

Marina berths in Swansea Yacht Haven.

Harbourmaster

Yachts are controlled by the marina master at the yacht haven.

Charges

There are marina fees, harbour dues and Tawe Barrage dues.

VHF radio telephone

Call *Swansea Yacht Haven* on Ch 80 and *Tawe Barrage* on Ch 18.

Facilities

Fuel Diesel from the marina between 0800–1800 (winter months) and 0800–2100 (summer months).

Water On all pontoons in the marina.

Slip In entrance basin to the marina.

Provisions Full range of shops in the town centre.

Showers Toilets and showers available 24 hours at the marina.

Laundry At Marine Reception.

Boatyard 18-ton marine travel-hoist. Boat storage and repair facilities.

Chandlery Cambrian Small Boat and Yacht Chandlery.

Engineers Swansea Marine – inboard and outboard engine repairs. Cambrian Yacht Repairs – hull and rigging repairs.

Electronics Marconi Marine.

Refuse disposal Refuse skips at bridgeheads.

Mumbles

A large area of yacht moorings drying to sand, shingle and firm mud. There is water at the two slipways in front of the Mumbles Yacht Club for 3 hours either side of HW. Visitors' moorings are provided by the yacht club. The easternmost moorings can be exposed to swell.

Mumbles Head

The outermost of two rocky islets, with a white octagonal tower lighthouse (Fl(4)10s35m17M). The Cherrystones are rocks creating broken water 2 cables east of Mumbles Head; they should be rounded to seaward. The Mixon Shoal is a drying sandbank SSW of Mumbles Head, with its south extremity marked by a red bell buoy. The channel to the north of the bank can be used in settled conditions, keeping 1 cable offshore.

Oxwich Bay

Lies between Oxwich Point and Pwll-du Head, a bold bluff 3½ miles west of Mumbles Head. There is good shelter from the north and west for yachts, anchoring in 6 metres sand. The northwest portion of the bay dries to firm sand.

Port Eynon Bay

Lies between Port Eynon Point and Oxwich Point. Anchor in 7 metres in the centre of the bay, sheltered from the north and west. In strong tidal conditions with contrary winds there are overfalls off Oxwich Point.

Helwick Sands

The sands, extending 7 miles west from a position 3 cables south of Port Eynon Point, are marked at either end by cardinal buoys. Tidal streams run (at up to 3 knots at springs) northeast and southwest across the bank. There is a narrow passage between the sands and Port Eynon Point which can be used in settled weather.

V. Worms Head to St David's Head

Burry Port

Waypoint 51°40'·0N 4°15'·0W ½M S of harbour
  entrance
Population 7,805 (1981)
Local High Water is Dover −0500
Charts Admiralty *1167, 1076, 1179*; Imray *C60*

General

A former commercial port, the harbour now provides good shelter for yachtsmen 3½ miles inland from Carmarthen Bay.

Warning

Burry Inlet should not be entered in strong onshore winds. The channel is not buoyed and is liable to change. The best time to enter the inlet is during the 2 hours before HW. The outer harbour at Burry Port dries to firm mud and should only be entered between 2 hours either side of HW.

Approach

By day The three chimneys of the power station at Burry Port are very conspicuous, although from the west they can appear as one. Burry Inlet is entered between The Nose and Burry Holms.

By night A night approach and entrance should not be attempted.

Entrance to Burry Port

Burry Port outer harbour, looking back at entrance

Anchorage in the approach

A good anchorage, with shelter from the south and east, may be had in 5·5 metres mud in Rhossili Bay, 5 cables northeast of Worms Head.

Entrance

The channels through Burry Inlet are liable to change and are best negotiated on a rising tide. Even in moderate west or southwest winds the bar can become quite turbulent on the ebb. A post with a Q.R.1M light lies 1 cable south of the harbour entrance. The west breakwater has a white lighthouse tower with a red cupola, displaying a F.R.7M light.

Moorings

The outer harbour is entirely filled with moorings.

Berthing

It would be possible for visitors to lie alongside in thick mud in parts of the inner harbour.

Facilities

Fuel Diesel fuel from Burry Port Yacht Services.
Slip On east side, by harbour entrance.
Provisions Adequate range of shops nearby.
Yacht club Burry Port Yacht Club.
Chandlery Burry Port Yacht Services, overlooking west dock.

BURRY
PORT

BURRY PORT

Old Harbour

Chys(conspic)

Power Station

☩

F.R ✲

✲Q.R

Sand

7₃

9.

10

Sand

2₁

51°40'N

2₇

7₃

N

10

Whiteford   Pool

✲ Whiteford
LtHo
Fl.5s7m7M
(occas)

Hooper   Sands

Whiteford
Point

0   1

Nautical Mile

4°16'W

Depths in Metres

There is a firing range in Carmarthen Bay, the limits of which are marked by DZ buoys. Red flags (and lights by night) are displayed on Pendine Burrows and Laugharne Burrows when practices are taking place.

Burry Port inner harbour

Approaches to Llanelli at low water

Burry Port outer harbour and conspicuous power station chimneys

Llanelli

A former commercial harbour, 3 miles east of Burry Port up the River Loughor. The entrance channels and the docks dry to soft mud. There are no facilities for yachtsmen.

Llanelli harbour

Ferryside

A small town on the east bank of the River Tywi, 5 miles beyond the Carmarthen Bar. The channels of the estuary are liable to change and should be entered on a rising tide within 2 hours of HW. Strong onshore winds can make the bar impassable. The River Towy Yacht Club has its premises at Ferryside, and visitors' moorings can be provided by prior arrangement with the club. The moorings dry to soft mud. There is room to anchor close by the moorings, but this should be done with care, as the river bottom shelves rapidly a little distance from the shore.

Ferryside on Afon Tywi

Saundersfoot, looking back at harbour entrance

Saundersfoot

Waypoint 51°42'·7N 4°40'·9W ½M E of harbour
  entrance
Population 2,373 (1981)
Local High Water is Dover −0510
Charts Admiralty *1482, 1076, 1179*; Imray *C60*

General

A popular holiday resort, its drying harbour providing good shelter for yachtsmen.

Warning

The harbour can only be entered for 2 hours either
side of HW. Shelter is good, although a swell can
enter the harbour in strong south winds.

Approach

By day Saundersfoot can be approached directly
from seaward. Monkstone Rock is the outermost
point of a rocky ledge extending from Monkstone
Point; it must be avoided.

By night The harbour can be approached at night
using the following lights, although local knowledge
is necessary prior to entering:

Caldey Island Fl(3)WR.20s65m14/12M
Tenby Pier head F.R.7m7M
Saundersfoot Pier head Fl.R.5s6m7M

Anchorage in the approach

Anchorage may be had in 4 metres sand to the east of the harbour in settled conditions.

Entrance

The harbour is entered directly between the two breakwaters.

Moorings

There are only a limited number of moorings in the centre of the harbour, although a space may be allocated by the harbourmaster. The moorings dry to firm sand.

Berthing

There is limited space alongside the breakwaters, and berthing must be with the permission of the harbourmaster. There are good ladders. The stream flowing through the harbour has cut steep banks which must be avoided.

Harbourmaster

Office on quay in northwest corner of harbour.

Charges

There are harbour charges.

Facilities

Water Tap at midpoint of south quay.
Slip In northwest corner of harbour.
Provisions Good range of shops in the town.
Post office On the main street, behind the sailing club.
Calor Gas and Camping Gaz Frost's Hardware, High Street.
Chandlery On the south quay.
Boat repairs Jones and Teague, Harbour Boatyard, on south quay.

Tenby

Waypoint 51°40'·65N 4°41'·0W ½M NE of Castle Hill
Population 5,657 (1981)
Local High Water is Dover −0510
Charts Admiralty *1482, 1076, 1179*; Imray *C60*

General

This popular holiday resort has terraces of Georgian and Regency buildings overlooking the harbour. Space within the harbour (which dries to firm sand) is limited, although shelter is good.

Warning

The harbour dries to firm sand, and can only be entered for 2½ hours either side of HW.

Approaching Tenby

Approach

By day Woolhouse Rocks lie 1·5 miles southeast of the harbour, and are marked at their south extremity by an unlit cardinal buoy. St Catherine's Island, to the south of the harbour entrance, should be given a wide berth to avoid Sker Rock (dries to 1 metre), ½ cable southeast of the island, and its associated rocky ledges.

By night The harbour can be approached at night using the following lights, although local knowledge is necessary prior to entering:
Caldey Island Fl(3)WR.20s65m14/12M
Tenby Pier head F.R.7m7M

Anchorage in the approach

There is a good anchorage (in 5 metres sand) northeast of Castle Hill, giving shelter from all directions except the east and southeast. An alternative anchorage is to the north of Caldey Island.

Entrance

The harbour is entered by rounding the pier.

Moorings

There are a number of moorings in the centre of the harbour, although space is limited. Private moorings lie to the northeast of the harbour, and beyond them is good holding ground for yachts to lie at anchor.

Berthing

There is limited space to lie alongside the pier (only with the permission of the harbourmaster). There are good ladders.

Harbourmaster

On the road leading up from the pier to the southeast of the harbour.

Tenby harbour

Charges

There are harbour charges.

Facilities

Water Tap by the sailing club.
Slip On the west side of the harbour.
Provisions A good range of shops in the town.
Post office Warren Street.
Yacht club Tenby Sailing Club, with premises on the harbour.
Chandlery Limited chandlery from Morris Bros, St Julian's Street.
Calor Gas and Camping Gaz Morris Bros.

Caldey Island

The island lies 2 miles south of Tenby, and is home to a thriving monastery of Cistercian monks. The round white tower of the lighthouse (Fl(3)WR.20s 14/12M) is conspicuous.

St Margaret's Island lies 2 cables west of Caldey Island, to which it is connected by a drying rocky reef.

There is a good anchorage (in 4 metres) 3 cables east of Eel Point, in Priory Bay, off the landing jetty. Landing requires the permission of the abbot at the monastery.

The landing jetty at Caldey Island

St Gowan light vessel

St Govan's Head

This is a prominent perpendicular cliff, 37 metres high, 10 miles southeast of the entrance to Milford Haven. In strong tidal streams with contrary winds overfalls build up off the headland. St Gowan Shoals lie 3·5 miles southwest of St Govan's Head, creating overfalls and breaking seas in heavy weather. St Gowan light vessel lies to the SSW of the shoals, 6 miles SSW of St Govan's Head.

Castlemartin Firing Range

There is live ammunition firing from the Castlemartin Range on most weekdays from April to November. The range extends from St Govan's Head in the east to Linney Head in the west. The range seaward is usually 3 to 4 miles, but can extend to 10M. Prior information regarding firing times can be obtained by telephoning Castlemartin (064 681) 321 ext 336. During firing, range safety vessels patrol the area. Both Castlemartin Range Control and the patrolling vessels operate on VHF radio.

Milford Haven

The magnificent natural harbour of Milford Haven consists of 25 miles of navigable waterway, offering shelter in all conditions. There is a major anchorage at Dale, the excellent Neyland Yacht Haven, moorings in picturesque surroundings at Lawrenny Yacht Station, and many other moorings and anchorages.

There is a constant movement of commercial traffic in the lower reaches, and it is imperative that yachts keep well clear of all commercial vessels. Yachts must keep a minimum of 90 metres away from oil terminals, ships alongside terminals, and ships under way and at anchor. This is a safety precaution that must be strictly adhered to.

The tankers operating in the lower reaches tend to manoeuvre relatively slowly. However, the B & I Ferry, operating from Pembroke Dock, can be moving quickly by the time it has reached the oil terminals.

Charts Admiralty *3274, 3275, 1478, 2878*; Imray *C60*

VHF radio telephone Milford Haven harbour is controlled by the Milford Haven Conservancy Board, operating from the port signal station at Hubberston Point. Yachts are not obliged to report their arrival and destination to the signal station (Milford Haven Radio), but doing this would help the harbourmaster to follow traffic movements.

The signal station is prepared to advise yachts regarding anchorages or traffic movements. A listening watch should be kept on VHF Ch 12 once inside the haven.

Weather forecasts for the haven and the neighbouring coastline are given by Milford Haven Radio on VHF Ch 12 and 14 at 0300, 0900, 1500 and 2100 UT. Gale warnings are broadcast on receipt.

Mill Bay buoy and leading marks, West Blockhouse Point, Milford Haven

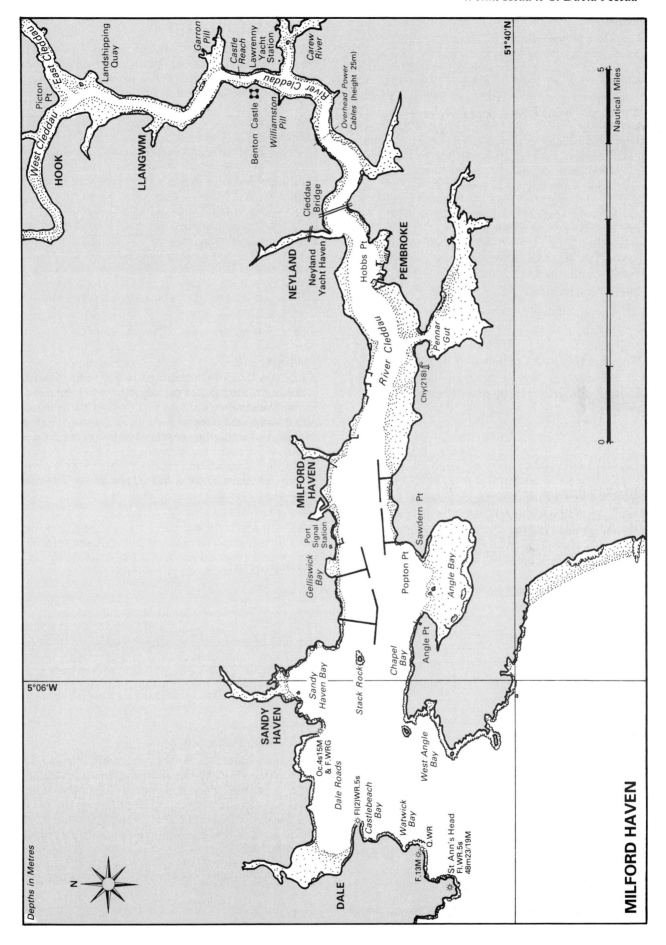

Depths in Metres

N

51°40'N

5°06'W

5
Nautical Miles
0

HOOK

West Cleddau

Picton
Pt

East Cleddau

Landshipping
Quay

LLANGWM

*Garron
Pill*

*Castle
Reach*

Lawrenny
Yacht
Station

Benton Castle

Williamston
Pill

*Carew
River*

River Cleddau

*Overhead Power
Cables (height 25m)*

Cleddau
Bridge

NEYLAND

Neyland
Yacht Haven

Hobbs Pt

PEMBROKE

River Cleddau

*Pennar
Gut*

Chy12181

MILFORD
HAVEN

Port Signal
Station

*Gelliswick
Bay*

Popton Pt

Sawdern Pt

Angle Bay

Angle Pt

*Chapel
Bay*

SANDY
HAVEN

*Sandy
Haven Bay*

Stack Rock

*West Angle
Bay*

Oc.4s15M
& F.WRG

Dale Roads

Fl(2)WR.5s

*Castlebeach
Bay*

*Watwick
Bay*

Q.WR

F.13M

St Ann's Head
Fl.WR.5s
48m23/19M

DALE

MILFORD HAVEN

Entrance

Entrance is possible in all weathers, although on-shore winds against the ebb meeting the cross-tidal stream can cause turbulence, especially around Middle Channel Rocks. St Ann's Head should be given a wide berth in unsettled conditions, in which the projecting rock ledge can give rise to confused seas.

St Ann's Head is a bold promontory, 37 metres high, with a light (Fl.WR.5s48m18/14M) shown from a white octagonal tower near the cliff edge.

Middle Channel lighthouse exhibits its light (Fl(3)G.7s18m8M) from a black round metal tower at the west end of Middle Channel Rocks, 6½ cables SSE of St Ann's Head.

Leading lights are exhibited from tall concrete towers on West Blockhouse Point and Watwick Point, and the harbour is sufficiently well lit to make night access straightforward as far as Westfield Marina.

Dale

Watwick Bay and Castlebeach Bay

Good anchorages for yachts at the entrance to the harbour, sheltered from all except east winds.

Dale

Position 51°42'·4N 5°09'·2W
Population 384 (1981)

General

Excellent anchorage, sheltered from all except northeast or east winds, with facilities for yachtsmen provided in the village.

Warning

Dale Roads, extending onto Dale Shelf and into Sandy Haven Bay, is a reserved anchorage for commercial shipping. Dale Flats is designated as an area of natural scientific interest. Yachts are prohibited from anchoring in either area.

Entrance

Dale harbour is entered by rounding Dale Point, with a light shown from a metal column (Fl(2)WR. 5s20m5/3M).

Moorings

There are numerous moorings in Dale. Visitors' moorings, for which there are charges, are allocated by Dale Sailing Co.

Anchorage

Anchorage is possible beyond the moorings, subject to the above-mentioned limitations.

Facilities

Fuel Diesel from Dale Sailing Co. Petrol from filling station at the head of the slip.
Water Dale Sailing Co.
Slip At west end of bay.
Provisions Limited provisions are available in the village.
Post office In the village.
Yacht club Dale Yacht Club. Open in the summer months, with showers, bar and restaurant.
Chandlery Dale Sailing Co.
Calor Gas Dale Sailing Co.

Sandy Haven

A beautiful, secluded anchorage on the north side of the haven, drying (except for a shallow stream) to firm sand. Entrance should be within 1½ hours of HW. The modern houses with slate roofs and timber-clad upper storeys should be kept open to avoid Bull Rock; then keep close to the moorings on the west side of the haven. Anchorage can be found above the landing beach at the small village. There are no facilities.

West Angle Bay

A good anchorage in settled conditions, it is subject to a southwest swell. The shoreline is rocky and care must be taken when anchoring. A reverse eddy tends to keep yachts pointing northeast on the flood and the ebb. Shelter is fair in strong east winds, but not as good as that off Popton Point, at the entrance to Angle Bay.

Chapel Bay

Good anchorage (close to the shore) in strong south winds.

5°08'W

51°42'·5N

Depths in Metres

Dale Shelf

10

5

6₇

Q(3)10s
BYB

Q Fl.Y.5s
Y

Dale Point
Fl(2)WR.5s20m5/3M

5

5

0

Cables

Dale Flats

25

50

25

25

25

*Mud
and
Stones*

2₇

2₄

3

2₄

Yacht Moorings

50

Chandlers

25— DALE

N

DALE

Milford Haven signal station

Pennar Park marina

Angle Bay

There is a floating anchorage to the northeast of Angle Point, with landing by the lifeboat slip. Angle Bay itself dries to soft mud. There is a good anchorage to use in east winds between Popton Point and Sawdern Point, although the water is shallow.

Gelliswick Bay

Home to the Pembrokeshire Yacht Club, the bay provides a good anchorage, but is exposed to southeast winds.

Milford Haven Conservancy Board

The Board's jetty is only to be used for alongside berths in an emergency, with permission from the signal station. The Board also have some moorings, which may be used by yachtsmen in similar extreme circumstances.

Milford Shelf

There is an area of shallow moorings close to Milford Docks that is exposed to the southwest. Yachts must keep clear of the dredged area that is used to allow vessels to swing.

MILFORD MARINA

A new 150-berth yacht marina in the E part of Milford Docks. Access is via the lock gates, which are open for the 2 hours before HW. There is a proposal to renew the lock gates, improving times of access.

All berths are provided with water and electricity. The marina office houses toilets, showers, a lounge and bar, and a chandlery. Cleddau Boatyard, on the W side of the dock, carries out boat and engine repairs, and has boat storage facilities ashore.

VHF radio telephone: call *Pierhead* on Ch 12, and they will contact the marina.

Pwllcrochan Flats

Yachts must keep clear of these flats, as there are uncharted obstructions.

Pennar Gut

There is limited anchoring space beyond the few laid moorings. A channel has been dredged to allow ships access to the power station, and although rarely used it should be left clear. The power station immediately to the west of Pennar Gut has a very conspicuous chimney (218 metres) with red lights.

Milford Marina

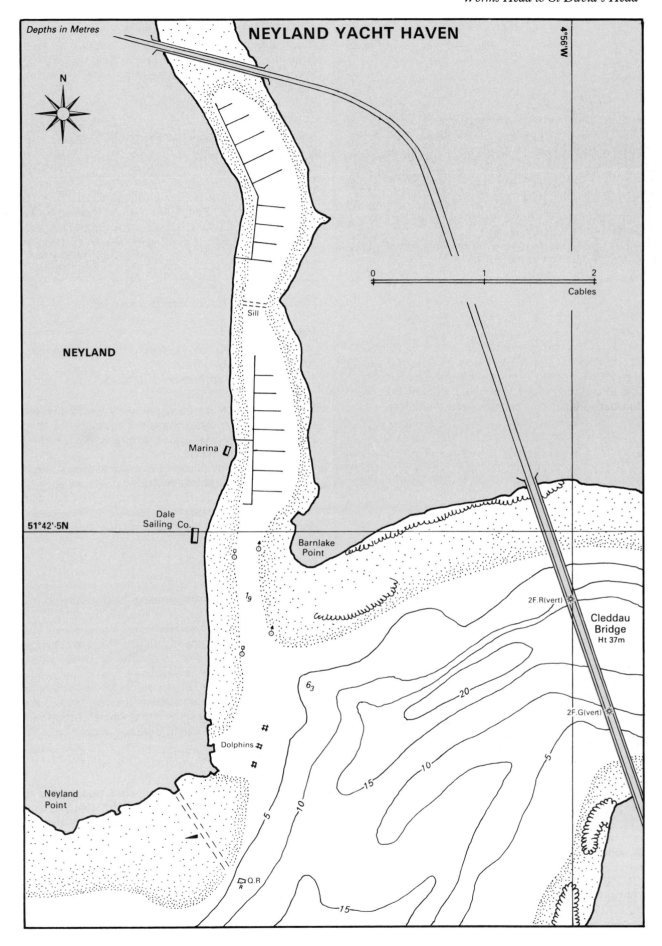

Depths in Metres

N

NEYLAND YACHT HAVEN

4°56'W

NEYLAND

Sill

0   1   2
Cables

Marina

51°42'·5N

Dale
Sailing Co.

Barnlake
Point

1₉

2F.R(vert)

Cleddau
Bridge
Ht 37m

6₃

20

2F.G(vert)

Dolphins

15

10

Neyland
Point

5

10

5

Q.R
R

15

Entrance to Neyland Yacht Haven

Neyland Yacht Haven

Neyland Yacht Haven

Neyland Yacht Haven

The excellent marina at Neyland, some 10 miles from the entrance to the haven, offers access at all states of the tide, and berths in an attractive setting for 450 boats.

Entrance

The dolphins at the entrance are to be left to port; the channel is buoyed.

Berthing

Berths in the lower marina basin are accessible at all states of the tide. The upper basin is entered over a sill which gives access to yachts drawing 1·5 metres for 3 hours either side of HW. Berths can be arranged in advance by telephoning (0646) 601601.

VHF radio telephone

Neyland Yacht Haven operates on Ch M.

Facilities

Fuel Diesel and petrol available from fuelling pontoon.

Water Water to all pontoons in lower basin, and to most in upper basin.

Electricity Electricity to all pontoons in the lower basin, and to most in the upper basin.

Provisions Good range of shops in Neyland, a short walk from the marina.

Toilets, showers and launderette At the marina centre.

Chandlery At the marina centre.

Boat repairs and engineers Dale Sailing Co., adjacent to the marina centre.

Sailmakers Brunel Quay Sails, at the rear of Dale Sailing Co.

Hobb's Point

There is a large area of moorings north of the point. Apply to Kelpie Boats for a visitor's mooring. Kelpie Boats operate a chandlery and a boat repair and engineering service from beside the slip. Yachts should not anchor close to Pembroke Dock, which is busy with commercial traffic.

From the Cleddau Bridge for 1·2 miles upstream to the overhead power cables is the only area in the haven allocated for use by water-skiers. Yachtsmen should recognise this right and not anchor between these points.

Williamston Pill

One of the best, and best sheltered, anchorages in the haven, although it is pretty full with resident moorings. There is limited space to anchor beyond the moorings without lying in the main stream.

Lawrenny Yacht Station

Moorings for 100 yachts at the entrance to the Carew River in a picturesque setting. Moorings can be arranged in advance by telephoning Carew (064 67) 212.

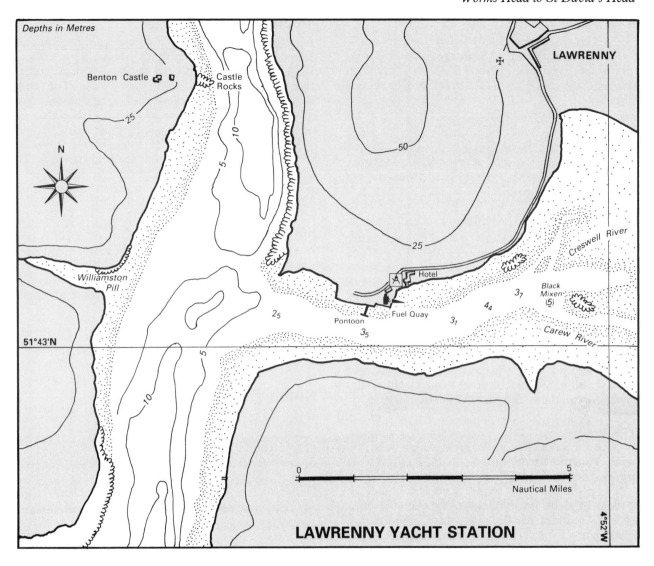

LAWRENNY YACHT STATION

The stream can run quickly through the anchorage, and it is the yachtsman's responsibility to ensure that the mooring he has taken is suitable for his yacht. Payment is made at the chandlery for the use of a mooring.

The yacht station has a floating pontoon, with a water tap, where yachts may tie alongside (stay limited to 10 minutes). Dinghies should tie to the inside of the pontoon. There is a fuel quay with diesel, petrol and water.

The station operates a chandlery (with *Calor Gas* available), a boatyard, boat repairs and a slip. There is a small café nearby, and the hotel offers a restaurant and bar meals. There are no other provisions available locally. The village of Lawrenny is ½ mile from the yacht station and has a sub-post office. There is little space to anchor beyond the moorings without drying out.

Castle Reach

To the north of Benton Castle and the offlying Castle Rocks is a delightful anchorage, although it is not a simple matter to find a position that will not

dry yet is out of the main stream. Garron Pill should be avoided, as there are obstructions and oyster beds.

Llangwm

Llangwm Pill dries to soft mud. There are moorings laid along the west bank of the River Cleddau above the pill, and a safe anchorage off the east bank, in a position just out of the main stream but not drying. Provisions and a post office can be found in Llangwm. There is a landing slip just to the north of Black Tar Point.

Above the moorings off Llangwm navigation becomes more difficult. The water off Fowborough Point is very shallow, and it is necessary to head over towards the Landshipping Quay, on the east bank of the river, before turning north to Picton Point and the confluence of the East and West Cleddau.

East Cleddau

There is an area of moorings beyond the quay to the north of Landshipping. Anchorage may be found beyond these moorings. This is the limit of practical navigation, as the channel then becomes narrow and winding.

West Cleddau

The moorings off Hook and the possible adjacent anchorage mark the limit of practical navigation, although vessels have historically made their way up the river to Haverfordwest.

Skomer Island

The island is a nature reserve owned by the Nature Conservancy Council and run by the West Wales Naturalists' Trust. A fee is payable to the warden on landing. Anchorage is in the North or the South Haven, depending on wind direction. When entering either bay, keep close to the west shore to avoid rocks on the east side of the bay.

The Wildgoose Race forms west of Skomer and Skokholm Islands during the strength of the streams in both directions. It is particularly dangerous near springs with a contrary or cross wind blowing, and must be given the widest possible berth.

Jack Sound

A narrow channel (about 1 cable wide) lying between Midland Island and Wooltack Point, with a stream that can reach 7 knots at springs.

Passage through the sound should be made in daylight at slack water, or by using the stream in settled conditions. At the strength of the stream a contrary wind will create turbulent water at the end of the sound from which the wind is blowing.

The south-going stream begins at Dover HW −0300 and the north-going stream at Dover HW +0300.

Approaching from the southeast, head directly for Blackstones (above-water rocks 2 cables south of Midland Island). Approximately 50 metres from Blackstones, turn NNE, heading for Tusker Rock (dries 2 metres, ¾ cable west of Wooltack Point). The passage is between the Crabstones (drying rocks 3·7 metres extending east from Midland Island) and Cable Rock (drying rock 1 cable northwest of The Anvil).

With contrary winds, the worst of the turbulence can be avoided by keeping close to the north shore of Midland Island when heading north, and by heading close over to the Blackstones as soon as clear of the Crabstones when heading south.

Grassholme Island

This is a rugged island 6 miles west of Skomer Island. Overfalls surround the island and extend up to 2 miles SSE at the strength of the tidal stream. There is a clear passage 5 miles wide to the east, between these overfalls and the Wildgoose Race off Skomer and Skokholm Islands.

The Smalls

A group of low rocks 13 miles west of Skomer Island. A light (Fl(3)15s36m25M) is shown from a white round tower with red bands. The light has a red sector (F.R.33m13M) overlooking Hats and Barrels, patches of shallow rock extending over 4 miles east from The Smalls. Hats and Barrels are generally alive with tide rips and overfalls.

At the strength of the tidal stream with a contrary wind turbulence can extend some distance west from The Smalls, and when passing in these conditions the islands must be left at least 2 miles to the east.

St Brides Bay

In south or east winds, anchorage may be had between Little Haven and Borough Head in the southeast corner of the bay. Porth-clais is a drying inlet 3 miles west of Solva, giving shelter to small craft.

Solva

Waypoint 51°51'·8N 5°11'·7W 2 cables S of harbour entrance
Local High Water is Dover −0450
Charts Admiralty *1478, 1973*; Imray *C60*

General

An attractive winding inlet providing good shelter for drying moorings in the inner harbour.

Warning

The inner harbour dries to a bottom of firm sand, and can only be entered for 2½ hours either side of HW. Strong south winds can make the entrance difficult.

Entrance to Solva harbour

Depths in Metres

N

5°16'W

51°44'N

10

20

20

Tusker Rock

Wooltack Point

Anvil Point

15

13

Crabstones

Cable Rock

The Anvil

.45
Midland
Island

Jack Sound

19

13

15

Blackstones
(1·5)

The Bench

(6·3)

(2·5)

(2)

SKOMER
ISLAND

20

10

The Neck

North
Haven

3

Little Sound

10

20

South
Haven

JACK SOUND

One Nautical Mile

0   1

Depths in Metres

N

Porth-y-Bwch

Dinas-fawr

.61

.55

5

10

14

12

7₃

16

Penthyn

SOLVA

Quay
Moorings
Slip

1₈

3₁

40

9,

Black
Rock (3₆)

14

The Mare

Green Scar

33

Black Scar

14

15

17

16

10

Cradle
Rock

.49

5°12'W

51°52'N

5

Cables

0

SOLVA

Solva harbour, looking back at Black Rock at the harbour entrance

Solva harbour

Solva harbour

Approach

By day Green Scar, Black Scar and The Mare are islets lying ½ mile south of the harbour entrance.

By night A night approach and entrance to the harbour should not be attempted.

Entrance

Black Rock, an islet with drying rocks that extend ¼ cable west, lies in the entrance to the harbour. The rock can be passed on either side, and anchorage may be had in 3 metres in the pool behind the rock, although this is not tenable in strong SW winds.

Moorings

The inner harbour around the dogleg of the inlet is well sheltered and crowded with moorings. Red buoys along the southeast side of the inlet indicate visitors' moorings .

Berthing

There is a small quay, with good ladders, for temporary alongside berthing.

Facilities

Water Tap in gents' toilets.
Slip At west end of quay.
Provisions Limited provisions may be found in the upper village.
Post office In the upper village.
Yacht club Solva Boat Owners' Association.

Ramsey Sound

A navigable channel lying between Ramsey Island and the mainland, with tidal streams running at up to 6 knots at springs.

Passage must be in daylight, and should ideally be made at slack water. At the strength of the tidal stream strong eddies can take a yacht off its heading; however, if it is correctly aligned away from the areas of danger this will not be a problem. At the strength of the tidal stream strong contrary winds will create some turbulence at that end of the sound from which the wind is blowing.

The south-going stream begins at Dover HW −0200 and the north-going stream at Dover HW +0400.

The Bitches are a ledge of rocks extending 2 cables east from the midpoint of the east side of Ramsey Island. There is a least width in the sound of 2 cables at this point, and passage should be made through the centre of this channel. Horse Rock (dries 0·9 metre, 5 cables to northeast of The Bitches) must be avoided.

There is a sheltered anchorage and landing place on Ramsey Island, close to the north of The Bitches.

Whitesand Bay, with St David's Head at its north end, provides an anchorage sheltered from the south and east in 6 metres sand.

Depths in Metres

N

5°19'.5W

Carreg-gafeiliog (3)

3₇

10   Gwaham (2)

42   Point St John

5₃

16

20   20   20

10   38

6₁

Ramsey   18   14   7₃

•95   Sound   53   Horse Rock
                              (dr.0·9m)
33•

50

17

3   66

4

The Bitches(4)

51°52'N

RAMSEY
ISLAND

•134   50   Pen Dal-aderyn

+   +   27   Shoe Rk
    +   (3)
10

20   64

Foel-
fawr

42

Ynys
Bery
            Pont yr Eilun
    Ynys
    Eilun (25)
70

Meni Duon   0   1
   (8)
                                        One Nautical Mile
20

The Bishops and Clerks

A group of islets and rocks lying within 2½ miles west and northwest of Ramsey Island. A light (Fl.5s44m24M) is shown from a white round tower on the summit of South Bishop, the southwesternmost islet of the group. North Bishop is the northernmost islet of the group, lying 3·2 miles NNE of South Bishop. Within the group are a number of dangerous rocks and islets which produce heavy overfalls and tidal rips. If not taking the passage through Ramsey Sound, the Bishops and Clerks should all be passed on the seaward side.

VI. St David's Head to Bardsey Island

Cardigan Bay lies between St David's Head to the S and Bardsey Island to the N. The majority of its harbours lie on a lee shore and are protected by bars, making for limited times of access and for dangerous conditions in strong onshore winds. To counter this the harbours are invariably attractive, in scenic surroundings.

The major ports of refuge are Fishguard, which can be entered at any state of the tide and in any conditions, and Pwllheli harbour, with access at most states of the tide and in most conditions. Limited shelter with access at all states of the tide can be found at New Quay and St Tudwal's Roads.

Sarn Badrig or St Patrick's Causeway, Sarn-y-Bwch and Cynfelyn Patches are three dangerous shoals extending to seaward in the north half of the bay.

Tidal streams for the most part follow the line of the coast. They are strong at St David's Head and

Bardsey Island, but become progressively weaker into the bay.

Firing exercises controlled from Aberporth take place in the southern half of the bay. Unlit targets and mooring buoys are frequently moved to accommodate these exercises.

St David's Head

A 30m-high headland extending NE from the entrance to Ramsey Sound. The coast to Strumble Head consists of perpendicular cliffs interspersed with sandy bays. Keep ¾M offshore between St David's Head and Porthgain to avoid outlying rocks.

Strumble Head

A conspicuous headland at the NW end of Pen Caer promontory. The lighthouse (Fl(4)15s45m 26M) has a white circular tower. When heading S, an inshore tidal eddy, beginning some 3 hours before the general tidal stream, can be used to assist passage through Ramsey Sound before the stream builds to full strength. There are overfalls on Strumble Bank, about one mile offshore, in contrary wind and tide conditions.

Fishguard

Waypoint 52°01'·0N 4°57'·9W 3 cables NNE of head of N breakwater
Local High Water is −0350 Dover
Charts Admiralty *1484, 1973*; Imray *C60, C61*

General

The main harbour was developed by the Great Western Railway as a terminal for transatlantic liners, but its trade was later taken by Southampton. Fishguard Harbour, now belonging to Sealink, subsequently became a main ferry port for trade with Ireland. Lower Fishguard is an attractive old fishing village that was used as the setting for the film version of Dylan Thomas's *Under Milk Wood*.

FISHGUARD

Pen Anglas

0   5
Cables

4°58'W

16

17

52°01'N

14

Fl.G.4·5s18m13M
Bell(1)8s

5

6_8

6_6

F.G.89m5M

F.G.77m5M

Lights in line 282°

6_2

5

1_4

2

3_8

Goodwick

1_6

Fl.R.3s10m5M

5_8

4_6

Goodwick

2

PFs

WC

Saddle Point

3

Castle Point

Sands

N

FISHGUARD

Lower Town

Depths in Metres

Fishguard harbour

Warning

The main harbour and the outer harbour at Lower Fishguard can be entered at any state of the tide and in any conditions. Strong winds from the N or NE can cause a heavy swell in both harbours, although some shelter can be obtained in the outer harbour behind Castle Point. The inner harbour at Lower Fishguard dries to firm mud and clay, and can only be entered for 1½ hours either side of HW.

Approach

By day Strumble Head, with its lighthouse, is conspicuous to the W of Fishguard, with the wedge-shaped Dinas Head to the E. There are drying rocks to the N of the root of the N breakwater, but no other dangers to the approach.

By night The harbour can be reached making use of the following lights:

Strumble Head Fl(4)15s45m26M
N breakwater Fl.G.4·5s18m13M
E breakwater Fl.R.3s10m5M

Entrance

The main harbour is entered between the two breakwaters. Lower Fishguard is entered between Saddle Point and Castle Point.

Moorings

There are private moorings laid to the SW of a line between the ro-ro terminal and the head of the E breakwater in the main harbour. There are private moorings laid in the outer harbour and inner harbour at Lower Fishguard.

Anchorage

Anchorage is prohibited NE of the line between the ro-ro terminal and the head of the E breakwater in the main harbour. If draft permits, anchorage may be obtained beyond the moorings laid to the SW of this line, or close to the moorings in the outer harbour at Lower Fishguard. The ends of the sewer outfalls at Lower Fishguard are marked with green triangular topmarks on poles. There are deeper anchorages off Saddle Point and between Saddle Point and the E breakwater.

Berthing

There are drying berths alongside the pier in the inner harbour at Lower Fishguard; however, priority is given to fishing vessels, and these berths should only be used with the consent of the harbourmaster.

Harbourmaster

Lower Fishguard ☎ 0348 5203

VHF radio telephone

None.

Lower Fishguard harbour

Facilities

Fuel Marine diesel from Goodwick Marine, behind PFS near slip at head of main harbour.

Water By toilets at head of main harbour, and from tap on wall of YC in Lower Fishguard.

Slip There are numerous slips in both harbours.

Provisions Provisions are obtainable in Goodwick for yachts in the main harbour, and in Fishguard (which is a short walk, but up a steep hill) from Lower Fishguard. EC Wednesday.

Post office There are post offices in Goodwick and Fishguard.

Yacht club Fishguard Bay Yacht Club, Lower Fishguard. Bar and showers.

Calor Gas From PFS at head of main harbour.

Chandlery Fishguard Yacht and Boat Co. Ltd, High Street, Fishguard, and Goodwick Marine.

Refuse disposal Bins on the quay.

Newport Bay

Shelter may be obtained from winds from S through SE to E by anchoring in 5m off the mouth of the Afon Nyfer, or by drying on the firm sand of the estuary in settled conditions only.

Cardigan

Waypoint 52°08'·0N 4°43'·0W 8 cables W of Cardigan Island

Local High Water is −0350 Dover

Charts Admiralty *1484, 1973*; Imray *C61*

Moorings off Teifi Boating Club, Cardigan

General

Formerly an important port; silting of the estuary has restricted its use to principally pleasure craft. Good shelter from all wind directions can be found on the drying moorings to the S of Pen yr Ergyd, and in the deep-water pool where the Afon Teifi narrows a mile further upstream.

Warning

The entrance is dangerous in strong W through NW to N winds. The bar dries, but there is over 2·5m at MHWS and 1·5m at MHWN. The channel between Pen yr Ergyd and Bryn-du is subject to continual change and is not buoyed. Entrance should be made on the flood when making for the deep-water moorings upstream.

Approach

By day Cemaes Head is a prominent headland, rising steeply to an elevation of over 180m. Approach is straightforward, with no offlying dangers. Cardigan Sound, between Cardigan Island and the mainland, should not be attempted without local knowledge.

By night There are lights: 2F.R(vert) to the S of the conspicuous hotel on the E side of the bay and Fl(2)5s on the steel beacon in the approach. There are no further lights at the river entrance, and approach without local knowledge is not recommended.

Anchorage in the approach

Shelter may be found from SW winds below Cemaes Head, and from E winds below the hotel on the E side of the bay.

Entrance

Approach on a SE course to leave the red can buoy to port and the steel beacon close to starboard before passing between the points, leaving Pen yr Ergyd to port.

Moorings

There are visitors' moorings (which mostly dry), belonging to the Teifi Boat Club, to the south of Pen yr Ergyd.

Berthing

Yachts that can take the ground can anchor close to the moorings S of Pen yr Ergyd. Deep-water anchorages can be found where the river narrows one mile to the S of the entrance, and in pools between St Dogmaels and Cardigan.

Facilities

Water From tap on wall of Teifi Boat Club.

Yacht club Teifi Boat Club.

Provisions Full provisions, post office, chandlery and petrol filling station can be found in Cardigan. EC Wednesday.

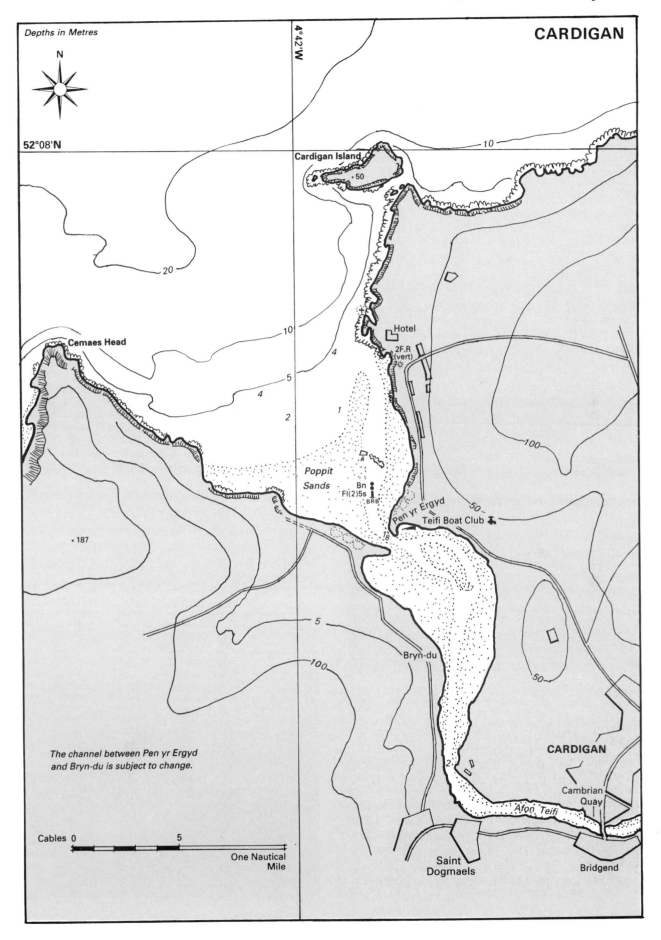

Depths in Metres

N

52°08'N

4°42'W

Cardigan Island

· 50

10

20

Cemaes Head

10

4

5

4

2

1

Poppit
Sands

R

Hotel

2F.R
(vert)

Bn
Fl(2)5s

BRB

Pen yr Ergyd

Teifi Boat Club

· 187

100

50

17

18

5

Bryn-du

100

50

The channel between Pen yr Ergyd
and Bryn-du is subject to change.

CARDIGAN

Cambrian
Quay

2

Afon Teifi

Cables 0   5

One Nautical
Mile

Saint
Dogmaels

Bridgend

Aberporth

Aberporth is a small fishing village to the east of Pencribach, the head providing some protection from SW or W winds. A Government missile test centre, airfield and research establishment are sited close to the village. A number of targets, moorings and buoys marking scientific instruments can be found within 20 miles of Pencribach, some marked with flashing lights. Their positions are frequently changed; the latest information may be obtained from the Marine Officer, RAE, Aberporth (☎ 0239 810205 ext 462).

New Quay

Waypoint 52°13'·4N 4°21'·3W 4·5 cables N of outer breakwater
Local High Water is −0330 Dover
Charts Admiralty *1484, 1972*; Imray *C61*

Approaching New Quay

General

A holiday resort and fishing village. The bay offers limited protection, although it can be entered at any state of the tide. There are floating moorings in New Quay Bay; to the S of the breakwater the harbour dries to firm sand. The pier was built in 1835, when there was a thriving shipbuilding trade.

Warning

The harbour is protected from winds E through S to W, although a swell can affect the moorings at any time. Strong winds from N or NW can produce a dangerous sea, making the moorings untenable,

with conditions only slightly improved in the shelter of the breakwater. An inner breakwater gives some additional protection, but this drying area is crowded with local small fishing boats.

Rounding the breakwater, New Quay

Approach

By day New Quay Head is the first conspicuous headland to the N of Cemaes Head. Carreg Ina are drying rocks extending 3 cables to the NW of Ina Point, on the E side of New Quay Bay. Their extremity is indicated by a N cardinal mark. Beacons ashore indicate alignment of a sewer outfall extending 7 cables NNW from Ina Point.

By night The harbour should be approached with care until the following lights are identified:
New Quay outer breakwater Fl.WRG.3s12m8-5M
New Quay inner breakwater Q.WR

New Quay harbour

NEW QUAY

52°13'N

4°20'W

N

Ina Point

Carreg Ina

BY

Green

White

New Quay Head

FI.WRG.3s12m8/5M

G

5

4₆

3₁

4₄

4₁

2₂

3₅

2₁

1₄

0₅

5

10

50

100

5

Cables

Depths in Metres

Entrance

New Quay Bay is entered between the end of the outer breakwater and the N cardinal mark off Carreg Ina. There is a further stone groyne running 50m SSE from the end of the outer breakwater. This affords some additional protection to vessels alongside the breakwater. Its extremity is marked by a green beacon, which must be left to starboard.

Moorings

There are private moorings in New Quay Bay, some of which dry to firm sand. Moorings for visitors, when available, may be allocated by the harbourmaster.

Berthing

Anchorage is possible close to the laid moorings in New Quay Bay and outside the breakwater in settled conditions. Berthing alongside the breakwater is only with the permission of the harbourmaster, and priority is given to fishing boats. The harbour inside the breakwater dries to firm sand.

Harbourmaster

Office at the head of the breakwater.

Facilities

Fuel Available from fishermen.
Water From tap on wall of yacht club.
Slip At head of outer breakwater.
Provisions Provisions are available in the town.
Post office On road looking down over the harbour.
Yacht club At head of outer breakwater.

Aberaeron

Waypoint 52°15'·0N 4°16'·35W 5 cables NW of harbour entrance
Local High Water is −0325 Dover
Charts Admiralty *1484, 1972*; Imray *C61*

General

A picturesque harbour, flanked by Regency houses painted in contrasting pastel colours, at the mouth of the Afon Aeron. Its development owes much to the foresight of a local landowner, the Reverend Alban Gwynne, at the beginning of the last century. Formerly a busy coastal port and shipbuilding centre, it is now a holiday resort, its drying harbour providing limited shelter for pleasure craft and small fishing boats.

Warning

The harbour mostly dries to a bottom of firm mud and small stones, and should only be entered between 1½ hours either side of HW. Strong onshore winds make the entrance dangerous, and the swell continues into the harbour, making it for the most part untenable.

Approach

By day The church tower 1·2M ENE of the harbour entrance is easily identified. There is foul ground with depths of 1·5m extending 3 cables offshore for ¾M to the SW of the harbour entrance. Carreg Gloyn, with a least depth of 0·3m, lies 3·5 cables to the SW of the harbour entrance. Sarn Cadwgan, with a least depth of 1·8m, extends ½M offshore from Cadwgan Point, ½M to the NE of the harbour entrance.

By night The harbour may be approached with care until the following lights are identified:
Aberaeron north pier Fl(4)R.15s6M
Aberaeron south pier Fl(3)G.10s6M

Harbour entrance Aberaeron

Aberaeron harbour

Anchorage in the approach

Anchorage is possible (in 5m off the harbour entrance) only in the most settled conditions.

Entrance

The harbour is entered between the two stone piers that extend WNW from the shore. The pierheads dry.

Moorings

The harbour is crowded with private drying moorings that may only be used with the permission of the harbourmaster.

Berthing

Limited space for visiting yachts against the NW wall of the harbour by the yacht club. Yachts may tie alongside the NE quay in settled conditions only.

Harbourmaster

Office by yacht club. No VHF radio telephone.

Facilities

Water From tap on wall of yacht club.
Slip In W corner of harbour.
Provisions Full provisions are available in the town.
Yacht club Aberaeron Yacht Club, on W side of the harbour.

Aberystwyth

Waypoint 52°24'·8N 4°06'·0W 5 cables NW of harbour entrance
Local High Water is −0325 Dover
Charts Admiralty *1484, 1972*; Imray *C61*

Approaching Aberystwyth

General

The principal holiday resort of West Wales, Aberystwyth houses the National Library of Wales and one of the colleges that form the University of Wales. The ruins of Aberystwyth Castle stand on Castle Point, the headland in the centre of the town. The castle was begun in 1277 by Edward I and later captured and held by Owain Glyndwr. The harbour, at the mouth of the Afon Rheidol, mostly dries, but affords good shelter. There is a proposal for a 105-berth marina located in the harbour.

Warning

Entrance to the harbour should only be made between 2 hours either side of HW. Entrance should not be attempted in strong onshore winds, and there can be a ground swell on the bar even on calm days. The harbour mostly dries to a bottom of stone and gravel overlaid with mud. It is well sheltered, although some swell can enter the harbour at HW with strong onshore winds.

Approach Aberystwyth harbour entrance

Approach

By day There is a conspicuous TV mast 3M to the S of the harbour entrance. The Wellington Monument (124m) on Pendinas, 5 cables to the SE of the harbour entrance, is also conspicuous. Rocky ledges extend 1½ cables offshore from Castle Point. The Wellington Monument in line with the head of the N breakwater on a course of 140° will keep a vessel clear of these rocks.

By night The harbour can be approached using the following lights:
Aberystwyth south pier Fl(2)WG.10s12m10M
Aberystwyth north pier Q.WR.4M
There are two F.R. leading lights within the harbour entrance on a bearing of 138°.

Depths in Metres

N

ABERYSTWYTH

4°06'W.

50

100

Craig Lais

Wellington Monument and head of
N breakwater in line 140°

Ldg lights 138°

Spire

Spire

Castle Point

Red

Tower

Castle
(ru)

White

ABERYSTWYTH

White

WG

PFS

10

Q.WR.4M

Fl(2)WG.10s12m10M

100

Ldg 2F.R

Afon Rheidol

52°24'N

Green

Obscd

5

Pendinas

Wellington
Monument

Afon Ystwyth

Note The leading lights are together on
the harbour wall not as shown
on Admiralty Chart.

0   5

Cables

Aberystwyth harbour entrance and leading marks

Aberystwyth harbour

Anchorage in the approach

Anchor off the harbour entrance only in the most settled conditions.

Entrance

The harbour is entered between the S stone pier and the N wooden pier. There are leading marks within the harbour entrance: a white pole in front of a white painted mark on the stone quay wall, in line at 138°. A patch of rocks extends some 20m N from the head of the S pier and a shingle bank extends W from the N pier. Once within the entrance, the deepest water can be found close to the N wooden pier. On passing the end of the N pier the channel turns sharply to the N, being marked initially by a W cardinal mark and then by port and starboard-hand marks on poles.

Moorings

Drying moorings, when available, may be allocated by the harbourmaster.

Berthing

The visitors' berth is marked midway along the Town Quay, along the W side of the harbour. Fin-keel yachts should lie alongside the quay, as berths dry at half-tide to a flat bottom of mud and small stones.

Harbourmaster

Office at head of Town Quay.

Charges

There are harbour charges.

VHF radio telephone

The harbourmaster operates a hand-held VHF radio; call Ch 16, work Ch 14.

Facilities

Fuel Diesel and petrol by cans from Moduron Anthony Motors filling station, on E side of harbour.
Water From taps on wall on Town Quay.
Slip On Town Quay.
Provisions Full provisions are available in the town.
Post office Great Darkgate Street, in town centre.
Yacht club Aberystwyth Sea Angling and Yacht Club, on Town Quay.
Calor Gas and Camping Gaz Aberystwyth Holiday Village, 10 minutes' walk from town centre on road heading S.

Sarn Cynfelyn and Cynfelyn Patches

Sarn Cynfelyn and Cynfelyn Patches, with a least depth of 1·5m, are stone and shingle spits extending some 6·5M WSW offshore from a point 2·5M N of Aberystwyth harbour entrance. There is a ½M-wide channel with a least depth of 4·9m between Sarn Cynfelyn and Cynfelyn Patches. The channel is not buoyed. The W end of Cynfelyn Patches is rock, and is known as Outer Patch, with a least depth of 1·5m. The Patches buoy is a W cardinal mark in clear water ¾M W of Outer Patch. In unsettled weather conditions passage should be to the W of the Patches buoy.

Aberdovey

Waypoint 52°31'·75N 4°06'·2W Aberdovey Outer
 buoy
Local High Water is −0320 Dover
Charts Admiralty *1484, 1972*; Imray *C61*

General

An attractive holiday resort at the mouth of the
Afon Dyfi, Aberdovey provides reasonable shelter,
with both floating and drying berths alongside the
jetty and quay in the heart of the town.

Warning

Aberdovey Bar is constantly changing and the buoys
are moved accordingly. The flood stream reaches
2–3 knots and the ebb 3–4 knots at springs. The
ebb stream at the jetty has been recorded at 6 knots.
Entrance should not be attempted before half-tide.
It is possible to enter after HW, but because of the
strength of the ebb any strong onshore wind will
quickly make the entrance impassable. Entrance is
possible in strong onshore winds just before HW,
but only recommended with local knowledge.

Approaching Aberdovey harbour

Approach

By day Aberdovey is the first major inlet S of Cader
Idris. On the N side of the estuary the hills rise
steeply to an elevation of 275m, with lower-lying
land to the S.

By night There are no official lights; a night entrance should not be attempted.

Entrance

The spherical RW Aberdovey Outer buoy should be
located. The Bar buoy, the first of 3 green conical
buoys, lies one mile to the ENE of the Outer buoy.

Follow the channel past the South Spit and Inner
green buoys, then head directly towards the harbour
jetty. A ruined iron refuge beacon stands to the
south of the channel.

Aberdovey harbour looking west

Moorings

There are a few moorings within the harbour, and
one may be allocated by the harbourmaster if required.

Berthing

Anchorage is not permitted within the harbour, as
there are submerged cables crossing the estuary.
Sandbanks continually shift within the estuary, and
all visiting boats should preferably berth alongside
the jetty or quay. Yachts wishing to remain afloat
should berth alongside the outer jetty; the inner
quay dries to firm sand. All berthing is at the direction of the harbourmaster.

Harbourmaster

Office on quay.

Charges

There are harbour charges.

VHF radio telephone

Call *Aberdovey Harbour* Ch 16, work Ch 12.

Facilities

Fuel Diesel fuel will be delivered by local yard depending on quantity required; contact harbourmaster. There are petrol filling stations 300m
 along the road heading E and that heading W out
 of the town.
Water Tap on jetty, or by container from toilets.
Slip Adjacent to the quay.

Provisions Adequate provisions are available in the town.

Post office On road fronting estuary, to W of the quay.

Yacht club Dovey Yacht Club, on quay. Bar and showers.

Chandlery Dovey Marine, behind Dovey Inn.

Calor Gas and Camping Gaz Dovey Marine.

Refuse disposal Bins on quay.

Borth

A channel on the S side of the Afon Dyfi estuary is freshly marked each year with buoys and withies to give access to the Aber Leri Boatyard, Ynys-las, Borth. There is a steel can fendered waiting buoy at the channel entrance. Approach should only be made between 2 hours either side of HW. Limited visitors' mooring space is available (both drying moorings and alongside berths). A deep-water berth is only available by prior arrangement. Water is provided on the quay, and repairs can be carried out. Boat storage facilities are available.

Sarn-y-Bwch

Sarn-y-Bwch, consisting of large stones and rocky boulders, extends 4M WSW offshore from Pen Bwch Point. It dries in patches for about one mile offshore, and depths of less than 5m extend for a further 2M. The outer end is marked by the Bwch buoy, a W cardinal mark.

Barmouth

Waypoint 52°42'·6N 4°04'·77W Barmouth Outer buoy

Local High Water is −0250 Dover

Charts Admiralty *1484, 1971*; Imray *C52, C61*

General

Barmouth is a holiday resort at the mouth of the beautiful Mawddach estuary. It is an excellent base for walking. Dinas Olan, which rises behind the town, became the first piece of land to be owned by the National Trust in 1895. It is the starting point for the Three Peaks International Yacht Race, held each June. Competitors race to Fort William, stopping en route to allow runners to reach the tops of Snowdon, Scafell Pike and Ben Nevis. The harbour offers good shelter, although strong onshore winds can make entrance impossible.

Warning

Entrance to the harbour should only be made between 2½ hours either side of HW. Tidal streams within the harbour can run at over 4 knots at springs, and a dangerous sea can build up with the ebb. With strong onshore winds, entrance becomes impossible. The bar is subject to change and the buoys are moved accordingly.

Barmouth harbour

Approach

By day Barmouth, viewed from seaward, lies on a well defined estuary, with land rising to the north and south of the harbour, and the peak of Cader Idris (890m) 5M to the ESE. Fegla Fawr, a small rounded hill, lies on the S side of the harbour.

By night The harbour can be approached using the following lights:

Barmouth Outer buoy LFl.10s

Y Perch Q.R.4m5M

SE end of Ynys y Brawd groyne Fl.R.5s5M

NW end of railway bridge 2F.R(hor)

Barmouth harbour

BARMOUTH

Depths in Metres

Anchorage in the approach
Anchor off the harbour entrance only in the most settled conditions.

Entrance
The spherical RW Barmouth Outer buoy should be located. The channel is marked by red port-hand buoys which are moved as necessary. Y Perch marks the S end of a stony ledge extending 3·5 cables SW from Ynys y Brawd, and is left to port. There is an offlying sandbank some 70m from the town quay, with its W end marked by a green buoy. On rounding the SE end of the Ynys y Brawd groyne, a sharp turn N towards the quay will avoid the sandbank, leaving the green buoy to starboard. Except at slack water, there will be a strong tidal stream running at the end of the groyne. The estuary is navigable for several miles beyond the railway bridge (5·5m clearance), although the channel is constantly changing and is not buoyed.

Moorings
There are both floating and drying moorings within the harbour; these may be used as directed by the harbourmaster.

Berthing
Anchorage is not permitted within the harbour because of the power cables laid across the estuary. Visitors may lie alongside the town quay as directed by the harbourmaster. The quay dries to firm sand and small stones.

Harbourmaster
Office on the quay.

Charges
There are harbour charges.

VHF radio telephone
Call *Barmouth Harbour* Ch 16, work Ch 12.

Facilities
Fuel Diesel may be delivered to the quay. Contact harbourmaster.
Water On wall of toilets on quay.
Slip E end of quay.
Provisions Full provisions are available in the town.
Yacht club Merioneth Yacht Club. Bar and showers.
Chandlery Seafarer Chandlery.

Sarn Badrig or St Patrick's Causeway
Sarn Badrig, or St Patrick's Causeway, extends 11M SW offshore from just S of Mochras Point, and dries in patches for most of its length. The inner portion is composed of small loose stones, whilst further to seaward there are extensive rock patches with large stones and rocks. The causeway is relatively steep-to on its S side and shoals to the N. The SW extremity is marked by the Causeway buoy, a W cardinal mark.

The East Passage is an inshore passage, about ½M offshore, between the NE end of the causeway and the mainland. This passage may be used between about 4 hours either side of HW, depending on draught and conditions. Moel-y-Gest, to the W of Porthmadog, in line with Mochras Point leads E of the NE end of the causeway; then keep some ¾M offshore as Mochras Point is approached in order to avoid Mochras Spit.

Mochras Lagoon

Waypoint 52°49'·83N 4°08'·33W 5 cables NW of harbour entrance
Local High Water is −0245 Dover
Charts Admiralty *1515, 1971*; Imray *C52, C61*

General
Well sheltered, mostly drying lagoon at the mouth of Afon Artro, with limited facilities. The S half of the lagoon is protected by Shell Island, a peninsula that was formed by the diversion of the Afon Artro in 1819. A leisure complex has been developed on the peninsula, with vehicular access via a tidal causeway.

Yacht moorings, Mochras Lagoon

Warning
There is a depth of approximately 1·2m over the bar for 2 hours either side of HW, and approach must be made within this period. Swell can make the bar dangerous even in calm weather, and in strong onshore winds entrance becomes impossible.

Approach

By day The entrance is one mile to the NE of Mochras Point. The ruins of Harlech Castle lie a further 2M to the NNE. When viewed from the SW, the castle is seen in silhouette and is conspicuous; when viewed from the W or NW it is more difficult to identify.

By night The harbour entrance displays a Fl.WRG. 4s sectored light, the white sector indicating the line of correct approach; however, a night entrance should only be attempted with local knowledge.

Anchorage in the approach

Anchor off the harbour entrance only in the most settled conditions.

Entrance

The entrance, between the sandhills, is marked by three green buoys on the S side and by three posts with red topmarks to the N. The bar lies to seaward of the first green buoy, extending N in a gentle arc. At HW and in settled conditions approach can be made directly from the NW. To avoid the worst of

the bar in alternative conditions, final approach should be made parallel to the N shore on a course of 185° towards the first red-topped post.

Once inside the lagoon, the channel to the N is initially marked with two red posts, then with red and green port and starboard can buoys, the course of the Afon Artro being marked as far as the railway station, where there are slips and water is available.

The channel to the S of the lagoon is marked by three red port-hand buoys leading into the lagoon. Good shelter may be found within the whole lagoon in all conditions.

Moorings

Private moorings are laid throughout the lagoon. There is a basin on Shell Island where shallow-draught boats may lie afloat. Leading marks indicate the line of entrance, in the shape of two poles ashore topped by black diamond markers. The basin is crowded with moorings belonging to local boats.

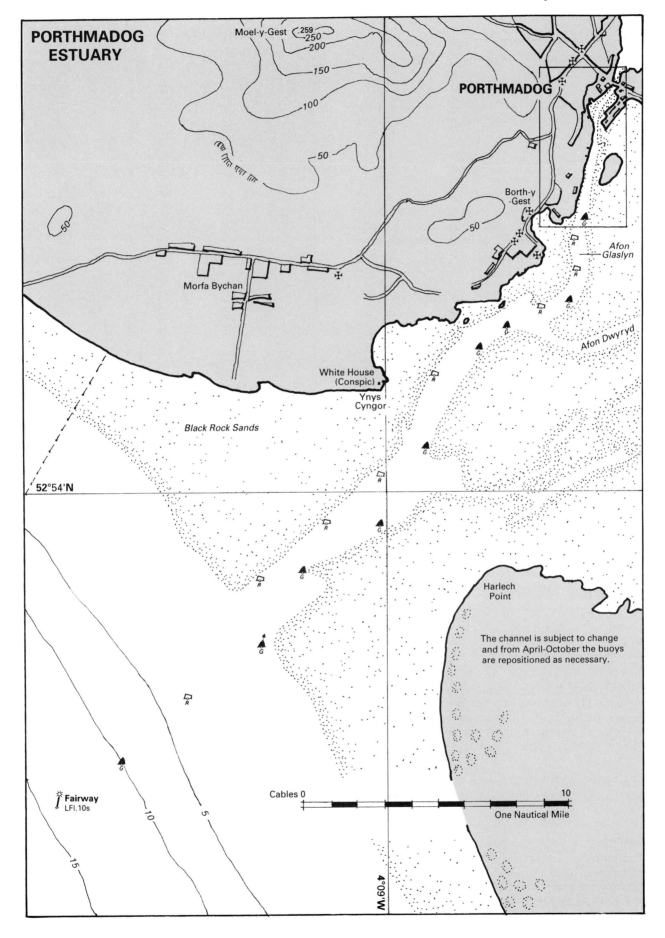

PORTHMADOG ESTUARY

Moel-y-Gest 259
250
200
150
100
50

PORTHMADOG

Borth-y-Gest

Afon Glaslyn

50

Morfa Bychan

Afon Dwyryd

White House (Conspic)

Ynys Cyngor

Black Rock Sands

52°54'N

Harlech Point

The channel is subject to change and from April-October the buoys are repositioned as necessary.

Cables 0   10
One Nautical Mile

Fairway
LFl.10s

10
5
15

4°09'W

Berthing

Anchorage for boats that can take the ground may be had on firm sand throughout the lagoon.

Charges

Harbour charges are levied by the Shell Island Leisure Centre on those boats that make use of their facilities.

Facilities

Water There are a number of water taps on Shell Island.

Slip There is a slip to the yacht club boathouse to the N of the harbour entrance. There are further slips in the Shell Island deep-water basin and to the N of the basin.

Provisions Provisions may be obtained at the Leisure Centre shop.

Yacht club Llanbedr and Pensarn Yacht Club.

Calor Gas and Camping Gaz From the Leisure Centre shop.

Porthmadog

Waypoint 52°52'·87N 4°11'·02W Porthmadog Fairway buoy

Local High Water is −0230 Dover

Charts Admiralty *1512, 1971*; Imray *C52, C61*

Approaching Porthmadog harbour

General

Porthmadog was created in the early 19th century, when the local MP, William Maddocks, built the mile-long embankment across the Glaslyn estuary to reclaim 7,000 acres of land. The town achieved

prosperity as the sea outlet for the local slate trade; the narrow-gauge Ffestiniog railway was built to transport the slate from the mines, the station being situated in the NE corner of the inner harbour. Local ships transported slate from Porthmadog to destinations all over the world.

The town is now a thriving holiday centre, and the harbour offers good shelter to those prepared to negotiate the 3·5M-long estuary channel.

Warning

Entrance to the harbour should only be made between 2 hours either side of HW. The channel is subject to change and the buoys are moved accordingly. An up-to-date chart showing the position of the buoys is obtainable from the harbourmaster. Strong onshore winds can build up a dangerous sea, particularly against the ebb, making the harbour impossible to enter. The inner harbour is well protected in all conditions; the outer harbour is more exposed to strong winds from the S or SW.

Porthmadog inner harbour

VHF radio telephone
Call *Porthmadog Harbour* Ch 16, work Ch 12 or 14.
Call *Madoc Yacht Club* Ch 80.

Facilities
Fuel Robert Owen Marine, on quay (adjacent to the chandlery).
Water Tap on yacht club wall; key required (from steward or a club member).
Slip On NW side of inner harbour.
Provisions Full provisions are available in the town. EC Wednesday.
Post office High Street, Porthmadog.
Yacht club Madoc Yacht Club. Bar and showers. Porthmadog and Transfynydd Sailing Club.
Calor Gas and Camping Gaz Gwynedd Caravans, Madoc Street.
Chandlery Glaslyn Marine, Oakley Wharf.
Marine engineer Robert Owen Marine, Oakley Wharf.

Approach
By day Porthmadog lies on the N side of the estuary formed by the confluence of Afon Dwyryd and Afon Glaslyn. Moel-y-Gest is a conspicuous, isolated hill (260m) to the north of the entrance, and Criccieth Castle, sited on a bold, grassed promontory, is conspicuous 2·5M NW of the Fairway buoy. Harlech Castle, to the S, forms an excellent navigational mark when approaching from the SW, although it may be difficult to identify against its background when approaching from the NW or W.
By night The Fairway buoy is lit (LFl.10s) and the buoys have reflective topmarks, but a night entrance should not be attempted without local knowledge.

Anchorage in the approach
Anchor off the harbour entrance only in the most settled conditions.

Entrance
The striped RW Fairway buoy must be located. The channel is marked for its full length with red and green lateral buoys, which are relocated as necessary.

Berthing
Drying berths for visitors are available alongside the yacht club quay. Yachts wishing to stay afloat should take a river mooring just before entering the inner harbour, at the direction of the harbourmaster.

Harbourmaster
Office on NW quay. ☎ 0766 512927.

Charges
There are harbour charges.

Pwllheli Harbour

Waypoint 52°52'·75N 4°23'·3W 5 cables SSE of harbour entrance
Local High Water is −0300 Dover
Charts Admiralty *1512, 1971*; Imray *C52, C61*

General
The biggest town on the Lleyn peninsula, Pwllheli has been an important market town and harbour since it was given its charter as a borough by the Black Prince in 1355. A street market is still held every Wednesday in the Maes. Substantial improvements have recently been made to the harbour, to improve access and to form Hafan Pwllheli, a well

Pwllheli Marina

PWLLHELI

sheltered marina with 415 alongside berths (May 1993) and excellent onshore facilities. It is one of only a few publicly owned marinas in the country, having been developed by Dwyfor District Council with financial assistance from the EC, and is managed by Yacht Havens Management Limited.

Depths in the channel are continually being monitored, and at present access is available at all states of the tide to yachts of moderate draft in virtually all conditions (one metre at MLWS).

Approach

By day Pwllheli harbour lies 3·5M NE of Llanbedrog Head, and can be identified by Carreg yr Imbill or Gimblet Rock, a 40m-high conspicuous mass of granite, to the S of the harbour entrance.

By night The harbour may be approached at night using the following lights:

St Tudwal's Island Fl.WR.20s46m15/13M

Pwllheli harbour entrance Q.G.3m3M and Q.R.3m 3M

It should be noted that the harbour entrance lights are obscured by the land to the W, and cannot be seen until a yacht is virtually due S. Sufficient offing should be maintained until these lights are identified. The training wall and the channel through to the marina are lit.

Anchorage in the approach

Anchorage may be found in 3m sand off the harbour entrance, giving shelter from winds from W through NW to N.

Entrance

Entrance is made between the new training wall to the N and Pwllheli Point. There is a groyne running NW from Pwllheli Point and an outfall running N; both are marked with beacons with red topmarks. The training wall is submerged after half-tide, and its position is marked with poles with green topmarks, all of which must be left to starboard. There are piled trot moorings to the S side of the channel.

Pwllheli Marina

Llanbedrog Head

Berthing

All yachts must report to the marina office, where they will be allocated a berth.

Harbourmaster

Office on S side of harbour.

VHF radio telephone

Call *Hafan Pwllheli* Ch 80.

Facilities

Hafan Pwllheli is a fully serviced marina, with water and electricity provided on the pontoons, and toilets, showers and a launderette ashore. There is a separate fuelling pontoon to the S of the pontoons, a slip and a 40-ton travel-hoist.

Slip There is a further slip to the S side of the harbour.

Provisions Full provisions are available in the town, although the centre is ¾M from the marina offices.

Yacht club Pwllheli Sailing Club. Bar and showers.

Boat repairs and engineers Partington Boatyard and Firmhelm Boatyard, both on S side of harbour.

Chandlery Firmhelm Boatyard, on S side of harbour.

Calor Gas and Camping Gaz Partington Boatyard.

Marine electronics Rowlands Marine Electronics, on S side of harbour.

Sailmakers JKA Sails (☎ 613266) and Tudor Sails (☎ 613141).

Trwyn Llanbedrog or Llanbedrog Head

A steep-sided, bold promontory, rising to an elevation of 131m. There are a small number of local boat moorings. Anchorage may be had to the N of the headland, close to and to seaward of the perch marking the end of the sewer outfall, in stones and sand, giving shelter from SW and W. Limited provisions may be obtained from the village ashore.

Abersoch

Waypoints 52°49'·46N 4°28'·05W one mile E of yacht club jetty, and 52°47'·26N 4°28'·7W 7 cables SSW of St Tudwal's Island lighthouse, at the S entrance to St Tudwal's Sound
Local High Water is −0315 Dover
Charts Admiralty *1512, 1971*; Imray *C52, C61*

General

A popular holiday and boating centre, Abersoch offers limited shelter to yachts in St Tudwal's Roads. There is a small drying inner harbour, formed by the channel of the Afon Soch, that can be accessed at HW, but has no space for visiting yachts. St Tudwal's Islands are privately owned, and landing is not allowed.

Warning

St Tudwal's Roads are sheltered from S through W to N. The anchorage is exposed to the E, and heavy seas can build in strong winds from this sector.

Approach

By day Overfalls can build ½M offshore off Trwyn Cilan in contrary wind and tide conditions. St Tudwal's Sound, between the West Island and the mainland, is clear of dangers. West Island has a white tower lighthouse (Fl.WR.20s46m15/13M) and white buildings. The islands themselves are steep-to except at their N ends, where shoals extend from both islands; these N ends should be given a clearance of at least 200m. Passage between the islands should be on a N-S course midway between the two. Careg-y-Trai is a dangerous patch of drying

ST TUDWAL'S ROADS

N

4°28'W

Trwyn
Llanbedrog

Cables 0   10
One Nautical Mile

3₁

4

3₇

5

Moorings

3₁

Jetty

10

ABERSOCH

2₈

3₇

4₃

Red

Obscd

Penrhyn Du

White

Red

East Island

Carreg-y Trai

Bell

St Tudwal's
Islands

West
Island

52°48'N

White

Fl.WR.20s
46m15/13M

20

5

White

5

20

Trwyn yr
Wylfa

Depths in Metres

rock, often used by seals, 3 cables ESE of East Island. It is marked at its seaward end by a red bell buoy.

There is a sewer outfall pipe running 1·5 cables ENE from Penbennar, close to the yacht club, its end being marked by a perch. This also serves to mark the low-water line of spring tides.

By night St Tudwal's Roads may be approached using the following lights:

Bardsey Island Fl(5)15s39m26M
St Tudwal's West Island Fl.WR.20s46m15/13M

Entrance to inner harbour, Abersoch

St Tudwal's Island West

Moorings

There are a large number of moorings laid to the SE and E of Penbennar. Contact the yacht club to arrange the use of a visitors' or vacant mooring. Anchorage may be found in sand and small stones clear of the moorings. There is a launch service arranged by the yacht club running to the yacht club

jetty. There is an anchorage midway along the NE side of St Tudwal's East Island, although the tidal stream can run through strongly at springs.

VHF radio telephone

Call *South Caernarfon Yacht Club* on Ch 80.

Facilities

Fuel Petrol and diesel from Abersoch Land and Sea Services.
Water By container from yacht club.
Provisions Full provisions are available in the town.
Yacht club South Caernarfon Yacht Club. Bar and showers.
Chandlery Abersoch Land and Sea Services, and Abersoch Boatyard Ltd.
Marine engineers Hookes Marine (☎ 2458).

Aberdaron

A small village, set in a fold in the rugged coastline. The bay offers limited protection as an anchorage, but is a convenient stopping place in settled weather when waiting for the tide in Bardsey Sound. The 12th-century church was originally built a respectable distance from the shore, but erosion by the sea has required the construction of a protective sea wall. The anchorage, off Aberdaron Church, is protected from W through N to NE winds, although

Aberdaron

a swell may find its way into the bay at any time. Anchor with care, as the holding ground is poor. Landing may be effected on the beach, and limited provisions and a post office can be found in the village.

Ynys Gwylan Fawr and Ynys Gwylan Fach are two islands lying at the SE entrance to Aberdaron Bay. There is a 3·5-cables-wide sound between Ynys Gwylan Fawr and the mainland, with a least depth of 5·8m through the centre of the sound. There is also a deep-water passage between the islands.

Bardsey Island

Bardsey Island, or Ynys Enlli, lies at the SW tip of the Lleyn peninsula. It is 1½M long and ¾M wide, and its S promontory is joined to the main part of the island by a narrow isthmus. The N coastline is about ½M long, and the cliffs are rugged and steep, rising to the heights of Mynydd Enlli (165m) in the E. Mynydd Enlli falls steeply into the sea on its E side. The remainder of the coastline is jagged but lower-lying. The lighthouse (Fl(5)15s39m28M) is a white square tower standing on the S promontory.

The island has long been a refuge for holy men; the earliest church is thought to have been begun in the 6th century. The ruins of the Abbey of St Mary of Bardsey, dating from the 13th century, still remain. The island is now managed as a farm and nature reserve, and visitors landing on the island are asked to respect the farming and wildlife interests.

There is an anchorage, for settled weather only, at the entrance to Henllwyn Cove, to the W of Pen Cristin, on the E side of the island. Smaller craft may anchor within the cove itself. Entrance to the cove must be made with great care, as there are isolated rocks and shoals extending from the shore.

Anchor with care, as holding is poor. There is a slip on the N side of the cove.

Passage to the S of Bardsey Island should be to the S of both Bastram Shoal and the Devil's Ridge, as heavy overfalls are created by the tidal streams and exacerbated by any contrary wind.

Bardsey Sound

Lying between Bardsey Island and the SW tip of the Lleyn peninsula, the 1·5M-wide Bardsey Sound allows daylight passage in suitable conditions of tide and wind. The only obstructions within the sound are Carreg Ddu, a small island on the N side, and Maen Bugail, a rock (drying 4·1m) on the S side of the sound.

The sound should preferably be passed through at or near slack water. The main tidal streams through the sound run NW and SE. The NW stream begins at +0500 Dover and the SE stream at −0100 Dover. During the last of the ebb, an eddy stream runs from Trwyn Cilan inshore along Porth Neigwl, passing through the sound between Ynys Gwylan Fawr and the mainland, anticlockwise around Aberdaron Bay, around Pen y Cil, and inshore of

Carreg Ddu to Braich y Pwll. This stream begins 2 hours before the main stream in Bardsey Sound turns to the NW. A similar stream sets in the opposite direction 2 hours before the main stream sets SE. Yachts can take advantage of these eddies in settled conditions.

There are races off Pen y Cil, Braich y Pwll and Maen Bugail at the strength of the tide, and strong winds can cause a confused and breaking sea in these localities. Strong winds contrary to the main tidal flow can cause heavy and confused seas, making the sound impassable.

Approaching the anchorage, Bardsey Island

VII. Braich y Pwll to Conwy

The coastline from Braich-y-Pwll to Caernarfon Bar is one of spectacular scenery, but with only Porth Dinllaen offering any realistic shelter, and that only from some of the prevailing winds, and with the often inhospitable Caernarfon Bar, it is a coast to be treated with respect. Tidal streams run N-S across the mouth of the bay, their strength lessening further into the bay as the stream follows the curve of the coast.

Anglesey offers an excellent cruising ground. Tidal streams are strong around the island and can be utilised to good effect.

Holyhead is an excellent port of refuge, with good shelter and access at all times and in all conditions. The variety of harbours and anchorages around the island between them offer shelter from all wind directions.

The Tripods

A shoal extending N for about 1½M and running about one mile offshore from a point ¾M N of Braich y Pwll. There is a least depth of 10m, but the bank produces overfalls at the strength of the tidal stream, and with a contrary wind builds up a considerable sea. Keeping Carreg Ddu open from the N side of Bardsey Sound leads S of the shoal.

Porth Dinllaen

Waypoint 52°57'·3N 4°34'·1W 5 cables WNW of
  Careg y Chwislen beacon
Local High Water is −0240 Dover
Charts Admiralty *1512, 1971*; Imray *C52, C61*

General

A small cove at the W end of the north-facing Dinllaen Bay, protected by a narrow promontory extending N on its W side. It was nearly chosen

instead of Holyhead as the road and rail terminal for the Irish ferries. The tiny hamlet comprises an inn and a row of cottages.

Approaching Porth Dinllaen

Trevor harbour

Warning

Dinllaen Bay can be entered at any state of the tide. Shelter is good in S to W winds, but N or NE winds can cause heavy seas and make the anchorage untenable.

Approach

By day When approaching from Braich y Pwll, an offing of ¾M will avoid the offshore rocks and islets. Carn Fadryn (369m), a cone-shaped mountain 3·5M S of Porth Dinllaen, is conspicuous; when approaching from the N, a bearing of 182° on Carn Fadryn will lead about one cable east of Careg y Chwislen. Approaching from the SW, Carreg-y-chad, a rock with a least depth of 1·6m, lying 7 cables SW of Trwyn Porth Dinllaen, must be left to starboard. Carreg Ddu are drying rocks extending one cable N of the headland. Careg y Chwislen, drying to 1·5m, lies 2 cables ENE of the headland. It is marked by an iron beacon with a globe top and should be left well to starboard, as there is a tendency for the stream to set on to Careg y Chwislen from inshore.

By night There are no official lights, apart from the F.R. displayed occasionally from the top of the lifeboat slip; a night approach is not recommended.

Moorings

There are a number of private moorings laid within the cove.

Berthing

Anchor in sand clear of the laid moorings, avoiding Carreg Oysters (rocks which dry 4·3m) on the S side of the cove.

Facilities

There are no facilities ashore for yachtsmen, apart from the inn, and provisions have to be carried from Morfa Bychan, up a steep road from the beach on the S side of the anchorage.

Trevor

A small cove 5 cables E of Trwyn-y-Tal, drying to sand with stone patches. The small harbour is protected from S through W winds, and a stone pier extending 100m E provides shelter from the NW. There is 2·5m alongside the pier at MLWN. There is a slip on the W side of the harbour, but there are no further facilities ashore. Provisions are available from the village, some 15 minutes' walk from the harbour.

Caernarfon Bar

Waypoint 53°07'·18N 4°24'·37W C1 buoy

Drying sandbanks extend for 3M W of the coast. The channel over the bar leads into the Menai Strait through the narrow entrance at Abermenai. The white tower of the lighthouse on Llanddwyn Island, to the NW of the bar, is conspicuous. The channel should only be used for 3 hours either side of HW. The depths and position of the sandbanks are subject to change, and the buoys are moved accord-

CAERNARFON BAR

Depths in Metres

N

4°24'W

53°07'N

Fl.WR.3.5s
6m3M

Abermenai
Point

Fort
Belan

Mussel
Bank

Fl(2)R.5s

15

10

5

2₈

C6
Fl.R.5s

SOUTH SANDS

1₃

2₅

0₆

NORTH SAND

0₉

3₄

C4
Q.R

C5
G

2₇

1₅

2₄

Llanddwyn
Bay

C3
Q.G

0₃

1₇

0₉

5

Mermaid Cove

Pilots Cove

YB

Fl.WR.2.5s12m7/4M

2₉

2₃

2₈

LLANDDWYN ISLAND

C2
Fl.R.10s

4₅

C1
Fl.G.10s

3₆

5₅

YB

0

0

Cables 0   One Nautical Mile   10

10

126

ingly. At springs, the tidal stream can exceed 5 knots at Abermenai Point, and use of a fair tide or slack water is necessary.

Contrary winds and tide can build severe seas on the bar, particularly when a swell has built up in the Irish Sea. Even moderately strong winds against the ebb can make the bar impassable. The buoys are mostly lit, but night entrance is not recommended without prior knowledge, and settled conditions would in any case be necessary.

Caernarfon harbour

Caernarfon

Waypoint 53°08'·53N 4°16'·82W C9 buoy
Local High Water is −0130 Dover
Charts Admiralty *1464, 1970*; Imray *C52, C61*

General

A totally sheltered, mostly drying harbour within the estuary of the Afon Seiont, 2M NE of the SW entrance of the Menai Strait. The harbour is domi-

nated by the magnificent 13th-century castle, the town having been a fortified centre since pre-Roman times. The drying tidal dock is currently being redeveloped with lock gates to allow half-tide access to pontoon moorings.

Warning

Entrance to the inner harbour and tidal basin should be made within 3 hours either side of HW. The tidal stream sets strongly across the entrances to the harbours, except at slack water, and strong winds contrary to the tide can create rough conditions. The inner harbour dries except for the bed of the river.

Entering Caernarfon tidal dock

Approach

By day The castle and town walls are conspicuous when approaching Caernarfon from either direction. It should be noted that the direction of buoyage changes in the Menai Strait, at the S cardinal mark to the NW of Caernarfon.

By night The only official lights are the 2F.G(vert) lights at the entrance to and to the N of the tidal basin; however, the proximity of the entrance channel to the lights of the town makes a night entrance feasible.

Anchorage in the approach

Anchorage may be had in 5m off the town, but the tide can exceed 3·5 knots at springs and the holding ground is uncertain. Yachts that can take the ground can anchor out of the tidal stream to the W of the entrance channel.

Entrance

The tidal basin is entered between the stone quays to the N of the town walls. The inner harbour entrance is marked with an E cardinal buoy, which must be left to starboard. Three green beacons mark the starboard side of the channel, and a red pole beacon marks the extremity of a stone pier to port. There is a pedestrian swing bridge across the channel which is manned when there is enough water to enter the harbour. It may be necessary to give a sound signal (using foghorn) in order to have the bridge opened.

Moorings

Private moorings are laid along the channel of the Afon Seiont.

Berthing

Drying wall berths may be available, as directed by the harbourmaster.

Harbourmaster

Office on quay.

Charges

There are harbour charges.

VHF radio telephone

Call *Caernarfon Harbour* Ch 16, work Ch 12 or 14 (office hours only).

Facilities

Fuel Diesel from Caernarfon Marine, on S side of Afon Seiont.
Water Hydrants on quay.
Slip Slip in tidal basin to Arfon Oceaneering.
Provisions Full provisions are avilable in the town. EC Thursday.
Post office Castle Square.
Yacht clubs Royal Welsh Yacht Club (bar). Caernarfon Sailing Club (bar).
Chandlery Caernarfon Marine and Owen Tudor, on quay.
Calor Gas and Camping Gaz Owen Tudor and Calor Gas Centre, Pool Street.
Marine engineers Arfon Oceaneering.

Abermenai

Temporary anchorage may be had at the SW entrance to the Menai Strait, within the shelter of Abermenai Point. The anchorage is protected from SW to NW but exposed to winds from the E sector. There are no facilities. A similar anchorage may be found on the S side of the entrance to the E of the fort at Belan.

Llanddwyn Island

Temporary anchorage may be found in suitable weather conditions off Pilot's Cove or Mermaid Cove, to the E of Llanddwyn Island. The attractive anchorages offer shelter from W through N to NE winds; in strong SW winds a swell runs round the headland into the cove. Small S cardinal buoys indicate the positions of rocks to the S and E of the headland. Approach to the anchorages should be made with care, as there are a number of drying rocks that are not buoyed, particularly to the S of the islet off Mermaid Cove. There are no facilities, but Pilot's Cove can provide an ideal anchorage in which to wait for the right conditions for entering the Menai Strait.

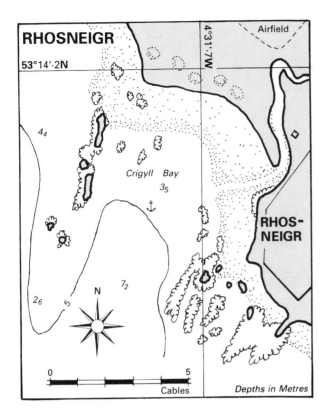

RHOSNEIGR

53°14'·2N

4°31'·7W

Airfield

Crigyll Bay

3₅

4₄

2₆ 5 7₂

N

RHOS-NEIGR

0   5

Cables

Depths in Metres

Rhosneigr

Shelter may be found from winds from N through E to SE off the village of Rhosneigr. Reefs extend in tongues offshore in a SW direction on either side of Crigyll Bay. Approach should be from a SW direction, in order to identify and avoid the reefs. Approach and anchor with care, as there are further isolated rocks within the bay. The bay is exposed to the SW. Provisions are available in the village.

Rhosneigr

Rhoscolyn

Rhoscolyn Bay offers shelter to yachts except in strong winds from the S or SE. A rock with a least depth of 1·8m at MLWS is situated at the midpoint of the narrow entrance to the bay. There is a limited amount of space in which to anchor close to the moorings laid within the bay. There is a small castellated tower on the islet to the S of the disused lifeboat station. Approach to the bay should be from the SE. Tidal streams set strongly across the entrance. Rhoscolyn Beacon marks the Beacon Rocks, lying 2 cables SW of Rhoscolyn Point and extending for ½M in a SW direction. Provisions are available in Rhoscolyn.

Trearddur Bay

Anchorage may be found on the S side of Trearddur Bay, giving shelter from winds from NW through N to SE. The bay is exposed to the SW. Maen Piscar (dries 1·8m) must be avoided when approaching from the S. There are conspicuous buildings on the N headland to help identify the bay. There are extensive patches of drying rocks in the N of the bay. Trearddur Bay is a popular holiday resort, and anchored yachts will have to contend with the wash from powerboats during the day in fine weather. Provisions are available in the village. Porth Diana, to the S of Trearddur Bay, is a small bay protected by offlying rocks. It is crowded with private moorings, and there is no space for a yacht to anchor.

TREARDDUR BAY

0   2   Cables

4°37'W

2₅ 4₇ 5

53°16'·5N

8₇

10

Porth Diana

N

Depths in Metres

Depths in Metres

4°36'.W

0   3
Cables

53°14'.5N

LB
(disused)

Small
tower

Bn

N

RHOSCOLYN

South Stack

A small island off the NW of Holy Island, to which
it is joined by a pedestrian suspension bridge at the
foot of a steep flight of cliff steps. The island is
topped with the white round tower and associated
buildings of South Stack lighthouse (Fl.10s60m
23M). A fog signal station is situated on North
Stack, one mile NE of the lighthouse. At springs,
tidal streams can run at over 5 knots off South
Stack. The N-going stream begins at +0530 Dover
and the S-going stream at −0030 Dover. During the
N-going stream, races extend 1½M NW of South
Stack and ½M W from North Stack. During the S-
going stream a race extends ½M W of South Stack.
In the most settled conditions, advantage may be
taken of the narrow passage inside the races, close
under the cliffs. In normal conditions the Stacks
should be given an offing of 2M, if passage is not
being made at slack water. Strong winds can extend
the race for up to 7M offshore. Strong contrary
winds can build a heavy and dangerous sea off the
headlands.

Conspicuous buildings to north of harbour entrance, Trearddur

Moorings at Porth Diana, Trearddur

Holyhead

Waypoint 53°20'·1N 4°37'·1W 3 cables N of end of
  breakwater
Local High Water is −0040 Dover
Charts Admiralty *2011, 1413, 1970*; Imray *C52, C61*

General

An excellent port of refuge, Holyhead can be entered in any conditions and is well sheltered from all
directions, although strong NE winds can raise an
uncomfortable sea in the harbour. The 1½M-long
breakwater which protects the New Harbour was
completed in 1873. The breakwater lighthouse is a
white stone tower with a black painted band. Holyhead is a busy commercial port, from which the
Sealink ferry runs regularly to Dun Laoghaire. Ap-
proval has been given for a 300-berth marina off
Soldier's Point in the outer harbour. It is intended
that this will include comprehensive haul-out, chandlery and boatyard facilities.

Approach

By day The races off North and South Stack have
been described above; the passages around Carmel
Head will be described later. There are no offlying
dangers when approaching the harbour from the
west. The 127m-high chimney 2M to the SSE of
the harbour entrance is conspicuous. When making
passage from Holyhead, departure should be timed
so as to reach Carmel Head or South Stack at slack
water.

By night The harbour may be approached at night
using the following lights:

South Stack lighthouse Fl.10s60m23M
The Skerries lighthouse Fl(2)10s36m22M + F.R.
  26m16M
Cliperau Rocks can Lt buoy Fl(4)R.15s

Breakwater Head lighthouse Fl(3)15s14M
Note that there are large unlit mooring buoys in
NW of harbour.

Entrance

The harbour is entered between the head of the
breakwater and Cliperau Rocks, marked with a red
can bell buoy. The breakwater should be given at
least 50m clearance. A small green buoy immediately within the harbour entrance should be left to
starboard. Yachts must use the New Harbour, within the confines of the breakwater. Keep parallel to
the breakwater until the small-craft moorings at the
head of the harbour are sighted.

Moorings

Small-craft moorings are laid at the head of the
inner harbour; these should be taken as directed by
the sailing club boatman. Alternatively, a vacant
mooring may be taken prior to reporting to the
sailing club. There is a sailing club launch service.
In the absence of a vacant mooring a yacht may
anchor close to the moorings. Anchorage in the
harbour entrance or approach is prohibited.

Charges

There are harbour charges.

VHF radio telephone

Call *Holyhead Harbour* Ch 16, work Ch 14.
Call *Holyhead Sailing Club* Ch 80.

Facilities

Fuel Holyhead Boatyard, on S side of the New Har-
  bour. Yachts may come alongside the fuelling
  quay after half-tide.
Water By container from sailing club, or alongside
  from Holyhead Boatyard, as above.
Slip On S side of New Harbour.
Provisions Full provisions are available in the town.
  EC Tuesday.
Post office In town centre.
Yacht club Holyhead Sailing Club. Bar and showers.
Chandlery Holyhead Chandlery, on Lower Shore
  Road facing harbour.
Calor Gas and Camping Gaz Holyhead Chandlery.
Marine engineers Holyhead Marine.
Refuse disposal Skip in sailing club yard.

Carmel Head and the Skerries

Carmel Head is a bold headland situated 6M NE of
North Stack at the N entrance to Holyhead Bay. To
seaward of Carmel Head are numerous rocks and
shoals, most prominent being the group of stacks
known as the Skerries. The Skerries lighthouse
(Fl(2)10s36m22M), a white round tower with a red
band, stands on the highest part of the group of
rocks. A fixed red light is shown below the main
light over the sector of dangerous rocks to the ENE.

In the channel between the Skerries and Carmel
Head the NE-going stream starts at +0500 Dover

HOLYHEAD HARBOUR

Fl(3)15s21m14M
Siren 20s

F.R.7m1M & F.W or R.10M

Aluminium Jetty

Fl(4)R.15s

2F.R(vert)

Ynys
Halen
or Salt
Island

4°38'W

53°19'·5N

Yacht Moorings

Perch

SC

Trwyn Llwyd

Soldier's
Point

HOLYHEAD

5
Cables

0

N

Depths in Metres

and the SW stream at −0100 Dover. At springs the stream can approach 6 knots. About one mile NW of the Skerries the NE-going stream starts at −0550 Dover and the SW-going stream at +0030 Dover.

Carmel Head can be passed close to at slack water to avoid the race between the headland and the Skerries. With even moderate contrary winds the tidal stream can cause confused seas in this area, and strong contrary winds can quickly build dangerous breaking seas. The rapid tidal stream causes heavy overfalls on East and West Platters, Middle Rock, Carmel Rocks and Passage Rock, and at all the inshore patches on this stretch of coast. At night or in unsettled conditions passage should be made at least one mile offshore of the Skerries. There are traffic separation zones to the N and NW of the Skerries and Holyhead Bay.

To the E of the Skerries are numerous dangerous rocks, although the area is well buoyed and they should not cause any significant danger in settled conditions. A passage 2M offshore will avoid all dangers. West Mouse is an island ¾M NNE of Carmel Head, marked with a white pyramidal beacon. There is foul ground stretching one mile to the W and SW of the island, and heavy, dangerous overfalls occur in this area on the ebb.

Cemlyn Bay

The bay, 2·5M E of Carmel Head, affords shelter in winds from SE through S to W. It is particularly exposed to the NE. It is an isolated anchorage with a bird sanctuary on its W side and no facilities ashore. The E side of the bay is dominated by the Wylfa Power Station. Passage from the W should be outside the green conical Harry Furlong buoy, which must be left to starboard on the approach.

Cemaes Bay

Shelter may be found from NE through S to SW winds in the attractive anchorage at Cemaes. There is an inner harbour (which dries) protected by a stone breakwater, although this is crowded with local boats.

Wylfa Power Station, Cemlyn Bay

Porth Bach, Cemaes Bay

There is a shoal patch extending for 3 cables off Llanbadrig Head, and entrance should be made by proceeding to the centre of Cemaes Bay before turning to the SE when the anchorage at Cemaes is open. Anchor in 3m sand in the centre of the bay. When going ashore by dinghy, note that the small stone breakwater at Porth Bach is awash at HW.

Water is available at the root of the inner harbour breakwater. Provisions are available in the town. There is a post office in the town, and *Camping Gaz* is available at Mona's Stores.

Temporary anchorage may be found at Llanbadrig Cove, to the N of Cemaes, and off Lamb Island, on the W side of the bay, offering protection from W winds.

Amlwch

Waypoint 53°25'·48N 4°19'·75W 5 cables N of breakwater head
Local High Water is −0030 Dover
Charts Admiralty *1977*; Imray *C52, C61*

Entrance to Amlwch harbour

General

Formerly an important commercial harbour exporting copper ore and building its own seagoing vessels. The harbour offers good shelter, although entrance is not possible in strong onshore winds. There are alongside floating moorings in the outer harbour and quayside moorings in the inner harbour, which dries.

Warning

The harbour can be entered at all states of the tide, although a yacht should be aware of the tidal set when approaching the narrow entrance. Strong N or NE onshore winds will build up a big swell at the harbour entrance; no approach should be made in these conditions. The shelter inside the harbour is good, but winds from the N sector can set up a scend in the outer harbour. The inner harbour can only be entered for 2½ hours either side of HW.

Amlwch harbour

Approach

By day There is a passage inshore of East Mouse to the W of the harbour entrance, although this is only recommended for use with local knowledge. The concrete wall forming the breakwater must be identified.

By night The 2F.R(vert) lights at the head of the breakwater must be identified. A night approach is not recommended without local knowledge.

Entrance

Enter the harbour round the head of the concrete breakwater, proceeding through the 50m-wide opening into the outer harbour.

Amlwch harbour

Berthing

Alongside berths in the outer harbour (as directed by the harbourmaster).

Harbourmaster

Office on quay.

Charges

There are harbour charges.

Facilities

Water Tap on quay.
Provisions Provisions are available in the town.
Chandlery Pilot's Store, in town.

Moelfre

Shelter may be found from S through W to N winds in Moelfre Roads. Ynys Moelfre should be passed to seaward. Anchor to the south of the end of the lifeboat slip, in 3m mud. Anchorage is very exposed to NE. Similar shelter may be found in the cove of Traeth Bychan, to the S of Moelfre Roads.

Red Wharf Bay or Traeth Coch

Shelter from all directions except NE may be found in this attractive bay, which mostly dries to firm sand. Entrance must be made between 2 hours either side of HW. The 15m-high, steep-sided rocky mass of Castell Mawr is conspicuous at the harbour entrance and the channel is buoyed by the sailing club. Limited provisions are available ashore. Water and showers are available at the Traeth Coch Sailing Club, although the opening hours are limited.

Approach Red Wharf Bay

Drying moorings Red Wharf Bay

Puffin Island

St Seriol's Tower is part of the ruins of a monastic settlement established on the island during the 6th century. The tower is conspicuous near the centre of the island, as is the ruined semaphore station at the N end. The island is a private bird sanctuary and landing is strictly by permission.

Access to the N end of the Menai Strait should be obtained between the S of the island and Trwyn-du. Entrance to the Strait to the SE side of the island should not be attempted without local knowledge.

Puffin Sound can be approached at any angle, the only danger being a shoal with a least depth of 2m between the green conical buoy marking Dinmor Bank and Trwyn-du lighthouse. Trwyn-du lighthouse (Fl.5·5s19m15M) is situated at the end of a rocky shelf extending from Trwyn-du, and has a white circular tower with three black horizontal bands. Entrance to the Strait should be made between Trwyn-du lighthouse and the red Perch Rock beacon. The channel running in a SW direction to Beaumaris is buoyed, although only a few of the buoys are lit. A night entrance should only be attempted with care and preferably with local knowledge.

At the entrance to the Menai Strait, contrary wind and tide can quickly build up a steep sea. Strong onshore winds against the ebb should be avoided. The S-going stream begins at −0600 Dover and the N-going stream at −0115 Dover.

Beaumaris

Waypoint 53°15'·6N 4°05'·18W B10 buoy
Local High Water is −0025 Dover
Charts Admiralty *1464*; Imray *C52, C61*

General

One of the main sailing centres on the Menai Strait; the laid moorings are fairly well sheltered. Beaumaris Castle is a moated fort built by Edward I.

Approach

By day Beaumaris is approached using the buoyed channel of the Menai Strait.

By night The channel buoys are not all lit, although there are a number of shore-based lights. A night approach should only be made with care and preferably with local knowledge.

Yacht moorings, Beaumaris

Moorings at Beaumaris looking towards Gallows Point

BEAUMARIS

Moorings

The moorings laid off Beaumaris are private, and whilst they are frequently made available to visitors, they must only be used by yachts with crew remaining on board or by prior consent. The yacht clubs may be able to allocate moorings to visitors. The moorings are well sheltered, although a NE wind can make them uncomfortable. Many of the moorings dry onto soft mud.

Berthing

Anchorage may be found in 2-3m in the pool to the SE of B10 buoy. Care should be taken to avoid the banks of the channel, which are steep-to. The pool is well sheltered to all wind directions except NE.

Facilities

Fuel By container from ABC (Anglesey Boat Co.) Boatyard, at Gallows Point.

Water Taps on Beaumaris Pier and on wall of yacht club on Gallows Point, and standpipe adjacent to the clubhouse.

Slip ABC Boatyard.

Provisions Full provisions are available in the town. EC Wednesday.

Yacht clubs Royal Anglesey Yacht Club, Beaumaris and North West Venturers Yacht Club, Gallows Point.

Chandlery ABC Boatyard.

Calor Gas and Camping Gaz ABC Boatyard.

Boat repairs and engineers ABC Boatyard.

The Swellies

The notorious narrow, rock-strewn reach begins 3M SW of Gallows Point and stretches for 9 cables between the Menai Suspension Bridge and Britannia Bridge. The complex nature of the tidal streams in the Strait can result in streams reaching 8 knots at springs.

The channel does, however, offer a perfectly safe passage to yachts arriving at or just before HW. Going against the last of a contrary tide will enable yachts without local knowledge to make a passage at a steady speed, in order to identify the necessary marks more easily. Making passage against the last of a foul tide can also assist a yacht further along the Strait as the tide becomes favourable.

THE SWELLIES

MENAI BRIDGE

FL.G

10_6

11_3

14

11

Q.R

Menai Suspension
Bridge (30·5m)

5

5

5

126

The Platters

Ldg Line

11_1

Swelly Rock
(dr 3·1m)

VQ(6)+
LFl.10s

$\cdot 8$

Beacon
Fl.WR.2s5m3M

5

5

8

Ldg Lts 231°

Gored Goch

Cottage

Gribbin Rock

5

2_8

Beacon (pyramid)

4°11'W

Iso.5s
at centre
of span

F

F

Britannia Bridge
(27·4m)

Britannia
Rock

8_3

10_8

5

53°13'N

N

3

Cables

0

Depths in Metres

138

The Swellies

It is possible to make the passage at LW slack on neaps. However, there is a least charted depth of 0·4m to the NE of Britannia Bridge, and whilst many rocks are exposed at LW, passage is easier at HW because there is then a depth of approximately 3m over the Platters; at this state of the tide these rocks can therefore safely be passed over. Passage should not be attempted at night. High water slack in the Swellies is −0150 Dover.

Heading from the NE at HW, a yacht should pass under the centre of the Menai Suspension Bridge and make to leave the S cardinal buoy, marking the Swelly Rock, close to starboard. The course should then be continued past the buoy towards the cottage on Gored Goch. This course is held until the metal pylon transit beacons on either side of Britannia Bridge are in line. The transit is followed until the white pyramidal beacon on the S shore is abeam, when the course is altered to pass under the centre of the south span of Britannia Bridge, leaving the centre pier of the bridge to starboard. These directions are reversed when heading from the SW.

Port Dinorwic

Waypoint 53°11'·2N 4°12'·63W red buoy at harbour entrance
Local High Water is −0105 Dover
Charts Admiralty *1464*; Imray *C52, C61*

General

The historic use of Port Dinorwic can be traced back to the 8th century, when the Vikings used this part of the Menai Strait as a secure anchorage. The harbour was developed in the 19th century to ex-

port slate from the quarries of Snowdonia. Total shelter can be found in the locked Yacht Harbour or the alternative tidal basin.

Warning

Access to the Yacht Harbour is via the lock gates, which are usually only opened (on request) between 2 hours before and 4 hours after HW. In an emergency, however, the gates can be opened at any time there is sufficient water. There is an average of 2m within the tidal basin at half-tide; berthing should be at the direction of the harbour office. Yachts using the tidal basin should be capable of taking the ground.

Approaching Britannia Railway Bridge from south

Approach

By day The harbour is approached following the buoyed channel of the Menai Strait.

By night Given the restrictions of the Swellies and Caernarfon Bar, it is unlikely that the harbour will be approached at night; however, the two red buoys at and to the N of the harbour entrance are lit, and a F.WR.5m2M is displayed from a pole on the N side of the entrance to the tidal basin.

Anchorage in the approach

Anchorage may be found in 4m soft mud close to and inshore of the moorings off the harbour entrance.

Entrance

The Yacht Harbour is entered from the red pillar buoy, keeping a minimum of 6m away from the quay between the entrance to the tidal basin and the lock gates. The tidal basin is entered between the stone quays; there is no sill.

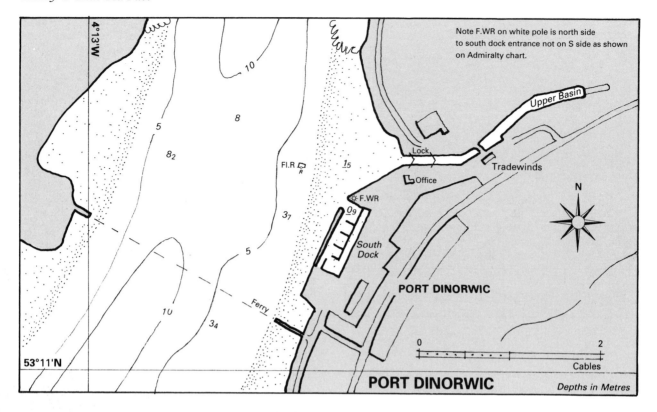

Note F.WR on white pole is north side to south dock entrance not on S side as shown on Admiralty chart.

PORT DINORWIC

Depths in Metres

Berthing

There are approximately 100 berths in the Yacht Harbour and a further 80 berths in the tidal basin. Berths can invariably be found for visitors. All berthing must be at the direction of the Yacht Harbour office.

Moorings

Deep-water moorings belonging to the Yacht Harbour are laid to the N of the harbour entrance. Private moorings are laid to the S of the entrance to the tidal basin.

Charges

There are harbour charges.

VHF radio telephone

Call *Dinorwic Marina* Ch 37.

Facilities

Port Dinorwic Yacht Harbour is a fully serviced yacht marina with water and electricity supplied to the berths. Fuel is available alongside the quay. There are toilets, showers and a restaurant.

Slip There is a slip in the tidal basin.

Provisions Limited provisions are available in the town. EC Wednesday.

Sailmaker J. Dawson (Sails).

Marine electronics M. J. Stallard.

Marine engineers P. D. Marine.

Bangor

Total shelter from all wind directions may be found alongside the quay in the drying harbours of Dickie's Boatyard, or in Penrhyn Dock. Approach should be made within 2 hours either side of HW. Water is available on the quay at Penrhyn Dock. Dickie's of Bangor is a fully equipped boatyard offering repair, servicing and ashore storage facilities. Water and diesel are available on the quay and *Calor Gas* from the shop. There is a comprehensive chandlery and yacht brokerage. Provisions are available in the town. EC Wednesday.

The Swellies looking northeast

Port Dinorwic harbour

Approaching Menai Suspension Bridge

Approaching tidal dock, Port Dinorwic

Approaching Port Dinorwic

Conwy

Waypoint 53°17'·96N 3°55'·49W Fairway buoy
Local High Water is −0015 Dover
Charts Admiralty *1977,1978*; Imray *C52, C61*

General

Conwy is probably the best-preserved medieval fortified town in Britain; the castle, its most dominant feature, was the most expensive of the chain built by Edward I. For decades the town has suffered from being the bottleneck through which all traffic along the North Wales coast must pass. The recently constructed tunnel under the river has alleviated this problem, and the casting basin for the tunnel sections has provided the setting for the construction of a new marina.

The new Conwy Marina provides excellent shelter in all conditions, and the moorings in the River Conwy itself are also well sheltered.

Approaching Conwy

Warning

The bar has about 0·6m at MLWS. The Scabs is a gravel patch which dries at LWS, lying between port-hand buoys C6 and C8. The channel is subject to change and the buoys are moved accordingly. The channel can be entered for up to 4 hours either side of HW; shallow-draught craft will be able to enter at any time on a neap tide. First-time entry should be made between 2 hours before HW and HW. The tidal stream can run at over 7 knots in the narrowest part of the channel at springs, and 2 hours after HW will be the latest practicable time to enter for most yachts. The channel can be entered in most conditions, although it is not advisable to do so in strong onshore winds, which will make the entrance difficult, especially on the ebb.

Approach

By day The Fairway buoy should be located. On approach from Puffin Island, the buoy lies on a line between the centre of the island and a jagged tooth of rock halfway up the N side of Penmaen-bach.

By night Only the perch beacon is lit in the channel, although the buoys have reflective topmarks. The marina entrance has fixed red and green lights. Entrance at night is not recommended without local knowledge.

Anchorage in the approach

Anchorage may be found off the entrance to the channel in settled conditions. Anchorage may be found between port-hand buoys C4 and C6 to wait for the tide, and at LW Conwy Sands will give some protection from NW winds.

Entrance

From the Fairway buoy, the channel is marked with lateral buoys which are repositioned as necessary. The inshore passage from the NW is unmarked and is not recommended. The perch beacon 3 cables N of Conwy Morfa should be left 30m to starboard. On rounding the perch beacon, Bonlondeb Point should be kept in line with the centre of the new road bridge. Conwy Marina is on the S bank of the river, to the NW of Bonlondeb Point.

Berthing

There are many private moorings laid throughout Conwy harbour, many of which dry. Visitors may be allocated a mooring by the harbourmaster. There is also a floating pontoon where visitors may lie alongside as directed by the harbourmaster. The harbour is well sheltered, although strong NW winds can make the harbour uncomfortable, especially on the ebb. Visitors may only stay in Conwy harbour for a maximum of 7 days, except in an emergency; this does not apply to the marina.

Conwy Marina is a new yacht marina, opened in 1992, providing berths and services for around 450 yachts.

Harbourmaster

Office on quay near to road bridge.

Charges

There are harbour charges and charges in the marina.

VHF radio telephone

Call *Conwy Harbour* Ch 16, work Ch 14 or 12.
Call *Conwy Marina* Ch 37.

Facilities

Conwy Marina is a fully equipped yacht marina, with water and electricity to the pontoons. There is a fuelling quay and a sewage pump-out facility. There are toilets, showers and a laundry ashore.

CONWY

Deganwy

River Conwy

Fl.G

Fl.R

Marina

Bodlondeb Point

Pontoon

Castle

Perch Fl.WR.5s 5m2M

White

Conwy Sands

Red

Red

3

2₁

0₉ ●3
G

3₃

0₆ □8
R

Burlingau Rock

⊛

□6
R

1₈

1₅

3₁

0₉

□4
R

▲1
G

Penmaen-bach Pt

Penmaen-bach

100

150

200

238

200

200

50

50

6₁

1₅

White

□2
R

0₉

0₉

0₉

2₅

Llys Elisap Clynnog

6₁

Fairway
RW

53°18'N

3°50'W

N

Depths in Metres

Cables 0

One Nautical Mile

10

Dickie's at Conwy provide chandlery and a yacht brokerage. Provisions are available in Conwy, although the centre is over a mile from the marina by land.

Conwy Quay Harbour provides fuel and water, alongside a drying berth.

Yacht clubs Conwy Yacht Club, Deganwy: bar and showers. North Wales Cruising Club: bar and showers.

Boat repairs, engineers and marine electronics Conwy River Boatyard.

VIII. Great Ormes Head to Silloth

Maryport

Workington

Harrington

Whitehaven

Ravenglass

Piel Island

River
Lune
Glasson
Dock

Fleetwood Marina

Ribble Estuary
and
Preston Marina

Liverpool

Rhyl

This stretch of coastline is predominantly exposed to the prevailing winds. Whilst good shelter is available in many harbours, the times of access are invariably restricted by conditions and by the state of the tide. There is no true harbour of refuge, and the coast should be cruised with a keen eye to the weather. Workington can be entered at any state of the tide, but it is a commercial harbour and its use by yachtsmen is not encouraged. The splendid scenery provided by Snowdonia and the Lake District is by way of compensation for the difficulties encountered.

Great Ormes Head

The headland is a prominent feature formed by a steep-sided mass of limestone rising to 203m. The lighthouse, a white square castellated tower (no longer lit), is on the N face of the headland. Temporary anchorage may be found in Ormes or Llandudno Bay, between Great Ormes Head and Little Ormes Head, in offshore winds or settled conditions.

Rhyl

Waypoint 53°20'·0N 3°30'·3W 5 cables N of outer perch
Local High Water is +0005 Dover
Charts Admiralty *1978*; Imray *C52, C61*

General

A popular seaside resort. At the SW end of the seafront is Foryd harbour, at the mouth of the River Clwyd. It is a well sheltered, mostly drying harbour, although rather small.

Warning

The harbour can only be entered for 2 hours either side of HW. First-time visitors are recommended to enter just before HW. Strong onshore winds make entrance impossible.

Approach

By day Rhyl Pavilion is a tall white tower with a domed top, conspicuous to the NE of the harbour. Rhyl Flats, to the N of the harbour entrance, have a

Approaching Rhyl

least charted depth of 0·1m, and the harbour should not be approached near LW.

By night The outer perch is lit with a Q.R, but a night entrance is not recommended without local knowledge.

Entrance

The perches marking the line of the river training wall must all be left close to port. On entering the harbour follow the centre of the channel before favouring the NW side of the harbour towards the quay and yacht club.

Berthing

Yachts must be able to take the ground and space in the harbour is limited. Visitors can invariably be found a mooring by a member of the yacht club, or they may tie alongside the yacht club quay. There is no harbourmaster and there are no harbour charges.

Facilities

Water Water tap on yacht club quay.
Slip Yacht club slip adjacent to the quay. Further slip by Foryd Bridge.
Provisions Full provisions are available in the town.
Yacht club Rhyl Yacht Club.

The Dee estuary

A large tidal estuary, mostly drying at LW. Reasonable shelter can be found in offshore winds, and the offlying banks give shelter from onshore winds at most states of the tide except for HW. Access to the estuary is via the Welsh Channel or the Hilbre Swash. The Welsh Channel is entered from the W; it runs round the Point of Air inshore of the extensive drying sands of the West Hoyle Bank. The Hilbre Swash is entered from the N and runs between the drying banks of the West and East Hoyle Banks. Both channels are well buoyed, but although most buoys are lit a night entrance is not recommended without local knowledge. The channels are liable to change and the buoys are moved accordingly. The streams run strongly in the estuary, especially when the banks are exposed and the streams are confined to the channels.

Mostyn Docks, on the S side of the estuary, is a privately owned commercial port, and yachts are only allowed to use the harbour in an emergency. There is an anchorage to the SE of the harbour where shelter can be found from NW winds behind the mole forming the entrance to the harbour. Approach must be after half-tide.

LIVERPOOL

Depths in Metres

0 5
Cables

Royal Liver Building

Port of Liverpool Pilots
Building (Dome)

Landing
Stage

Canning Dock

Salthouse Dock

13

*Albert
Dock*

Wapping Basin

53°24'N

Dukes
Fl(2)R.6s
R

Wapping Dock

15₉

River

Mersey

*Queens
Dock*

17₈

3₄

*Coburg
Dock*

6₉

Office — *Marina*

17₄

10

0₅

*Brunswick
Dock*

1₆

Lock
control
office

Lock

Red/Green
docking
signals

15₂

**Pluckington
Bank**
VQ(9)10s
YBY

Fl(2)G.6s

3°00'W

There are drying moorings laid in sand off the foreshore at Hoylake, with access from the Hilbre Channel, although these are very exposed to onshore winds. Similar drying moorings are laid off West Kirby and further up the estuary off Caldy and Heswall, drying onto mud. These are a little better protected from onshore winds than Hoylake, being in the lee of Hilbre Island and the associated rocks. There is plenty of space to anchor between the laid moorings in the sand off West Kirby and Hoylake. Hoylake Sailing Club has a slip at the N end of the town. West Kirby Sailing Club has good facilities and provisions are available ashore.

Drying moorings, Heswall, River Dee

Liverpool

Waypoint 53°31'·35N 3°15'·4W Queen's Channel Fairway buoy
Local High Water is +0015 Dover
Charts Admiralty *3490, 1951, 1978*; Imray *C52, C62*

General

The construction of the new yacht marina in the Brunswick and Coburg Docks has provided sheltered and well serviced moorings for yachts in the heart of this historic city. The restoration of the Albert Dock, with its Maritime Museum, quayside shops, bars and restaurants, and the arrival of the Tate Gallery have brought new life to the waterfront of what was one of the world's biggest and most prosperous ports.

Warning

The marina is accessed via lock gates, which are opened for approximately 2 hours either side of HW, the exact timing depending on the height of the tide. There is a waiting berth on the south side

of the lock entrance, but this can be uncomfortable in other than settled conditions. Tides are strong, reaching 5 knots at springs, and strong onshore winds make the entrance to the channel dangerous, particularly against the ebb, when there are steep, breaking seas.

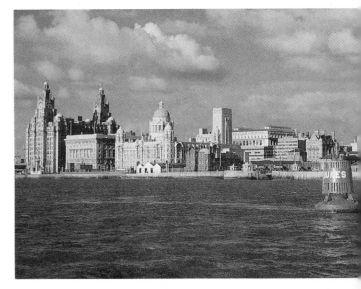

Dukes buoy, Liver Building and entrance to Albert Dock

Approaching Liverpool Marina, entrance on right side of building with grey slate roof

Approach

By day From the W or NW, there are no offlying dangers to the approach to Queen's Channel.

By night Queen's Channel, Crosby Channel and the River Mersey are all well lit and a night approach does not present any difficulty. Contact the marina in advance if requiring access through the lock gates at night.

Entrance

The approach is via the buoyed Queen's Channel, Crosby Channel and the River Mersey, which are navigable at all states of the tide. There are training walls on either side of the fairway, and yachts should take care not to pass beyond the lines of buoys. Rock Channel, to the N of New Brighton, is not buoyed and should not be attempted without local knowledge. Yachts should be aware of the strength of the ebb, and will have to time their approach according to the opening times for the lock gates when intending to pass into the marina. The marina lock gates are approximately one mile upstream of the Liver Building. The buoyed channel is followed as far as the W cardinal buoy marked 'PB', denoting Pluckington Bank, when the marina entrance will lie directly to port. Three vertical red/green docking signals indicate the availability of the lock; the lock control building is conspicuous, with a grey slate roof.

Liverpool Marina, Coburg Dock

Entering the lock, Liverpool Marina

Berthing

Liverpool Marina has an ultimate capacity of around 450 berths. Berths can always be found for visiting yachts. Access to the Albert and Canning Docks is only by prior arrangement and must be during the 2 hours before HW. Access to the inland waterway system is via Eastham Channel and the Eastham Locks, on the SW side of the river.

VHF radio telephone

Call *Mersey Radio* Ch 12. Traffic movements, local navigational warnings and weather reports are broadcast on Ch 09 at 3 and 2 hours before HW. Call *Liverpool Marina* Ch 80.

Facilities

Liverpool Marina is a fully serviced yacht marina with water and electricity supplied to the pontoons. There are showers, toilets, a restaurant, a bar and a

chandlery ashore. *Calor Gas* is available adjacent to the marina entrance.

Marine electronics Robbins Marine, Coburg Dock.
Admiralty chart agents and chandlery Dubois Phillips and MacCallum.

Anchorage

A drying anchorage offering good shelter is available to shallow-draught yachts on the River Alt. The

Douglas Boatyard, Hesketh Bank

access, from the Crosby Channel in the region of the C17 or C19 buoys, is subject to change and is marked each year by members of the Blundellsands Sailing Club. A further anchorage may be had in settled weather off New Brighton. Anchorage must be outside the fairway and yachts must be aware of the strength of the tidal stream.

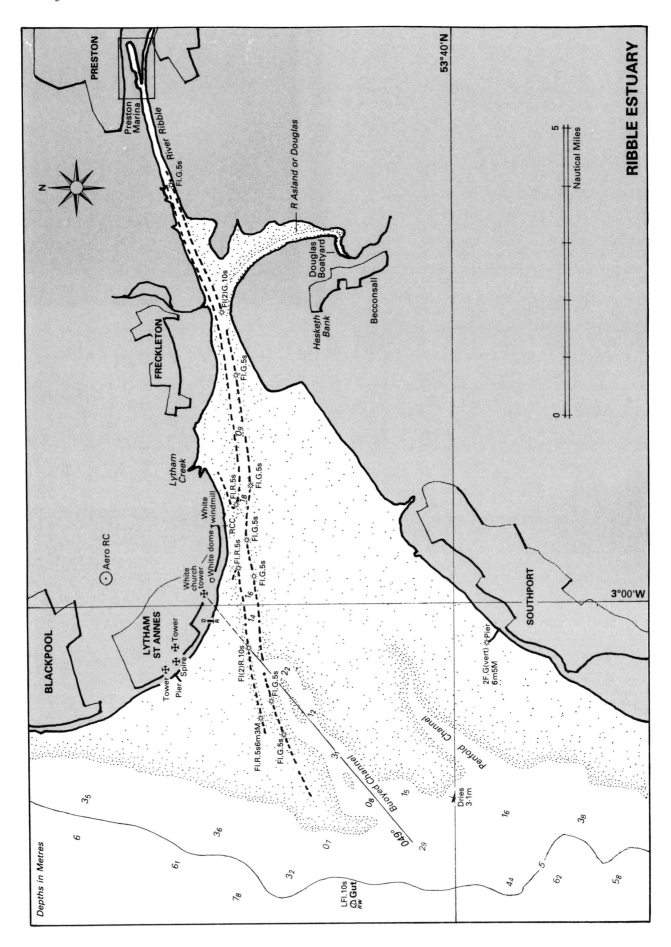

Depths in Metres

RIBBLE ESTUARY

The Ribble estuary

Preston was once a prosperous port, but its trade declined over the years and it was closed to commercial traffic in 1981. The construction of the new Preston Marina, in the old Albert Edward Dock, and the associated Riversway Docklands commercial and residential developments have breathed new life into the port.

Additional facilities for yachts are to be found at Lytham and Freckleton, on the N bank of the estuary, and at the Douglas Boatyard at Hesketh Bank on the River Asland or Douglas, which enters the estuary on its S side.

Entrance

The original navigable channel of the River Ribble from the Gut buoy between the training walls has silted and the main channel now runs from a breach in the training wall through South Gut. From the Gut buoy (waypoint 53°41'·75N 3°08'·8W) an ESE course for 1·5M will lead to the entrance to the South Gut. Whilst the channel is accessible for 2 hours either side of HW, ideally a yacht should leave the Gut buoy at around 2 hours before HW. Local High Water is +0025 Dover. There is water in the South Gut at most states of the tide. The training wall is not covered before half-tide; early arrivals can find shelter from NW winds by anchoring to the S of the training wall. Anchorage is available at all times in the '11-mile hole'·

The channel of the South Gut is marked by local interests with unofficial buoys. The red and yellow buoys should be left to port as the main channel is approached. The first two starboard-hand marks on the training wall of the original (now silted) channel are grey lattice towers. The third starboard-hand mark is a green-painted steel post. The fourth mark

Quayside moorings, River Ribble, Preston

is again a lattice tower with a radar reflector, and the opening in the training wall is to the E of this tower. A bearing of 049° on the tower of the white church at Lytham St Anne's will lead directly from South Gut to this opening. The remainder of the channel is marked with perches on the training wall. Although a number of the buoys are lit, a night-time entrance without local knowledge is not recommended. Entrance should not be attempted in strong onshore winds.

Douglas Boatyard

The boatyard lies on the River Asland or Douglas and can be accessed for 2 hours either side of HW. The river is reached by means of the Ribble estuary channel, turning to starboard immediately before the 5-mile perch. There is a comprehensive chandlery and engineering and repair facilities. Visitors' berths are always available, as are winter storage facilities. Many berths dry, although there are pontoon berths with 1·8m at LW.

Entrance Dock, Preston Marina

PRESTON MARINA

The new marina has been constructed at the entrance to the old Albert Edward Dock, one of the largest of its kind in Europe. There is an ultimate provision for around 350 berths, and spaces are always available for visitors. Entrance into the dock is through the new lock gates, which are open for approximately 1½ hours either side of HW Liverpool between 0700 and 2100 local time during the months of April to September. During the winter months the gates will be opened on any reasonable tide, given 24 hours' notice. There is a waiting berth, in which yachts of moderate draught will lie afloat at LW, alongside the south quay of the entrance channel out of the tideway. Yachts should not be left unattended in the waiting berth.

PRESTON MARINA

Depths in Metres

N

Lt Ho (replica)

Floating wave breakers

Albert Edward Dock

Marina

Marina office

Lock 2

Lock 1

Waiting quay

River Ribble

0   3

Cables

Preston marina is a fully serviced yacht marina with electricity and water on the pontoons. There are toilets and showers ashore, a chandlery and yacht brokerage. *Calor Gas* is available at the marina. Fuel is available alongside during lock gate operation between the hours of 0900 and 1800. Winter storage facilities ashore are available. The Riversway Docklands development itself includes restaurants, cinemas and shopping areas. There are marina fees, but no charge is made for any lock-gate or docking activity. There are two VHF radio telephone stations covering marina activities. Call *Riversway* Ch 16, work Ch 14, between 2½ hours before and 1½ hours after HW for information regarding lock-gate operation, and call *Preston Marina* Ch 37 between 0900 and 1800 for information regarding berthing.

Freckleton Creek

Lytham St Anne's and Freckleton

There are drying moorings in sand off the Ribble Cruising Club at Lytham St Anne's, although these are exposed to the S through W to the NW. Local boats find shelter in the drying Lytham Creek. Similar berths can be found at Freckleton Creek, where there is a boatyard. There is a slip, limited chandlery is available, and there are winter storage facilities.

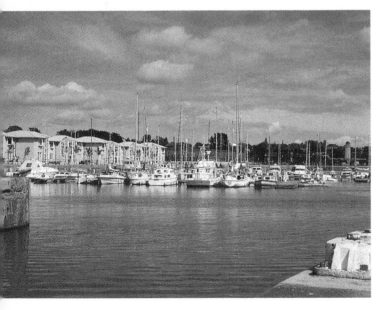

Preston Marina

Morecambe Bay

The bay is an extensive inlet, mainly drying to sand and mud, whose entrance stretches from Rossall Point in the south to the Isle of Walney. The bay is exposed to the prevailing SW and W winds. There are access channels into the bay, intersected by linking channels which are subject to change.

The Lune Deep is the principal channel into the bay. The River Wyre runs into the Lune Deep from the S and forms the entrance to the new marina at Fleetwood. Further anchorages on the River Wyre can be found at Knott End, Skippool Creek and Wardley's Creek. The marina at Glasson Dock is entered via the River Lune, which flows into the Lune Deep from the E.

The main channel of the Lune Deep runs to Heysham. This is a commercial harbour and yachts are only permitted to enter it in an emergency. There is no buoyage beyond Heysham; although yachts may reach Morecambe in settled conditions and on a rising tide, the drying anchorage is totally exposed to onshore winds.

At the N end of Morecambe Bay is the entrance channel to Barrow-in-Furness, which includes the anchorages off Piel Island and Roa Island.

Entrance to the Lune Deep

The Lune Deep S cardinal buoy (waypoint 53°55'·75N 3°10'·8W) must be located 4·5M WNW of Rossall Point. The channel is marked with lateral buoys and runs on a straight course to the Fairway No. 1 N cardinal buoy (waypoint 53°57'·7N 3°02'·2W) at the entrance to the River Wyre. Yachts must keep to the marked channel, as the sides are steep-to, rising from depths of over 40m, and there are dangerous shoals extending 4M W of Rossall Point. The buoys are lit to allow for a night entrance. The stream can run at over 3 knots at springs, and onshore winds against the ebb can create short, steep seas.

FLEETWOOD MARINA

The creation of the new yacht marina is the first part of the proposed comprehensive development of a 70-acre area around the well sheltered Wyre Dock at Fleetwood which, it is hoped, will help to revive the fortunes of this formerly busy fishing port. It is proposed that Fleetwood Harbour Village shall include residential developments, shopping facilities and leisure amenities.

So far, the channel to the Wyre Dock has been dredged, but only the first phase of the projected 350-berth development has been completed, with services provided ashore in Portacabins. Once the overall scheme has been completed no doubt the marina will provide an excellent haven, but at present the surroundings and lack of amenities leave a lot to be desired. The shelter within the marina is excellent, although the fishing boats passing through into the Fish Dock create a wash.

Approach is via the buoyed channel of the River Wyre from the Fairway No. 1 N cardinal buoy. The disused Wyre Lighthouse is a steel structure on the W side of the river channel. Leading lights are displayed approaching Fleetwood on a course of 156° from a stone tower ashore and from a taller brick tower beyond. The channel should be followed past the ferry terminal on the W bank of the river. The channel, dredged to 1·1m above chart datum, begins close to the end of the terminals and should be followed in a SSW direction until the lock entrance to the Wyre Dock is sighted. The channel is lit to allow for night access.

The locks are operated at present for 1½ hours either side of HW Monday to Friday and for 3 hours either side of HW on daytime tides at weekends. Local High Water is +0015 Dover. Signals are

Entrance to Wyre Dock, Fleetwood

Fleetwood Marina, Wyre Dock

displayed at the dock entrance; one black ball indicates that it is clear for inbound traffic and two black balls that it is clear for outward-bound vessels. There is a waiting quay at the entrance to the lock on the SE side of the channel. Yachts approaching the marina should use VHF radio telephone and call *Fleetwood Dock* Ch 16, work Ch 12.

Water and electricity are provided on the pontoons; showers, toilets, and laundry and waste disposal facilities are provided ashore. Provisions are available in the town (EC Wednesday), a good 20 minutes' walk through the dock area.

River Wyre

There are laid yacht moorings and an anchorage off Knott End, out of the main channel to the E of No. 20 and No. 22 port-hand buoys. Many of the moorings dry, and yachts wishing to stay afloat should anchor in the pool to the S of No. 22 buoy, away from the ferry manoeuvring area. The anchorage is well sheltered except to strong N winds. Limited provisions are available ashore, or the ferry may be taken to Fleetwood.

The channel of the River Wyre can be followed upstream to Wardleys Creek and Skippool Creek. First-time visitors should begin off Knott End 1 hour before HW and follow the channel midstream to the NW end of the ICI pier at Burn Naze, leaving the two green buoys to starboard. Wardleys Creek lies on the E bank of the river. There are drying moorings, belonging to Wardleys Marine; there is also a chandlery, and water is available. There is a slip and landing jetty.

Skippool, the home of the Blackpool and Fleetwood Yacht Club, is 5M above Fleetwood on the W bank of the river. Visitors may tie alongside the drying jetties on either side of the yacht club; there is no charge. There is a slip, and water is available on the jetties. There are toilets, showers and a bar at the yacht club. Private alongside moorings can be found in Skippool Creek.

Wardleys Marina, River Wyre

River Lune

The river flows into the Lune Deep 1½M NE of the Fleetwood Fairway No. 1 cardinal buoy, and the confluence is marked by a W cardinal buoy. The channel to Plover Scar is marked with lateral buoys and is subject to change, the buoys being moved accordingly. There are leading lights from the white stone tower of Plover Scar (Fl.2s6m6M) and a framework tower near Cockersand Abbey beyond (F.18m8M). The lights are in line on a bearing of 084°, although this does not necessarily follow the deepest-water channel. The lateral buoys themselves are lit as far as Glasson Dock to allow for night access. There are drying moorings to the E of Sunderland Point and N of No. 10 buoy which are sheltered from all directions except S and SW, when a swell sets up the river. A pipeline crosses the river to the S of No. 10 buoy; anchorage is not permitted in this locality.

It is possible for shallow-draught craft to reach Lancaster, 5M beyond Glasson Dock, approaching HW, although the unmarked channel is narrow and should only be attempted with local knowledge.

Entrance to Glasson Dock

GLASSON DOCK

A well sheltered yacht marina with 260 berths, some of which are always available for visitors, offering good facilities for yachts. The entrance to the outer basin is via lock gates that are only opened for one hour before HW. Local High Water is +0030 Dover.

The approach is via the buoyed channel of the River Lune, leaving the Lune W cardinal buoy at up to 2 hours before HW to arrive at the lock gates at the appropriate time.

The outer dock is a commercial dock; yachts may lie alongside the quay of this dock as directed whilst waiting for entry through the lock gates into the inner basin containing the marina. The inner lock gates are only opened between sunrise and sunset. Yachts leaving the marina should present themselves at the upper lock gates 2 hours before HW. The dock connects with the British Waterways network of the Lancaster canal.

There are dock gate signals. By day a red flag and black ball and by night two red vertical lights indicate that the gates are open and that vessels in the dock are clear to leave. By day a red flag only and by night a red light over white indicates that the gates are open and that vessels are clear to enter the dock. Vessels must stand by and await the correct signal.

Glasson Dock Marina

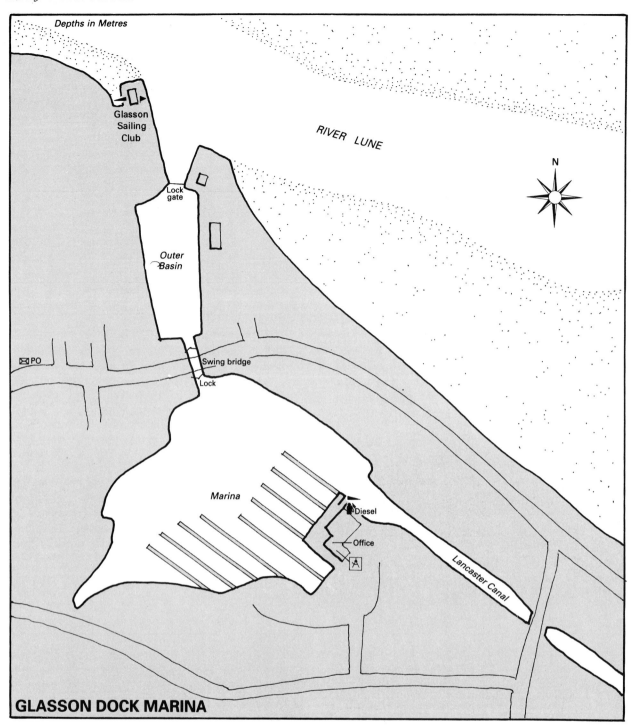

GLASSON DOCK MARINA

VHF radio telephone watch is kept from 2 hours before HW to 1 hour after HW; call *Glasson Dock* Ch 16, work Ch 08 for information regarding locking operations, call *Glasson Dock Marina* Ch 80 for information regarding berthing.

Yachts berth alongside the fixed marina pontoons. Water and electricity are available on the pontoons. There are toilets, a bathroom and showers ashore. Fuel is available alongside the quay, and a chandlery forms part of the marina complex. There is a boatyard, with boat, engineering and electronic repair facilities as well as winter storage. There are mooring charges, but no further fees for locking operations.

Glasson Sailing Club operates from premises close to the lock gates, where there is a slip. There is a post office, and provisions are available from the shops close to the outer basin, some 10 minutes' walk from the marina.

Piel Island and Barrow-in-Furness

The Walney Channel begins about one mile S of Hilpsford Point, at the S end of Walney Island. Walney Island lighthouse (Fl.15s23M) is a stone tower situated near the SE extremity of the island. Lightning Knoll Fairway Buoy (LFl.10s) is a RW spherical bell buoy (waypoint 53°59'·73N 3°14'·2W) 3·3M SSW of Hilpsford Point. A course from the buoy of 041° on the leading lights will leave the Halfway red buoy (Q.R) and Outer Bar red buoy (Fl(4)R.10s) to port. The leading lights are No. 1 beacon (Q.10M), a black pile structure with a white daymark, and the rear No. 2 beacon (Iso.2s10M), a red brick structure with a white face. The course indicated by the leading marks is followed until the Bar red buoy (Fl(2)R.5s) is abeam, when leading marks Nos 3 and 4 are followed on a course of 006°. The structures and light characteristics are the same for leading marks Nos 3 and 4 as for marks Nos 1 and 2. This course is followed until the Piel red buoy (F.R.5s) is abeam. The channel to Barrow is marked with lateral buoys.

Morecambe Bay itself should only be crossed by shallow-draught yachts with great care after half-tide. Allowance should be made for the strong tidal currents running into and out of the bay. The Walney Channel should be entered before the Bar buoy after crossing the bay.

The ruined castle, Piel Island

The ruins of the castle on Piel Island are conspicuous, the only other buildings on the island being a public house and a row of pilots' cottages. There are moorings laid off the E side of Piel Island and a landing jetty ashore. Anchorage can be found clear of the moorings out of the main channel. Tidal streams can run at up to 2½ knots at springs, and care must be taken when using a tender between boat and shore. The anchorage is well sheltered from all directions except the SE, when a swell sets in across the bay.

A similar anchorage and moorings can be found off Roa Island, which has the advantage of being connected to the mainland, so that provisions are more readily available. There is less room to stay afloat out of the channel than at Piel Island, but there are drying moorings and an anchorage for yachts that can take the ground between Roa Island and Foulney Island.

The commercial docks at Barrow are about a further 3M NW of Piel Island. There are moorings laid in the Walney channel beyond the commercial dock entrance and to the S of the bridge at Barrow. Shelter is excellent, although many of the moorings dry. Anchorage may be found clear of these moorings. Full provisions are available ashore.

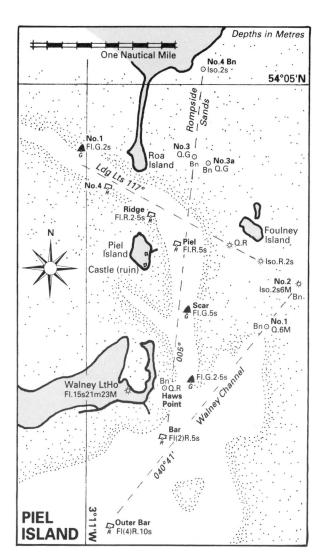

Duddon Mouth

The estuary is exposed to onshore winds and mostly dries. The channel beyond the Duddon Bar is unmarked and constantly changing; it should only be used with the benefit of local knowledge. There is an anchorage off Haverigg. Yachts that can take the ground can anchor off Askam, where there is a pier, or off Hodbarrow, where there is a pier and a small drying harbour.

Ravenglass

Waypoint 54°19'·7N 3°28'·8W 2M WSW of estuary
   mouth
Local High Water is +0020 Dover
Charts Admiralty *1346*; Imray *C62*

General

A large, well sheltered, mostly drying harbour formed by the estuaries of three rivers: the Irt, the Mite and the Esk. Formerly a Roman fortified harbour, it is a peaceful and unspoilt anchorage. The dunes at the mouth of the estuary are a bird sanctuary that can only be visited by prior appointment. Ashore, Ravenglass is the terminus for the Ravenglass and Eskdale Railway, a narrow-gauge steam railway originally built in 1875 to carry iron ore down the Eskdale Valley.

Warning

The harbour can only be entered between 2 hours either side of HW; first-time entry should preferably be made during the hour before HW. Strong onshore winds make entrance impossible.

Approach

By day The tall cooling towers of the Calder Hall reactors at Sellafield, 5M NW of the harbour, are conspicuous. Approach must be made 2M offshore to avoid Drigg Rocks (awash at LW) to the N of the entrance, and Selker Rocks (which dry at MLWS) to the S. A green conical bell buoy (Fl(3)G.15s) is positioned to the W of Selker Rocks. The harbour entrance lies in a break in the coastal sandhills. To the S of the harbour entrance is Eskmeals Firing Range, where guns are occasionally fired up to 5M out to sea. Red flags are shown at either end of the range when firing is about to begin or in progress. Vessels have right of passage through the area when firing is taking place.

By night The harbour is unlit; night approach should not be attempted.

Anchorage in the approach

Anchor off the harbour entrance only in the most settled conditions.

Entrance

It is necessary to identify the small green hut with a white square shutter to the S of the harbour entrance. The hut lies above and to the E of a concrete blockhouse, painted with a white horizontal band, at the NW end of the firing range. To find the entrance channel, the hut should be aligned with Yoadcastle Peak (a conical peak, 490m high, 4½M to the E of the harbour) on a bearing of 083°. About 2 cables from the shore, turn on a bearing of 035° towards the village of Ravenglass.

Moorings

Private drying moorings are laid throughout the harbour.

Anchorage

Anchorage for yachts that can take the ground can be found close to the laid moorings in or between the channels of the rivers Irt and Mite. The banks of the River Esk are relatively steep-to and should be avoided.

Harbourmaster

No harbourmaster or harbour charges.

Facilities

Water Tap by butcher's shop on the main street, to the N of the Pennington Arms.
Slip At S end of main street.
Provisions Provisions are available in the village. EC Wednesday.
Post office On the main street.
Yacht club Ravenglass Boating Association.

St Bees Head

The headland is a 95m-high sandstone perpendicular cliff. The lighthouse (Fl(2)20s102m21M) has a white round tower.

Whitehaven

Waypoint 54°33'·22N 3°36'·2W 2 cables WNW of
   head of W pier
Local High Water is +0020 Dover
Charts Admiralty *2013, 1346*; Imray *C62*

General

A large, well sheltered drying harbour which was developed during the 17th century as a port for shipbuilding and the exportation of local coal. By the early 18th century Whitehaven was one of the major ports in the country. Trade has dwindled since then, but Queen's Dock, which is entered through lock gates, still handles cargo vessels of up to 3,000 tons.

Warning

The harbour dries, and can only be entered for 2½ hours either side of HW. Entrance can be made in most conditions, only strong onshore winds against the ebb causing difficulty. Keep close to the W pier when entering with the flood, as a strong E tidal stream sets across the harbour mouth.

3°36'W

Depths in Metres

N

0   2
Cables

Fl.G.5s16m13M

2F.R(vert)8m9M

Outer Harbour

North Harbour

Lock

2F.R(vert)

Queens Dock

2F.G(vert)

54°33'N

Inner Harbour

South Harbour

WHITEHAVEN

WHITEHAVEN

Entrance Whitehaven harbour

South harbour, Whitehaven

Approach

By day The harbour is 2·6M NNE of the conspicuous St Bees Head, and is easily identified by the tall chimneys and towers to the S of the entrance. There are no offlying dangers.

By night The harbour can be approached and entered using the following lights:

St Bees Head Fl(2)20s102m21M
Whitehaven West Pier Fl.G.5s16m13M
Whitehaven North Pier 2F.R(vert)8m9M
North Harbour Quay head 2F.R(vert)8m2M
Old Quay head 2F.G(vert)8m2M

Anchorage in the approach

Anchorage may be found off the harbour entrance in settled conditions.

Entrance

The harbour is entered between the stone-built West and North Piers. Both have lights at the head displayed from white round towers. Yachts should pass through the outer harbour, then turn SW along the SE side of the Old Quay into the South Harbour.

Moorings

There are private drying moorings laid in the South Harbour.

Berthing

Visiting yachts should tie along the SE side of the Old Quay, or as directed by the harbourmaster. Yachts not wishing to dry out may be accommodated in Queen's Dock, but only by prior arrangement.

Harbourmaster

Office overlooking Inner Harbour.

VHF radio telephone

Call *Whitehaven Harbour* Ch 16, work Ch 12.

Facilities

Fuel On Old Tongue, E side of South Harbour.
Water On Old Tongue.
Slip Alongside New Tongue.
Provisions Full provisions in town. EC Wednesday.
Yacht club Whitehaven Sailing Club.

Harrington

Waypoint 54°36'·75N 3°35'·2W 3 cables W of harbour entrance
Local High Water is +0025 Dover
Charts Admiralty *2013*, *1346*; Imray *C62*

General

One of the smaller Cumbrian ports, Harrington reached its zenith at the turn of the last century. Many ships were built in the harbour; coal, iron and steel were the principal exports. Developments at Workington heralded the decline of the harbour. In 1932 the Harbour and Dock Board was wound up and in 1940 the harbour entrance was sealed with a concrete blockship. Local pressure resulted in the harbour being re-opened in 1966.

Entrance to Harrington harbour

Inner harbour, Harrington

Anchorage in the approach

Anchor off the harbour entrance only in settled conditions.

Entrance

Entrance is made between the stone S pier and the loose-rock N breakwater. The breakwater is covered at half-tide; its position is marked by two red perches. The deepest water is to be found close to the N breakwater. There is a concrete projection at the end of the stone breakwater; when this is awash there is 1·8m of water at the entrance to the inner harbour. Yachts should pass through into the inner harbour, the deepest water being found on the S side of the inner harbour entrance.

Moorings

There are private moorings laid in the inner harbour; these may be used by visitors as directed by the harbourmaster.

Berthing

The visitors' berth is clearly marked at the far end of the NE quay in the inner harbour. There are good ladders. Anchorage may be found in the outer harbour in suitable conditions. Do not anchor in the inner harbour.

Harbourmaster

Lives close to harbour.

Charges

There are no charges for visitors.

Facilities

Water Standpipe by visitors' berth.
Slip Slips on N and S sides of outer harbour.
Provisions Provisions are available in the town.
Yacht club Harrington Sailing and Fishing Club. Bar and showers.

Warning

Both the inner and outer harbours dry to mud. Entrance is possible for 2 hours either side of HW for a yacht with 1·2m draught, although dredging is improving the situation. The inner harbour is well sheltered, although a swell is experienced in strong W or NW winds. Entrance should not be attempted in strong onshore winds.

Approach

By day The harbour lies 3·8M N of the conspicuous towers and chimneys at Whitehaven. There are no offlying dangers.

By night Entry is only recommended with the of local knowledge.

Workington

Waypoint 54°39'·45N 3°35'·2W 2 cables NW of harbour entrance
Local High Water is +0025 Dover
Charts Admiralty *2013, 1346*; Imray *C62*

General

A sheltered commercial port at the mouth of the River Derwent that can be entered at any state of the tide and in most conditions. Yachtsmen are not actively encouraged to use the harbour, although they will be assisted in an emergency.

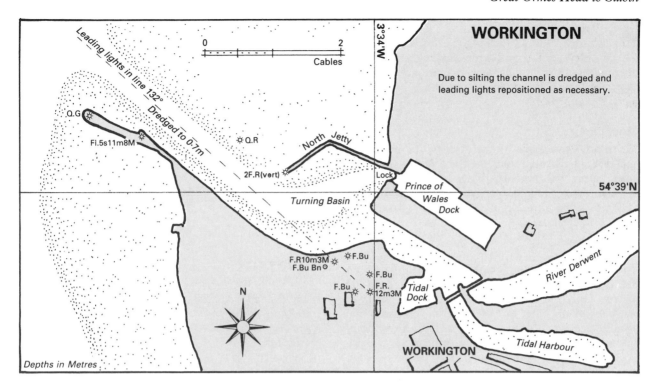

WORKINGTON

Due to silting the channel is dredged and leading lights repositioned as necessary.

Bush perch Q.R
Workington N jetty 2F.R(vert)
Leading lights F.R.10m3M and F.R.12m3M indicating channel on a bearing of 131·5° with F.Bu lights marking the NE and SW extremities of the channel.

Anchorage in the approach
Anchorage may be found to the W of the harbour entrance in settled conditions.

Outer Tidal Dock, Workington

Approach
By day There are no offlying dangers for yachts when approaching from the S or W. Approach from the N should be at least one mile offshore to avoid drying rocky shoals. Strong winds with contrary tides can raise a difficult sea over Workington Bank, which can be avoided by using the inshore English Channel. There is a conspicuous chimney (68m) to the S of the harbour entrance.

By night The harbour can be approached and entered using the following lights:
Workington S Pier head Q.G
Workington S Pier Fl.5s11m8M

Inner Tidal Dock, Workington

Entrance

The entrance channel is dredged, and is marked by the conspicuous red and white leading marks on a bearing of 131·5°. The stream can run strongly across the harbour entrance and must be allowed for in the approach.

Moorings

There are private moorings, drying to soft mud at half-tide, in the tidal dock on the S side of the harbour before the inner harbour bridge. These are maintained by the local Vanguard Sailing Club. The bridge into the inner drying basin is now fixed, with only 1·8m clearance.

Berthing

Yachts which need to go alongside should tie up on the N jetty, with the permission of the berthing master. Only the E end of the N quay has water at all states of the tide, but the sheeting on the piling does not go down to water level at LW. Temporary anchorage may be found in the turning basin, with the permission of the berthing master, but the boat must not be left unattended during the hours of commercial movement. The lock gates to the Prince of Wales Dock operate between 2½ hours before and 2 hours after HW. VHF radio telephone watch is only maintained between these hours. Call *Workington Harbour Radio* Ch 16, work Ch 14 or 11. There are no facilities for yachtsmen.

Maryport

Waypoint 54°43'·07N 3°31'·22W 2 cables W of harbour entrance
Local High Water is +0040 Dover
Charts Admiralty *2013, 1346;* Imray *C62*

General

The new marina in the Senhouse Dock has brought life back to this formerly bustling port at the mouth of the River Ellen. The docks were built by a local landowner, Humphrey Senhouse, to export the local coal. Iron and steel also became principal exports, and at one time over a million tons of cargo left the docks every year. The decline of trade saw the docks suffer from silting. The channel is now dredged to allow access to the new marina. There are currently (1992) 240 deep-water pontoon berths, with a number of berths reserved for visitors. There is also good shelter in the drying commercial Elizabeth Dock.

Warning

The channel is dredged to one metre above chart datum, allowing access to the entrance channel and holding basin for a yacht of 1·3m draught for 4 hours either side of MHWS and 5½ hours either side of MHWN, and for a yacht of 1·75m draught for 3½ hours either side of MHWS and 4½ hours either side of MHWN. The lock gates into the marina are open for a minimum of 2½ hours either side of HW. The harbour can be entered in most conditions.

Approach

By day Approach from the S should be made at least one mile offshore to avoid drying rocky shoals. The pier is conspicuous when approaching from the S. When approaching from the Scottish coast, the sandbanks and strong tidal streams of the Solway Firth must be avoided by passing to the S of the Two Feet Bank W cardinal buoy. Allowance should be made for the tidal streams which run strongly off the harbour entrance.

By night A light (Fl.1·5s10m4M) is displayed from the head of the S pier, but given the absence of any further lights, night approach is only recommended with the benefit of local knowledge.

Anchorage in the approach

Anchor off the harbour entrance only in settled conditions.

Entrance

The harbour is entered between the S pier (a concrete breakwater) and the stone-built N pier, which has timber piling at its W end. The dredged channel is approximately 25m wide. It can be found by using a transit of the N end of the Elizabeth Basin quay and the middle windows of a large, conspicuous cream-painted house at the bottom of the shipping brow. Turn towards the lock gates as they come abeam. There is a waiting berth to the E of the lock gates, although this will have less water than the entrance channel. Yachts waiting for the gates to open may anchor in the approach to the lock.

Marina facilities

Maryport Marina is a fully equipped yacht marina, with water on the pontoons and electricity supplied to most pontoons. Fuel is available from a fuelling berth, and there are showers, toilets and a launderette ashore. There is a chandlery on site, and *Calor Gas* is available. There are extensive boat and mechanical repair facilities and a yacht brokerage. VHF radio telephone watch is kept; call *Maryport Marina* Ch 37. There is a slip and hard standing for winter storage. Provisions are available in the town. EC Wednesday.

Silloth

Yachts may use the outer harbour at Silloth, or, with the permission of the harbourmaster, be locked into the inner basin, although this is principally for commercial traffic and there are no facilities for yachts. The outer harbour dries to mud. The harbour maintains a listening VHF radio telephone watch from 2½ hours before HW to 1½ hours after HW; call *Silloth Harbour* Ch 16, work Ch 12. Approach must be made during the 2 hours before HW. The tidal streams run strongly, and off the harbour entrance can reach 7 knots at springs, when the channels narrow. The banks and channels are constantly shifting, and the buoys are laid for the use of the pilots and do not necessarily mark the navigable channel. Consequently, approach can only be recommended with the benefit of local knowledge. Provisions are available in the town.

Approaching Maryport

Maryport Marina

Silloth outer harbour at low water

Silloth outer harbour at high water

IX. Solway Firth to Portpatrick

This chapter covers the Scottish coast from the shifting sandbanks of the Solway Firth, round the Mull of Galloway with its attendant races, to Portpatrick. All the harbours on the south coast of Scotland dry at low water; they are generally small, although there are anchorages in which a yacht may lie afloat. Portpatrick harbour may be entered at most states of the tide, and the outer harbour at Isle of Whithorn at any state of the tide, but not in adverse conditions. There are deep-water anchorages where limited shelter may be found in the Fleet estuary, the Dee estuary and Rough Firth.

Tides are of moderate strength, increasing round the headlands. In Luce Bay and Wigtown Bay there is a circular flow during the ebb and the flood, and there is often a slight counter-current close to the coast.

The Nith estuary

A navigable channel follows the course of the River Nith up to Kingholm Quay, one mile to the S of Dumfries. There is also a stone quay at Glencaple. Access is through the Dumfries Channel, where the banks and channels are constantly moving. The tidal streams are very strong, and the channel of the river itself is liable to change and is not buoyed. Navigation of the estuary can only be recommended with the benefit of local knowledge.

Kippford

Waypoint 54°49'·65N 3°47'·9W 2 cables SE of Hestan Island lighthouse
Local High Water is +0035 Dover
Charts Admiralty *1346*; Imray *C62*

General
The popular sailing centre of Kippford lies on the E bank of Urr Water, 2½M from the entrance to the beautiful Rough Firth or Urr estuary. Wooded hills shelter this small, attractive resort. Yachts may use a rising tide to pass beyond Kippford to the former small commercial harbour at Palnackie, although the channel is not buoyed.

Warning
The estuary dries at LW, except for the river bed, which is not navigable until after half-tide. All the moorings and the new yacht club pontoon dry, so yachts must be capable of taking the ground. Tidal streams run quickly, in excess of 3 knots at springs.

Approach
By day Approach from the S or SE must be to seaward of the sandbanks of the Solway Firth, passing to the W of the Two Feet Bank W cardinal buoy.

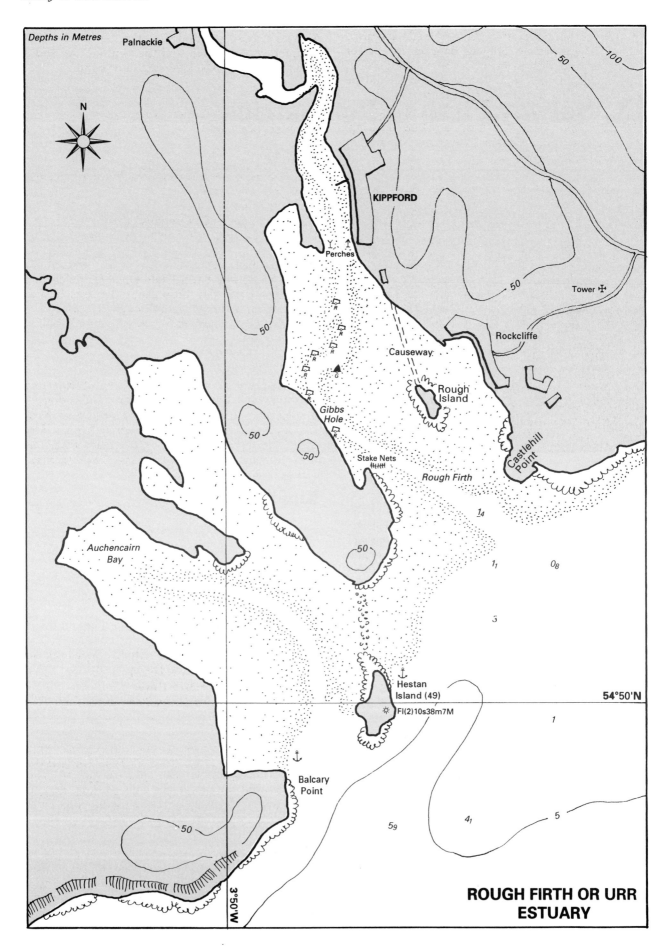

Depths in Metres

Palnackie

N

KIPPFORD

Tower

Rockcliffe

Perches

Causeway

Rough
Island

Castlehill
Point

Gibbs
Hole

Stake Nets

Rough Firth

Auchencairn
Bay

Hestan
Island (49)

Fl(2)10s38m7M

Balcary
Point

**ROUGH FIRTH OR URR
ESTUARY**

54°50'N

3°50'W

Approach from the SW will be through the Ministry of Defence firing range off Abbey Head, described below. There are no offlying dangers except for Craig Roan, drying rocks to the S of Castle Point. Approaching from the S, Rough Island should be kept open of Castle Point to clear these rocks.

By night There is a light (Fl(2)10s38m7M) on Hestan Island, displayed from a white building. There are no other lights, and entrance should not be attempted at night.

Kippford

Anchorage in the approach

Shelter may be found in the anchorages off Hestan Island whilst waiting for the tide. The anchorage close to the W of the island is exposed to winds from the S and SW. Anchorage to the NE of the island, sheltered from SW through W to N winds, should be found as close to the land as draught will allow in order to be out of the tidal stream. There is a very well sheltered anchorage, drying to soft mud, in Horse Isles Bay. A further anchorage can be found in Gibb's Hole, where shallow-draught yachts may stay afloat at LW, but the stream runs quickly and settled conditions are necessary.

Entrance

The estuary is entered to the S of Castle Point. There are stake nets off Horse Isles Bay, marked by withies, which can be cleared by keeping the lighthouse on Hestan Island open until the bay itself starts to open. Beyond Gibb's Hole to Kippford the channel is marked in the summer by buoys laid by the yacht club. The channel is subject to change and the buoys are moved accordingly. Keep to the centre of the channel on approaching the village.

Moorings

There are many private moorings laid off Kippford. A visitors' mooring may be allocated by the yacht club if required.

Berthing

Visitors should tie alongside the new yacht club pontoon. All moorings and the pontoon dry and a yacht must be capable of taking the ground.

Charges

There is a charge payable to the yacht club for the use of the pontoon.

Facilities

Fuel Marine diesel by cans from Kippford Slipway Ltd, on main street.
Water By yacht club slip.
Slip Slips by yacht club and by chandlery.
Provisions Limited provisions are available in the village.
Post office On main street.
Yacht club Solway Yacht Club. Open for toilets and showers every day throughout the season. Bar open every Saturday night throughout season.
Chandlery, boat and mechanical repairs Kippford Slipway Ltd.

Ministry of Defence firing range

A danger area extends 14 miles to the S from the four-mile-long firing range between Kirkcudbright and Abbey Head. Vessels wishing to pass through this area should liaise with the Range Safety Boat which will be on duty at firing times and then pass as close inshore as possible. Call *Kirkcudbright Range Control* Ch 16, work Ch 73.

Kirkcudbright

Waypoint 54°45'·67N 4°04'·53W 4 cables SE of lighthouse on Little Ross Island
Local High Water is +0025 Dover
Charts Admiralty *1344, 1346, 2094;* Imray *C62*

General

Complete shelter can be found in the elegant county town of Kirkcudbright. Coasters and fishing boats use the town quay, although space is usually available for visiting yachts. The 16th-century McLellan's Castle, by the quay, has been partially restored and is open to the public.

Warning

The estuary dries at LW, except for the river channel, and should not be entered until after half-flood. Tidal streams can run strongly, and a favourable stream should be used when navigating the estuary. The estuary can be entered in most conditions.

Approach

By day The firing range to the E of the bay has been described above. There are no further offlying dangers, although the tidal stream runs strongly along the coast. The sound to the W of Little Ross Island should only be used after half-tide. Richardson's Rock, on the W side of the sound, shows at HW.

By night Little Ross lighthouse shows Fl.5s50m12M from a white tower. The buoyed channel of the River Dee is well lit and entrance by night should not be a problem.

Kirkcudbright

Leading marks, Little Ross Island

Anchorage in the approach

Anchorage whilst awaiting the tide may be found in Kirkcudbright Bay, although this is exposed to onshore winds. Anchoring in Ross Roads, close to the N end of Little Ross Island, will provide more shelter from winds from the S or SW. A well sheltered drying anchorage may be found in Ross Bay, sheltered from all winds except those from the E; the anchorage dries to sand and mud. At the entrance to the channel there is a depth of 0·1m over the bar. If there is sufficient water over the bar for a yacht to reach the lifeboat slip, then anchorage may be found in this area, away from the end of the slip itself.

Entrance

The white tower of the lighthouse on Little Ross Island and the pyramidal beacon on the N side of the island are leading marks which when in line astern on a bearing of 201° will lead to the bar. The channel passes close to the lifeboat house on the E bank of the bay. This is a light brown, rendered building which may be difficult to locate when approaching from the SW. There are two white flagstaffs attached to the S side of the building which should help identification. The remainder of the

Kirkcudbright

channel to the town is marked with easily identified lateral buoys and perches.

Moorings

There are private moorings, which mostly dry, laid in the channel off the town. Moorings may be allocated to visiting yachts by the harbourmaster if required.

Berthing

As directed by the harbourmaster. The town quay dries to soft mud, and visiting yachts can usually be accommodated alongside. The ebb may run strongly if excessive rainfall leads to the sluice gates of the upstream power station being opened.

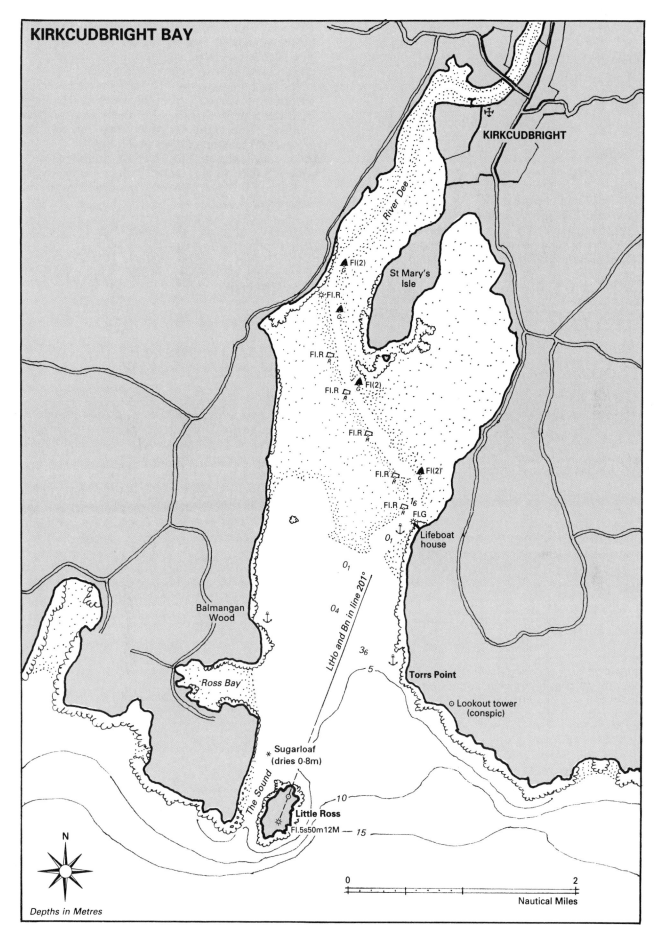

KIRKCUDBRIGHT BAY

KIRKCUDBRIGHT

River Dee

Fl(2)
G.

Fl.R.

G.

Fl.R
R

Fl.R
R

Fl(2)
G.

St Mary's
Isle

Fl.R
R

Fl.R
R

Fl(2)
G.

Fl.R
R

*1*6
Fl.G

*0*1

Lifeboat
house

*0*1

*0*4

LtHo and Bn in line 201°

Balmangan
Wood

*3*6

Ross Bay

5

Torrs Point

⊙ Lookout tower
(conspic)

The Sound

✳ Sugarloaf
(dries 0·8m)

10

Little Ross
Fl.5s50m12M — 15

N

Depths in Metres

0

Nautical Miles

2

Harbourmaster
Office on quay.

Charges
There are harbour charges.

VHF radio telephone
Call *Kirkcudbright Harbour* Ch 16, work Ch 12.

Facilities
Fuel Contact harbourmaster for supply.
Water Taps on town quay.
Slip At W end of town quay.
Provisions Full provisions are available in the town. EC Thursday.
Post office In square overlooking town quay.
Yacht club Kirkcudbright Sailing Club.

The Fleet estuary
There are attractive anchorages with limited shelter off the Islands of Fleet at the mouth of Fleet Bay. The islands are National Trust for Scotland property and are home to colonies of seabirds.

The anchorage to the NW of Ardwall Island, in 3m mud, is sheltered from all winds except those from the S to W. To the N of the island complete shelter can be found for yachts that can take the ground (the anchorage dries to soft mud).

The anchorage to the E of the main island of Murray's Isles, in the bay below the ruined cottages, is exposed to the S. There is good holding in the anchorages.

Garlieston

Waypoint 54°47'·0N 4°20'·9W ½M SE of end of pier
Local High Water is +0035 Dover
Charts Admiralty *2094*; Imray *C62*

General
Garlieston is a neat, small town on the W side of Wigtown Bay, offering good shelter in the drying inner harbour. Some commercial vessels and a small fishing fleet operate from the harbour.

Approaching Garlieston

Warning
The approach bay to the harbour dries, and entrance should only be made between 2½ hours either side of HW. Approach is not recommended in strong SE winds.

GARLIESTON

Approach

By day The harbour lies at the head of a ½M-wide inlet to the W of Eggerness Point. The pole carrying the lights on the end of the concrete pier must be identified. There is a rocky reef to the S of Eggerness Point, and there are further rock outcrops on the W side of the bay. Approach should be made on a course of 295° from at least ½M out from the pierhead.

By night The lights (2F.R(vert)8m3M) on the end of the pier must be located when making a night entry. Approaching from the S, the lights of the town will not be visible until the harbour is open; this makes the pier lights easy to identify.

Anchorage in the approach

Anchorage may be found in moderate holding ground ½M SE of the pier light. The anchorage is exposed to winds from the S and SE.

Entrance

The harbour is entered by leaving the concrete pierhead to port after approaching on a course of 295°.

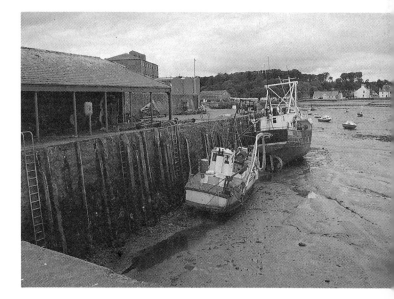

The harbour, Garlieston

Moorings

There are a few private small-boat moorings.

Berthing

Yachts should tie up alongside the quay, where there are good ladders. On the N-facing quay to the E of the slip the river has cut steep-to banks some 6m away from the quay, and these banks continue 8m away from the W-facing quay. There are outfall pipes and isolated rock patches within the harbour, and yachts should not attempt to anchor.

Harbourmaster

Lives in town and will visit yachts.

Charges

There are harbour charges.

Facilities

Water Tap on quay.
Slip On N-facing quay by warehouse.
Provisions Provisions are available in the town. EC Wednesday.
Post office In the town.
Calor Gas From caravan park on road into town.

Isle of Whithorn

Waypoint 54°41'·3N 4°21'·35W ½M SSE of St Ninian's Tower
Local High Water is +0035 Dover
Charts Admiralty *2094*; Imray *C62*

General

A popular and convenient port for yachtsmen, as the outer harbour can be entered at any time, although it is exposed to onshore winds. There is good shelter in the drying inner harbour.

Warning

The inner harbour dries, and can only be entered after half-tide. The outer harbour can be entered at any state of the tide, but is exposed to onshore winds, which will bring in an uncomfortable sea. Entrance can be made in most conditions, particularly at HW, but is inadvisable in strong onshore winds.

Approach

By day There is a radio mast that is conspicuous from all directions 2M to the W of the harbour. St Ninian's Tower is a white square tower on the promontory to the E of the harbour, close to the ruins of the 13th-century St Ninian's Chapel.

By night The leading lights are Oc.R.8s7m7M and Oc.R.8s9m7M on a bearing of 335°. The pierhead light is Q.G.4m5M.

Conspicuous white tower to east of entrance, Isle of Whithorn

Entrance

The harbour is entered to the W of the promontory on which is situated St Ninian's Tower. Rocks extend a short distance W from this promontory, and there is a larger reef of rocks extending E from the mainland to the W of the entrance. This reef was formerly marked by an iron perch which is no longer in place. It is essential to identify the leading marks on a bearing of 335°; this course will avoid the offlying dangers. The marks are conspicuous Dayglo orange diamonds on poles in a field on the W side of the harbour. The tidal stream sets strongly across the harbour entrance and must be allowed for, taking particular care not to be set on to the rocks at the harbour entrance.

Moorings

There are drying moorings in the inner harbour; these may be allocated to visitors by the harbourmaster.

Berthing

Visitors' alongside berths are marked on the quay at the root of the pier, where there are good ladders. Anchoring is not allowed in the inner harbour.

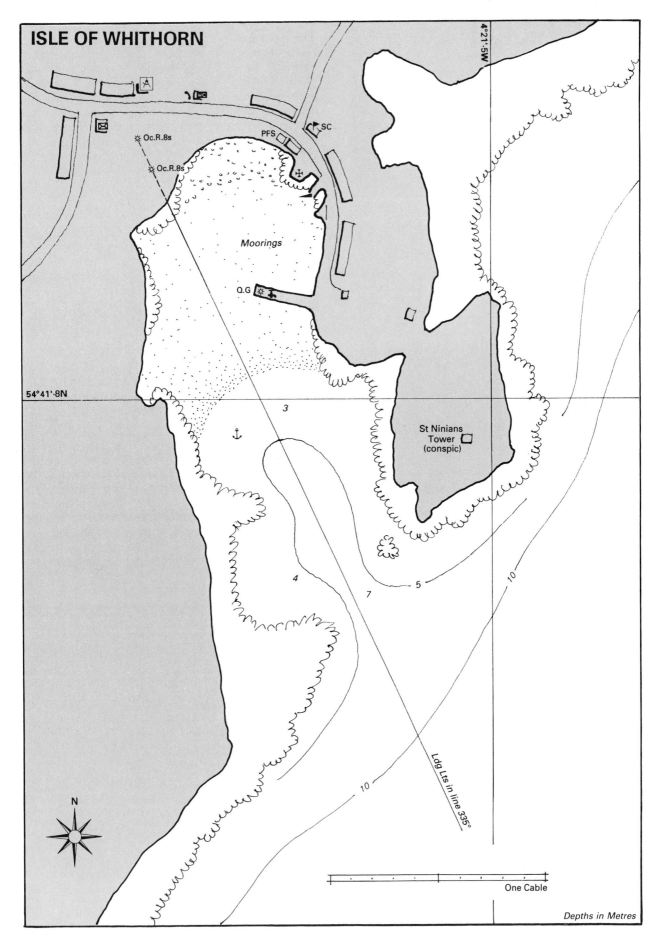

ISLE OF WHITHORN

4°21'·5W

WC

Oc.R.8s

Oc.R.8s

PFS

SC

Moorings

Q.G

54°41'·8N

3

St Ninians
Tower
(conspic)

4

5

7

10

10

N

Ldg Lts in line 335°

One Cable

Depths in Metres

Leading marks Isle of Whithorn

Isle of Whithorn

Harbourmaster

At McWilliam's Stores, in NE corner of harbour. There are harbour charges.

Facilities

Fuel By can from John's Petrol, in NE corner of harbour.
Water Tap on quay.
Slip In inner harbour.
Provisions Provisions are available in the village. EC Thursday.
Post office NW corner of harbour.
Yacht club Wigtown Bay Sailing Club. Showers.
Chandlery Rowley Marine, on road at N end of the harbour. Rowley Marine also have launderette facilities.

Burrow Head

The headland is a prominent steep cliff off which tidal streams run strongly. The E-going stream begins at +0430 Dover and the W-going stream at −0130 Dover. The spring rate is about 4 knots in both directions. A heavy race builds up off the headland, especially when the W-going stream is against a strong W wind. The race can be avoided by keeping well inshore, or well offshore into the Firth.

Port William

Waypoint 54°45'·65N 4°35'·9W 4 cables W of harbour entrance
Local High Water is +0015 Dover
Charts Admiralty *2094*; Imray *C62*

General

A small drying harbour on the E side of Luce Bay where reasonable shelter may be found. The harbour is formed by a dog-leg quay which is protected by a stone causeway on its NW side.

Warning

The harbour dries, and can only be entered for 2½ hours either side of HW. There is more water in the outer harbour, and a further wait may be necessary before moving up into the inner harbour. The inner harbour is well sheltered, while a swell enters the outer harbour with strong onshore winds. Entrance to the harbour should not be attempted in strong onshore winds. Space is limited within the harbour.

Entrance to harbour, Port William

Depths in Metres

1₅

PORT WILLIAM

N

Breakwater

⊙ Perch

Fl.G.3s ☼

54°45'·7N

4°35'W

Half of One Cable

PFS

Approach

By day The harbour is the only one on the E side of Luce Bay; the pier with its flagstaff is easily identified. There are rocks close inshore to the S of the entrance; approach, from about ½M offshore, should be in an E direction.

By night The harbour has no lights, and a night approach should not be attempted.

Anchorage in the approach

Anchorage may be found off the harbour entrance in 5m stones and mud, although this area is exposed from S through W to NW. Temporary anchorage may be found in Back Bay or Monreith Bay, to the S of the harbour entrance. These bays are also exposed to onshore winds.

Entrance

The harbour has a narrow entrance between the concrete pier and the stone causeway, the end of which is marked by a perch. Enter close to the pier, as a shingle bank tends to build up close to the perch.

Moorings

There are some private small-boat moorings in the NE part of the harbour.

Berthing

Yachts should tie up alongside the quay of the inner harbour, which dries to soft mud. Anchoring is possible close to the slip on the NE side of the harbour, which dries to muddy clay, but space is limited.

Harbourmaster

Office on quay.

Charges

There are harbour charges.

Facilities

Fuel By arrangement with the harbourmaster.
Water Tap at toilets in the square.
Slip On NE and SE sides of harbour.
Provisions Provisions are available in the village. EC Thursday.
Post office On Main Street.
Calor Gas and Camping Gaz Dewar's, in main square.

Drummore

Waypoint 54°41'·5N 4°51'·6W one mile E of harbour entrance
Local High Water is +0015 Dover
Charts Admiralty *2094*; Imray *C62*

General

Scotland's southernmost village has a drying harbour, offering good shelter. It is a convenient spot in which to wait for the tide or suitable weather when planning to round the Mull of Galloway.

Warning

The harbour dries, and can only be entered for 2½ hours either side of HW. Levels of silting in the harbour can vary, and the harbour should not be used by deep-draught yachts.

Approach

By day The harbour lies 3½M to the N of the Mull of Galloway. The Scares are a group of unlit rocks 6½M to the ESE of the harbour; they are home to a colony of gannets. Luce Bay is used as a bombing range by the Royal Aircraft Establishment.

By night The harbour is unlit, and should not be approached at night.

DRUMMORE HARBOUR

Anchorage in the approach

Anchorage may be found in 3m off the harbour entrance, although this area is exposed to winds from the N through E to S.

Drummore harbour

Entrance

The harbour is entered leaving the concrete pier to port and the loose stone breakwater to starboard; the deepest water is to be found close to the pier. There are shingle banks to the N of the stone causeway and from the end of the pier. Final approach should be made from the NW on a course of 140°.

Moorings

There are some private small-boat moorings close to the stone causeway.

Berthing

Visiting yachts may lie alongside the pier, although the ladders are poor. There is good shelter; the harbour dries to soft mud.

Harbourmaster

No harbourmaster, and no harbour charges.

Facilities

Water Tap at root of pier.
Slip On S side of harbour.
Provisions Available in the village. EC Thursday.
Yacht club Kirkmaiden Boating Club.

East Tarbet Bay

Anchorage may be found in the bay when waiting for the tide or suitable weather to round the Mull of Galloway. Anchor in 6m sand 8 cables WNW of the lighthouse, off the little jetty on the beach. Good shelter is to be found from the W or SW, although the race can extend for some distance to the NE of the Mull on the E-going stream and (especially in unsettled conditions) make the approach to the bay difficult.

Mull of Galloway

A bold headland rising to 82m that is steep-to on its S and W sides. The light (Fl.20s99m28M) is shown from a white tower near the SE extremity of the headland. A heavy race extends for 3M off the Mull, SW and W during the W-going stream and NNE during the E-going stream. The race can be dangerous to yachts, especially when there is a contrary wind.

To make passage round the Mull, a yacht must arrive at slack water and pass either close inshore or several miles offshore in order to avoid the race. Tidal streams can reach 4·5 knots at springs. The E-going stream begins at −0545 Dover and the W-going stream at +0020 Dover. There is a further race off Crammag Head, 3M to the NW of the Mull; this is at its worst on the flood when the wind is from the S. In these circumstances the race must be given a wide berth.

Port Logan

An attractive small village 4M N of Crammag Head that was abandoned as a port in the 19th century. There is a temporary anchorage off the breakwater in 6m, exposed to winds from the S and W. Additional shelter may be found, for yachts that can take the ground, behind the breakwater that extends for 180m from the S side of the bay. Enter between 1½ hours either side of HW, leaving the breakwater at least 50m to starboard to clear the loose rocks at its extremity. There are no facilities for yachts.

Port Logan

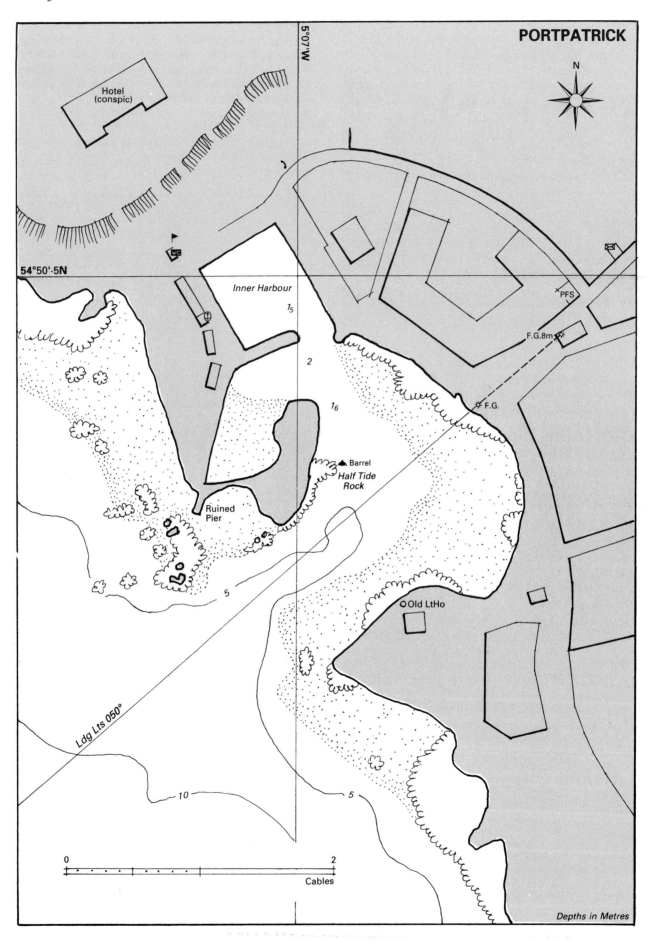

PORTPATRICK

N

5°07'W

Hotel
(conspic)

WC

54°50'·5N

Inner Harbour

1₅

2

1₆

Barrel

*Half Tide
Rock*

Ruined
Pier

5

Ldg Lts 050°

10

5

PFS

F.G.8m

F.G.

O Old LtHo

0   2

Cables

Depths in Metres

Portpatrick harbour and conspicuous hotel

Portpatrick harbour

Portpatrick

Waypoint 54°50'·0N 5°08'·0W 7 cables SW of the harbour entrance
Local High Water is +0030 Dover
Charts Admiralty *2198*; Imray *C62*

General

This popular cruising port was once the main ferry port for the short crossing to Northern Ireland, until a series of accidents resulted in the service being transferred to Stranraer in 1862. The harbour can be entered at most states of the tide, and good shelter can be found in the inner harbour.

Warning

The harbour can be entered at most states of the tide, but deep-keel yachts should not enter at LW if there is a swell running into the harbour. Strong tidal streams run across the entrance, and an approach should not be attempted in fresh to strong onshore winds.

Approach

By day The harbour is 2M S of the white tower of Kilantrigan lighthouse. There is a conspicuous radio mast to the E of the harbour. Approaching from the S or W, the large hotel above and to the N of the harbour is conspicuous.

By night Kilantrigan lighthouse (Fl(2)15s49m25M) is 2M to the N of the harbour. There are leading lights on a bearing of 050·5°; the front light (F.G) is on the sea wall and the rear light (F.G.8m) on a building in the small square.

Entrance

Entrance is made between the ruined N and S piers. There is a disused lighthouse on the S quay. Rocks shoal from the S shore, and there are isolated rocks off the N shore. It is necessary to identify the leading marks on a bearing of 050·5°. The front mark is a painted orange stripe on the sea wall, below the orange pole carrying the front leading light; the rear mark is also an orange stripe, painted at eaves level on the left-hand side of the three-windowed gable of the building in the small square. Once inside the entrance, the barrel marking Half Tide Rock should be identified and left close to port. Turn for the inner harbour as soon as the entrance opens.

Moorings

There are private small-boat moorings in the shallow bay to the W of the inner harbour entrance.

Berthing

Visitors should moor alongside the N wall or the N part of the E wall in the inner harbour.

Harbourmaster

Office on the quay.

Charges

There are no harbour charges, except for the use of the water hose.

Facilities

Fuel By can from Portpatrick Filling Station, off Main Street.
Water Tap on quay in inner harbour.
Slip From S side of bay onto shingle beach, for small craft only.
Provisions Provisions are available in the village. EC Thursday.
Post office On Main Street.
Calor Gas Portpatrick Filling Station.

X. Isle of Man

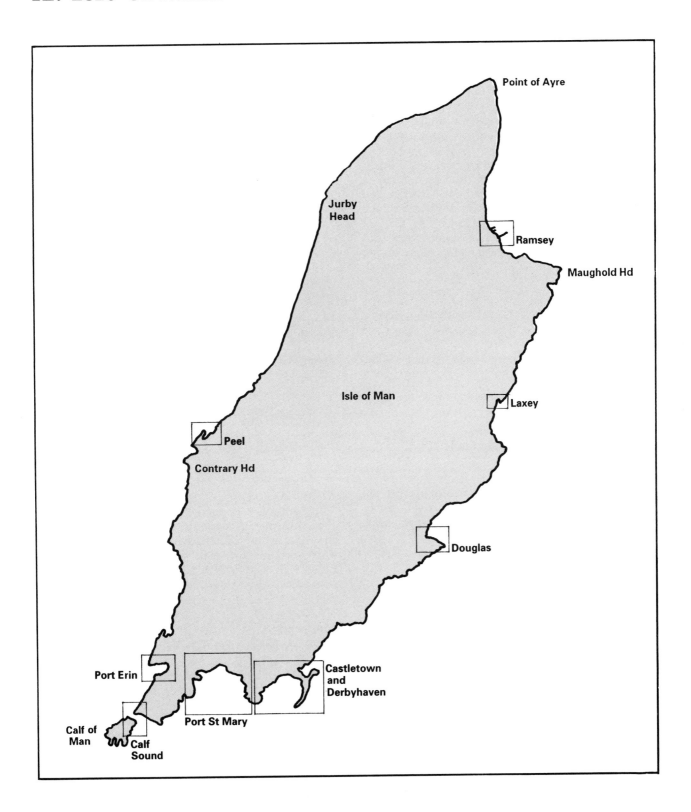

By virtue of its position in the middle of the N Irish Sea, the Isle of Man not only provides an excellent cruising ground in its own right, but is also a useful resting point for yachtsmen crossing the Irish Sea, allowing full use to be made of the tidal streams.

The tidal streams around the island are complex. The streams to the W and NE of the island are controlled by the flow through the North Channel; on the flood the streams divide in NE and S directions at Contrary Head, to the S of Peel. The streams to the S and SE of the island are controlled by the flow through St George's Channel. The streams meet on the E side of the island at Maughold Head, to the S of Ramsey. The streams on the E side of the island are stronger than those on the W side, and run strongly round the headlands, particularly at the Point of Ayre, Langness Point and the Calf of Man.

There are ports of refuge at Douglas and Port St Mary which give fair shelter and can be entered in most conditions. The outer harbours at Peel and Port Erin can both be entered at any state of the tide, but provide only limited shelter.

The harbours are generally well maintained, and the harbourmasters are invariably accommodating to visiting yachtsmen.

Port St Mary

Waypoint 54°03'·6N 4°43'·22W 8 cables SSE of head of outer breakwater
Local High Water is +0020 Dover
Charts Admiralty 2696, 2094; Imray Y70, C62

General

A busy fishing port and popular yachting centre on the W side of Bay ny Carrickey. The drying inner harbour offers good shelter for yachts that can take the ground; the outer harbour and anchorage are subject to swell in strong E or SE winds.

Warning

The inner harbour dries to firm sand, and can only be entered for 3 hours either side of HW. Strong S winds make entrance difficult.

Approach

By day The harbour lies 2M ENE of Spanish Head and 4M WNW of Langness Point. There is a conspicuous TV mast (133m) above the town. The Carrick is a rock drying to 4·3m in the middle of Bay ny Carrickey, marked with an iron tripod beacon, and should be left to starboard on the approach. There are rocky ledges extending to the S of Kallow Point and the outer pier; these may be cleared by keeping at least 2 cables offshore when

approaching from the SW. Tidal streams run strongly off the harbour and must be allowed for in the approach.

By night The harbour can be approached and entered using the following lights:
Chicken Rock lighthouse Fl.5s38m13M
Calf of Man lighthouse Fl.15s93m28M
Dreswick Point Fl(2)30s23m21M
The Carrick Q(2)5s6m3M
Port St Mary outer pier Oc.R.10s8m6M
Port St Mary inner pier Oc.R.3s8m5M

The light on The Carrick can be difficult to identify. Keeping the lights of the outer and inner piers in line on a bearing of 301° leaves The Carrick to the NE.

Approaching Port St Mary

Entrance

The harbour is entered between The Carrick and the outer pier. A drying rocky shoal extends from the shore within the outer harbour and close to the outer pier, marked at its seaward end with a green perch with a triangular topmark. This must be left to starboard when berthing at the root of the outer pier.

Moorings

There are private moorings laid in the inner harbour and off Gansey Point, and private drying moorings in the inner harbour. There are visitors' moorings laid off Gansey Point, the red buoys being capable of taking yachts of up to 5 tons and the white buoy of taking a yacht of up to 10 tons. These buoys should be used as directed by the harbourmaster. Yachts may anchor off Gansey Point close to the laid moorings, although the holding is indifferent due to the number of stone patches and the quantity of kelp.

PORT ST MARY

Depths in Metres

N

4°42'W

54°04'N

Pylon

Black Rocks

BAY NY CARRICKEY

The Carrick

BRB

Q(2)5s6m3M

Carthure
Rocks
G

Pylon Spire
Tower

Oc.R.3s8m5M

WC
C

Oc.R.10s8m6M
Bell(3)12sIoccas

Cables 0   One Nautical Mile

Quayside moorings, inner harbour, Port St Mary

VHF radio telephone

Call *Port St Mary Harbour* Ch 16, work Ch 12.

Facilities

Fuel Contact harbourmaster.

Water Taps on inner and outer piers.

Slip On W side of outer harbour.

Provisions Provisions are available in town. EC Thursday.

Post office On Bay View Road, on N side of town.

Yacht club Isle of Man Yacht Club. Bar and showers.

Calor Gas Manx Gas Service Centre or the Fishermen's Association.

Chandlery Limited chandlery from the Fishermen's Association.

Marine engineers Ballasalla Marine and Auto Engineers.

Calf Sound

Given the right weather conditions and a favourable tide, the sound provides a convenient daytime short cut round the SW corner of the island. In bad weather or at night, a yacht must pass well S of the Calf of Man and Chicken Rock to avoid the tidal race. The passage between the Calf and Chicken Rock should only be used with settled weather and a favourable tide.

Calf Sound lies between Thoulsa Rock, clearly marked with a white round beacon, and Kitterland, a low, barren, grass-covered island. The other passages, Little Sound to the E of Kitterland and the passage to the W of Thoulsa Rock, should only be used with local knowledge.

The N-going tidal stream begins at −0130 Dover and the S-going stream at +0400 Dover. The stream runs strongly, at up to 4 knots at springs, and the sound should not be attempted with a strong contrary wind against the tide. There are overfalls to the N and S of the sound; the worst of these can be avoided by keeping to the E side of the disturbed water once clear of Kitterland.

Berthing

Alongside berths may be found as directed by the harbourmaster. Yachts that wish to stay afloat may moor alongside the root of the outer pier; the remainder of the pier is used by the fishing fleet. Yachts that can take the ground can find complete shelter in the inner harbour, although space is limited.

Harbourmaster

Office at root of inner pier.

Charges

There are harbour charges.

Calf Sound looking south

CALF SOUND

N

4°48'W

27   17

Heifer
Rocks
(3)

27

24   27   19

15

24   20   10

18   13

10

Thousla
Rock
Fl.R.3s9m4M ⊙ Bn   17

Kitterland
Island

**Grants
Harbour**   15

10

Fold
Point   15

16

20

15

19   19   54°03'·3N

50   20

The
Cletts   22   21

CALF OF MAN

10

0   3

Cables

Depths in Metres

Port Erin

Waypoint 54°05'·3N 4°46'·92W 4 cables WNW of
green buoy at head of ruined breakwater
Local High Water is +0020 Dover
Charts Admiralty *2696, 2094*; Imray *Y70, C62*

General

An attractive holiday resort at the head of a bay
sheltered by two headlands. The outer breakwater
protecting the harbour was destroyed by a storm in
1884, and as a consequence protection is limited in
onshore winds.

Warning

The harbour is exposed to winds from SW to NW,
although some additional shelter may be found in
the small drying harbour to the E of Raglan Pier.

Approach

By day The approach from the S, through Calf
Sound or to seaward of the Calf of Man, has been
described above. Milner's Tower is a dark, square
tower standing at an elevation of 131m on Bradda
Head, to the N of the bay; it is conspicuous when
approaching from the S or W.

By night The harbour may be approached and entered using the following lights:

Chicken Rock lighthouse Fl.5s38m13M
Calf of Man lighthouse Fl.15s93m28M
Raglan Pier Oc.G.5s8m5M
Port Erin front leading light F.R.10m5M
Port Erin rear leading light F.R.19m5M

The leading lights are in line on a bearing of 099·1°,
which will clear the unlit green buoy marking the
extremity of the ruined breakwater.

Approaching Port Erin

Port Erin

Entrance

The harbour is entered to the S of Bradda Head.
The leading lights are displayed from a white, round
light tower with a red band, situated above the
beach in the centre of the bay, and a white pole with
a red band on the promenade above. There is a
white triangle painted on the cliff face below the
rear mark. The leading marks are in line on a bearing of 099·1°. On a daytime approach the marks are
not as important as they are at night, so long as the
green conical buoy marking the N extremity of the
ruined breakwater can be identified. This must be
left to starboard.

Moorings

There are two black visitors' buoys lying between
Raglan Pier and the lifeboat slipway.

Bradda Head

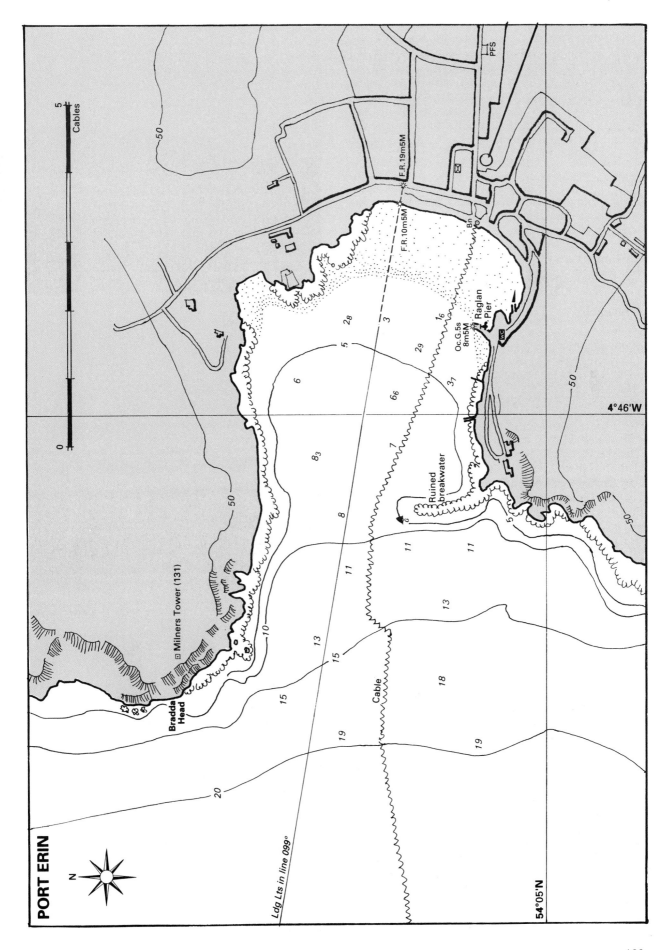

PORT ERIN

N

Cables

5

0

50

50

50

50

50

50

Ldg Lts in line 099°

Cable

Bradda
Head

Milners Tower (131)

Ruined
breakwater

Raglan
Pier

Oc.G.5s
8m5M

F.R.10m5M

F.R.19m5M

Bn

WC

PFS

4°46'W

54°05'N

20

19

19

18

15

15

13

13

11

11

11

11

10

8₃

6

6₆

5

5

7

8

9

6

2₅

3₁

2₉

2₈

3

16

Anchorage

Good anchorage may be found in 3m sand and gravel to the N of Raglan Pier, taking care to avoid the line of the telegraph cable which runs from the beacon on the shore, passing ½ cable N of Raglan Pier. Dinghies going ashore may use Raglan Pier or the jetty to the W of the pier. Note that the head of the jetty is covered at HW. Yachts that can take the ground can find additional shelter by anchoring to the E of Raglan Pier.

Berthing

Yachts that can take the ground may be able to berth alongside Raglan Pier, but this space is usually taken up by local fishing boats.

Harbourmaster

The harbour is controlled by the Port St Mary harbourmaster, who visits once a day. Charges are levied; VHF radio telephone contact should be made with Port St Mary.

Facilities

Water Tap on Raglan Pier.
Slip To the E of Raglan Pier.
Provisions Full provisions may be found in the town. EC Thursday.
Post office In town centre.

Approaching Peel

Peel

Waypoint 54°13'·83N 4°42'·05W 3 cables NW of head of outer breakwater
Local High Water is +0010 Dover
Charts Admiralty 2696, 2094; Imray Y70, C62

General

The harbour of this tourist resort and fishing port is at the mouth of the River Neb. Peel Castle dominates the harbour from its site on St Patrick's Isle. The castle, whose main walls date back to the 14th century, houses the ruins of the 13th-century St German's Cathedral. St Patrick's Isle is an island in name only; it is connected to the mainland, and provides the harbour with good shelter from the W.

Warning

The inner harbour mostly dries, and can only be entered for 2½ hours either side of HW. The outer harbour is exposed to winds from the NW to NE, when swell can also enter the inner harbour. Entrance to the harbour should not be attempted in strong NW to NE winds.

Rounding Peel breakwater

Peel outer harbour

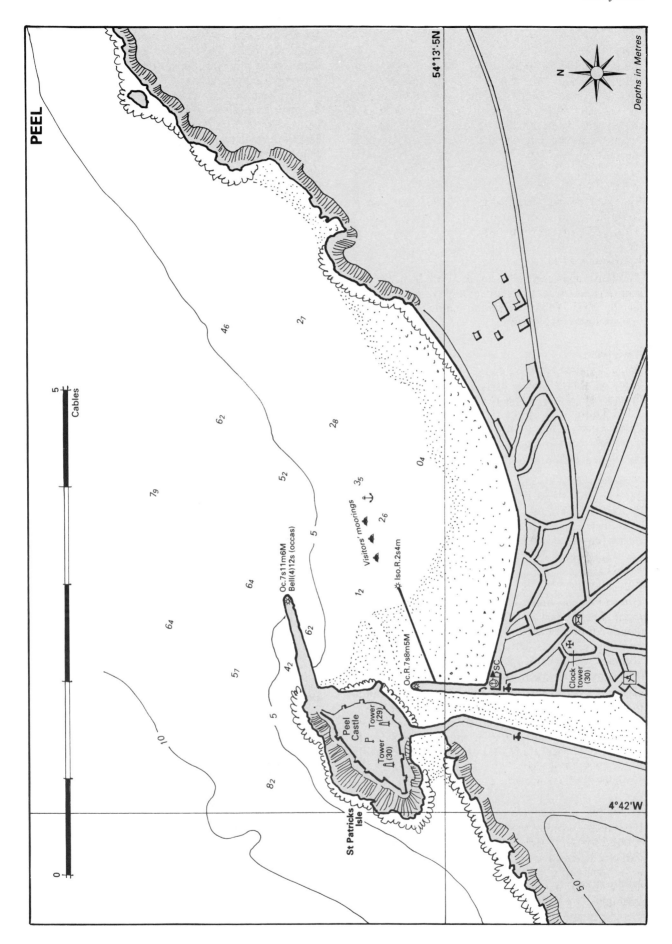

PEEL

54°13'.5N

Depths in Metres

N

Cables

5

0

Oc.7s11m6M
Bell(4)12s (occas)

Visitors' moorings

Iso.R.2s4m

Oc.7s8m5M

St Patricks Isle

Peel Castle

Tower (29)

Tower (30)

Clock tower (30)

SC

4°42'W

Peel inner harbour at low water

Approach

By day Corrin's Folly is a conspicuous square stone tower standing at an elevation of 150m at the summit of Contrary Head, 1M to the S of the harbour. Peel Castle, on St Patrick's Isle, is conspicuous on the approach. Rocks shoal for a short distance N of St Patrick's Isle, and must be cleared on the approach from the SW.

By night The harbour can be approached and entered at night using the following lights:

Peel outer breakwater head Oc.7s11m6M
The Groyne head Iso.R.2s4m
Castle Jetty Oc.G.7s5m4M
East Quay Oc.R.7s8m5M

Entrance

The harbour is entered to the N of the outer breakwater, which has a white light tower at its head. The inner harbour is entered between Castle Jetty and East Quay. Castle Jetty extends a short distance from the E side of St Patrick's Isle, and has a white light tower with green bands. East Quay has a white light tower with a red band, over an office building at the N end of the quay. The Groyne runs 150m NE from near the outer end of East Quay, with its extremity marked by a black and white beacon; it must be left to port. There is deeper water along the bed of the River Neb, close to the W quay in the inner harbour.

Moorings

There are three red visitors' mooring buoys in line one cable NE of the Groyne; these are marked 'at your own risk'!

Anchorage

Anchor in 3m sand close to the visitors' moorings, keeping clear of the head of the outer breakwater.

Berthing

Yachts that can take the ground can be accommodated alongside the quays in the inner harbour, as directed by the harbourmaster. Yachts wishing to stay afloat may be able to lie alongside the outer end of the breakwater, where there is always water; however, priority is always given to fishing boats.

Harbourmaster

Office on E quay of inner harbour.

Charges

There are harbour charges.

VHF radio telephone

Call *Peel Harbour* Ch 16, work Ch 12, between 0830 and 1630.

Facilities

Fuel Contact harbourmaster to arrange supply.
Water Taps on quays of inner harbour.
Slip Cobbled slip on W quay of inner harbour. Slip on E quay only by arrangement with the harbourmaster.
Provisions Full provisions are available in the town. EC Thursday.
Post office In town centre.
Yacht club Peel Sailing and Cruising Club. Showers are available at the club; the key, for which there is a nominal charge, is obtained from the harbourmaster.
Calor Gas Manx Gas Service Centre.
Chandlery Fishermen's Association, Station Place.
Electricity Electricity is available on the quay if needed for repair or in an emergency; contact the Fishermen's Association.

Jurby Head

There is an active bombing range off Jurby Head. Yachts are advised to pass well to seaward of the yellow buoys and lights, or to pass inshore, keeping between ½M and 1M off the headland and passing close to Jurby Rock. There is 3·5m over Jurby Rock at MLWS.

Point of Ayre

The Point of Ayre is the N extremity of the island, and lies at the N end of a low-lying plain. The High Light (Fl(4)20s32m19M) is shown from a white tower with two red bands, situated ¼M SW of the point; the Low Light (Fl.3s10m8M) is shown from a tower with the upper part red and the lower part white, 2 cables NE of the High Light.

There are dangerous shoals off the point: to the NW the Strunakill Bank, with a least depth of 5·5m; to the E the Ballacash Bank, with a least depth of 2·4m, and the King William Bank, with a least depth of 3·7m; and to the SE the Whitestone Bank, with a least depth of 0·6m, and the Bahama Bank, with a least depth of 1·5m. The sea can break heavily over all the banks in bad weather.

Tidal streams around the point can reach 3·5 knots at springs. The E-going stream begins at +0600 Dover and the W-going stream at −0015 Dover. During the W-going stream an eddy forms W of the point, resulting in the tide running nearly continuously E between the point and Strunakill Bank. A race forms off the point when the eddy meets the W-going stream. To the SE of the point, the E-going stream forms an eddy which causes a race when the eddy stream meets the tidal stream.

Strong contrary winds can create heavy seas off the point and on the offlying banks. Ideally, a yacht should try to round the point at slack water.

Ramsey

Waypoint 54°19'·5N 4°21'·9W 3 cables ENE of harbour entrance
Local High Water is +0020 Dover
Charts Admiralty *2696, 2094*; Imray *Y70, C62*

General

Set in the centre of the long sweep of Ramsey Bay, the harbour of this popular yachting centre and commercial and fishing port is at the mouth of Sulby River. Queen's Pier, to the S of the harbour entrance, was originally built for excursion steamers, but has since been condemned. It offers no shelter, and is in the slow process of being demolished. There is a proposal for a half-tide 160-berth yacht marina to be located in the N basin above the swing bridge.

Approaching Ramsey harbour

Warning

The harbour mostly dries, and can only be entered between 2½ hours before and 2 hours after HW. The inner harbour is well sheltered, although a swell comes in through the harbour entrance in strong onshore winds. Entrance should not be attempted in strong E winds.

Ramsey outer harbour looking north

Ramsey inner harbour

Anchorage in the approach

Anchorage may be found in 4m sand to the N of the end of the derelict Queen's Pier in settled conditions or offshore winds. Landing on Queen's Pier is prohibited; dinghies should be taken to the steps inside the E end of the South Pier.

RAMSEY

54°19'.3N

4°22'W

Depths in Metres

N

6

4₅

5

5₉

Fl.R.5s
R

2₆

5₆

Y

3₆

4₃

Queen's Pier

(condemned-landing prohibited)

0₄

4₂

2₃

0₄

15

0₄

Oc.G.5s9m5M

Oc.R.5s8m4M
Bell(2)10s (occas)

North Pier

South Pier

Mast

Flats
(conspic)

WC

2
G

2F.R(hor)

Iso.G.4s

Town Quay

West Quay

WC
YC

Swing Bridge

RAMSEY

Sulby River

3

Cables

0

Approach

By day The harbour lies at the transition point between the low-lying plain to the N and the cliffs which run S along the remainder of the E coast. The ten-storey block of flats immediately to the S of the harbour entrance is conspicuous. Approach from the N should be close inshore to avoid Whitestone Bank.

By night The harbour can be approached and entered using the following lights:

Maughold Head Fl(3)30s65m21M
Ramsey North Pier Oc.G.5s9m5M
Ramsey South Pier Oc.R.5s8m4M
Queen's Pier buoy Fl.R.5s
Dolphin light Iso.G.4s
Swing bridge 2F.R(hor)

Entrance

The harbour is entered between the North and South Piers. Tidal streams can run quickly, invariably in a N direction, off the entrance, and must be allowed for in the approach. Both piers have white light towers on a black base; the South Pier light tower has a horizontal red band. Within the entrance the channel bears S, leaving the dolphin and the green perch with topmark to starboard.

Berthing

Berth as directed by the harbourmaster, usually alongside the SW quay below the swing bridge. Yachts that can take the ground may moor on the bank between the dolphin and the N quay, although this bank is subject to swell in onshore winds.

Harbourmaster

Office on East Quay.

Charges

There are harbour charges.

VHF radio telephone

Call *Ramsey Harbour* Ch 16, work Ch 12.

Facilities

Fuel Contact sailing club.
Water Tap on West Quay.
Provisions Full provisions are available in the town. EC Wednesday.
Post office Court Row, in town centre.
Yacht club Manx Sailing and Cruising Club, on West Quay. Bar and showers.
Calor Gas Manx Gas.

Laxey

Waypoint 54°13'·2N 4°22'·6W 4 cables SE of harbour entrance
Local High Water is +0015 Dover
Charts Admiralty *2696, 2094*; Imray *Y70, C62*

Approaching Laxey

Laxey outer harbour at high water

Laxey outer harbour at low water

General

A small drying harbour at the N end of Laxey Bay, at the mouth of the Laxey River. The Wheel of Laxey, above the main town, is one of the island's best-known sights. The mighty water wheel was constructed in 1854 to pump water out of the lead workings below Snaefell.

Warning

The harbour dries, and can only be entered for approximately 1½ hours either side of HW. There is a minimum of 2m in the harbour at MHWN, and 3·5m at MHWS. The harbour is only suitable for yachts that can take the ground. The inner harbour is well sheltered, but is full of local boats. The outer harbour is well sheltered from winds from SW through N to NE, but SE winds will bring an intolerable swell into this part of the harbour.

Approach

By day The harbour lies on the E side of Laxey Head, at the N end of Laxey Bay. Approach is straightforward, with no offlying dangers. There is a conspicuous TV mast (142m) 3 cables W of the harbour.

By night It is necessary to identify the lights on either side of the entrance when making a night approach; the E jetty is lit Oc.G.3s7m5M and the W quay Oc.R.3s7m5M. The W quay light is obscured when bearing less than 318°.

Anchorage in the approach

Anchorage may be found in 3m sand to the S of the harbour entrance. There is a further anchorage in 3m sand in Garwick Bay, 1·2M to the S of the harbour. Both anchorages offer good holding in settled conditions or offshore winds.

Entrance

Entrance is made between the E jetty, which has a white light tower with a green band, and the W quay, which has a white light tower with a red band. Keep close to the W quay on entering to avoid the patch of rocks extending S on the N side of the harbour entrance. Green perches mark the line of the river training wall; these must all be left to starboard.

Berthing

Berth alongside the W quay, which dries to a flat, firm bottom of sand and shingle. The inner harbour lies beyond this quay, but is likely to be crowded with local boats.

Harbourmaster

Office above inner harbour.

Charges

There are harbour charges.

VHF radio telephone

There is no VHF radio telephone at Laxey, although Douglas Harbour will advise the Laxey harbourmaster if a call is made to them.

Facilities

Water Tap on quay.
Slip On N side of inner harbour.
Provisions Limited provisions may be obtained close to the harbour. Full provisions are available in the main town, some 20 minutes' walk from the harbour. EC Thursday.
Post office There is a post office close to the harbour.
Yacht club Laxey Sailing Club, overlooking inner harbour.

Douglas

Waypoint 54°09'·03N 4°27'·53W 3 cables NE of harbour entrance
Local High Water is +0010 Dover
Charts Admiralty *2696, 2094*; Imray *Y70, C62*

General

The island's capital and chief port extends along the curve of Douglas Bay, with the harbour at its S end, at the mouth of the Douglas River. There is a considerable volume of ferry and commercial traffic. The outer harbour has water at all states of the tide, and is well sheltered, except that strong NE winds can send in a heavy swell. The inner harbour dries and is well sheltered.

Approaching Douglas from south

Douglas harbour entrance

Warning

The volume of traffic using the harbour demands that a yacht should follow the displayed light signals and the directions of the harbourmaster at all times. The inner harbour dries, and can only be entered for 2 hours either side of HW. The recently extended breakwater has improved shelter in the outer harbour, but strong NE winds will send in a heavy swell.

Approach

By day Douglas Head is seen as a bold headland when viewed from the NE or SW. The light is shown from a white tower near its extremity. The harbour entrance lies to the N of the headland. Conister or St Mary's Rock is a detached, drying ledge to the NNW of the harbour entrance; a castellated refuge tower stands on the highest part of the ledge. The approach to the harbour entrance is indicated by two leading marks to the W of the lifeboat house. The marks are white posts with red triangular topmarks, and are in line on a bearing of 229°. This course will leave the green conical buoys, Channel Markers Nos 1 and 2, to starboard.

There are International Port Traffic Signals shown by night or day as necessary from a mast at the head of Victoria Pier. Three red vertical lights indicate that a vessel shall not proceed; two greens with a central white light shown vertically indicate that only specifically permitted vessels may proceed, and three green vertical lights indicate that vessels generally may proceed. Supplementary signals are shown below the lights, the panels having flashing amber lights on each top corner; a red cross indicates that vessels unless specified shall not proceed, and a white arrow indicates that vessels may proceed in the direction shown.

By night The harbour may be approached and entered using the following lights:

Douglas Head Fl.10s32m24M
Channel marker No. 1 QG(3)5s4M
Channel marker No. 2 Fl.G.3s5M
Dolphin light 2F.R(vert)2M
Breakwater head light Fl.R.5s16m8M
Battery Pier lighthouse Q.R.12m1M
Victoria Pier light Oc.G.8s10m3M
Ldg Lts 229·3° Oc.10s9/12m5M synchronised

Entrance

The harbour is entered between the new breakwater and Victoria Pier. The dolphin at the end of the breakwater is left to port. The inner harbour is entered between King Edward VII Pier and Fort Anne Jetty; the harbourmaster will arrange for the pedestrian swing bridge to be opened between 3 hours either side of HW.

Berthing

All berthing must be as directed by the harbourmaster. There is a black communal mooring buoy on the S side of the outer harbour; anchor off and take a stern line to the buoy. There is a landing pontoon at the inner end of Battery Pier where yachts may lie alongside. The inner harbour is for yachts that can take the ground; visitors will usually be directed to lie alongside the N quay.

Harbourmaster

In the Sea Terminal building, at the root of Victoria Pier.

Charges

There are harbour charges, which will be collected by the Harbour Patrol launch.

VHF radio telephone

Call *Douglas Harbour* Ch 16, work Ch 12.

54°13'.4N

4°23'W

N

5

2

Cables

0

50

Oc.G.3s7m

Oc.R.3s7m5M

G

G

G

WC

WC

SC

Training wall

Inner Harbour

Laxey River

LAXEY HARBOUR

DOUGLAS HARBOUR

Depths in Metres

Ldg Lts 229°

Fl.G.3s3M

2F.R(vert)10/8m2M
(vis 038°-310°)

Fl.R.5s16m8M
Whis(2)40s

Princess Alexandra Pier

Oc.G.8s10m3M
Bell(1)2s

Q.R.12m1M
(vis 038°-218°)

Outfall

Refuge
tower

Conister or St Mary's
Rock

Victoria Pier

Oc.G.4s
6m2M

Mooring pontoons
(Battery Pier)

2F.R(vert)4₃

White spire
(conspic)

King Edward VIII Pier

2F.R
(vert)

Moorings

Ldg Lts

Oc.10s9/12m5M

Douglas Head

Fl.10s32m24M

Swing bridge

SC

Oc.R.6s (tidal)

WG

Yacht Basin

PFS

Cables

N

Facilities

Fuel Contact harbourmaster to arrange supply.
Water Taps on Battery Pier and on the N quay of the inner harbour.
Slip Alongside Fort Anne Jetty.
Provisions Full provisions are available in the town. EC Thursday.
Post office Regent Street, in town centre.
Yacht club Douglas Motor Boat and Sailing Club. Bar and showers.
Calor Gas J. R. Riley Ltd.
Chandlery Manx Marine Ltd, on N side of inner harbour.

Derbyhaven

Good shelter may be found in winds from S through W to N in the anchorage between St Michael's Island and Ronaldsway Airport. There is a ruined fort on the NE end of the island, which is connected to the shore by a causeway. Rocky ledges shoal from the N side of St Michael's Island, which must be given a wide berth on the approach, as the tidal stream (which is S-going for 9 hours) will invariably be setting a yacht in this direction. Anchorage should be in 3m sand and mud 2 or 3 cables E of the S end of the breakwater. The anchorage is untenable in E or NE winds, when a heavy swell sets into the bay. Some additional shelter may be found behind the detached breakwater for yachts that can take the ground. Entrance should be made round the S end of the breakwater, which has a white light tower with a green band (Iso.G.2s5m5M), leaving the perch marking the NE end of a rocky ledge to port. There is a depth of 3·5m at MHWN, and 5m at MHWS, at the entrance, gradually shoaling within. There are no facilities for yachts.

Inner harbour, Douglas

Langness Point

The promontory extends S along the E side of Castletown Bay. A light (Fl(2)30s23m21M) is shown from a white tower situated on Dreswick Point, the SE extremity of Langness. Tidal streams run strongly off the point, and overfalls develop with a contrary wind. With the E-going stream, a clockwise current develops in Castletown Bay and an anticlockwise current to the S of Santon Head. A race develops off Langness Point when these eddies meet the strength of the stream. With the W-going stream, there is a further eddy to the E side of Castletown Bay, causing a race as it meets the main stream to the S of the point.

Castletown

Waypoint 54°02'·82N 4°38'·83W 1·5M S of harbour entrance
Local High Water is +0025 Dover
Charts Admiralty *2606, 2094*; Imray *Y70, C62*

General

Good shelter can be found in the drying harbour at Castletown, which was the capital of the island until 1874. The medieval fortress of Castle Rushen, formerly the home of the Viking kings of Man, dominates the harbour. The excellent Manx Nautical Museum is situated on the N side of the harbour.

Warning

The harbour dries, and should be entered between 2½ hours either side of HW. Strong SW winds will bring a swell into the outer harbour, reaching into the inner harbour above the bridge.

Approach

By day Castletown Bay is entered between Scarlett Point and Langness Point. The race and overfalls off Langness Point have been described above. The Skerranes are drying rocks extending SW from Langness Point. The Lheeah-rio Rocks are drying rocks on the W side of Castletown Bay; Boe Norris and Sandwick Boe are drying rocks on the N side of the bay. A red bell-buoy (Fl.R.3s) lies to the SE of the Lheeah-rio Rocks, and must be left to port. A straight course from this red buoy to the head of the breakwater will leave the other drying rocks to starboard.

By night The harbour can be approached and entered using the following lights:
Dreswick Point Fl(2)30s23m21M
Lheeah-rio Rocks buoy Fl.R.3s

CASTLETOWN AND DERBYHAVEN

Outer breakwater Oc.R.15s8m5M
North side of entrance Oc.G.4s3m
Irish Quay Oc.R.4s5m5M
Swing bridge 2F.R(hor)

Anchorage in the approach

Anchorage may be found 2 cables SE of the harbour entrance, to the N of Lheeah-rio Rocks in 3m sand and gravel. The anchorage is exposed to SE to SW winds.

Entrance

The harbour is entered leaving the outer break-water, with a white light tower with a red band, to port. The outer harbour dries to firm sand and small stones. The inner harbour is entered between Irish Quay, which has a white light tower with a red stripe at its head, and the white perch with a green band marking the extremity of the rocks to the NE of the entrance, leaving the perch to starboard. The inner harbour is divided by the pedestrian swing bridge. Contact the harbourmaster to have the bridge opened.

Berthing

Berth as directed by the harbourmaster. Yachts can dry out alongside the quay of the outer harbour in suitable conditions. There are berths alongside Irish Quay and through the bridge in the inner harbour.

Harbourmaster

Office on Irish Quay.

Charges

There are harbour charges.

Approaching Castletown

Castletown harbour entrance

VHF radio telephone

Call *Castletown Harbour* Ch 16, work Ch 12, between the hours of 0830 and 1630. Port St Mary harbourmaster will reply to the call if the office at Castletown is not occupied.

Facilities

Fuel The harbourmaster can arrange to have fuel delivered from Port St Mary.

Water Taps on Irish Quay and by the Castle Arms, in inner harbour.

Slip Outer harbour.

Provisions Full provisions are available in the town. EC Thursday.

Post office Parliament Square.

Showers Castletown Swimming Pool.

Calor Gas J. J. Clague Ltd, Arbory Street (near Town Hall).

Appendix

I. CHARTS

British Admiralty charts

Chart	Title	Scale
34	Isles of Scilly	25,000
777	Land's End to Falmouth	75,000
1076	Linney head to Oxwich point	75,000
1121	Irish Sea with Saint George's Channel and North Channel	500,000
1123	Western approaches to St George's Channel and Bristol Channel	500,000
1149	Pendeen to Trevose Head	75,000
1152	Watchet to Weston-super-Mare and Barry to Newport	50,000
1156	Trevose Head to Hartland Point	75,000
1160	Plans on the coast of Somerset and Devon	
	Ilfracombe	12,500
	Lynmouth. Porlock. Minehead. Watchet	20,000
	Barnstaple and Bideford	25,000
1161	Swansea Bay	25,000
1164	Hartland Pt to Ilfracombe incl. Lundy	75,000
	Lundy	25,000
1165	Worms Head to Watchet	75,000
1166	River Severn: Avonmouth to Sharpness	25,000
1167	Burry Inlet	25,000
1168	Harbours on the north coast of Cornwall	
	Newquay Bay	12,500
	Approaches to Padstow. St Ives Bay. River Camel to Wadebridge	25,000
1169	Approaches to Porthcawl	25,000
1176	Severn estuary: Steep Holm to Avonmouth	40,000
	Newport	20,000
	Clevedon to Redcliff Bay	25,000
1178	Approaches to the Bristol Channel	200,000
1179	Bristol Channel	150,000
1182	Barry and Cardiff Roads with approaches	25,000
	Barry Docks	12,500
	Cardiff Docks	15,000
1320	Fleetwood to Douglas	100,000
1344	Kirkcudbright bay	15,000
1346	Solway firth and approaches	100,000
	Ravenglass	15,000
1410	St George's Channel	200,000
1411	Irish sea – western part	200,000
1413	Approaches to Holyhead	25,000
1464	Menai strait	25,000
	The Swellies	10,000
1468	Arklow to the Skerries islands	100,000
1478	St Govan's Head to St David's Head	75,000
1482	Plans on south and west coasts of Dyfed	
	Jack Sound	12,500
	Tenby and Saundersfoot with approaches: Ramsey Sound with the Bishops and Clerks	25,000
1484	Plans in Cardigan bay	
	New Quay	12,500
	Fishguard bay	15,000
	Aberystwyth: Aberaeron	18,000
	Aberdovey: Barmouth	25,000
	Aberporth	30,000
	Approaches to Cardigan: Newport bay	37,500
1512	Plans on the Lleyn peninsula	
	Porthmadog harbour	7,500
	Mochras lagoon	10,000
	Pwllheli	12,500
	Porth Dinllaen, Saint Tudwal's roads	18,000
	Approaches to Porthmadog	25,000
1552	Ports in Morecambe bay	
	Fleetwood: Heysham	10,000
	Glasson	12,500
	River Lune and approaches to Heysham; Approaches to Fleetwood	25,000
1826	Irish sea – eastern part	200,000
1859	Port of Bristol	
	City docks	5,000
	King Road; River Avon	10,000
	City docks to St Anne's Bridge	25,000
1951	Approaches to Liverpool	25,000
1953	Approaches to the River Dee	25,000
	Mostyn quay	12,500
1961	Rossall point to St Bee's head	75,000
1970	Caernarvon bay	75,000
1971	Cardigan bay – northern part	75,000
1972	Cardigan bay – central part	75,000
1973	Cardigan bay – southern part	75,000
1977	Holyhead to Great Orme's head	75,000
1981	Approaches to Preston	75,000
	Preston riversway docklands	10,000
2010	Morecambe bay and approaches	50,000
2011	Holyhead harbour	6,250
2013	Saint Bee's head to Silloth	50,000
	Workington harbour	7,500
	Whitehaven harbour: Harrington harbour: Maryport harbour: Silloth docks and approaches	10,000
2093	Southern approach to North channel	100,000
2094	Kirkcudbright to Mull of Galloway and Isle of Man	100,000
2198	North channel – southern part	75,000
	Portpatrick	4,000
2649	Western approaches to the English Channel	500,000
2635	Scotland – west coast	500,000
2675	English Channel	500,000
2696	Plans in the Isle of Man	
	Douglas bay	7,500
	Ramsey bay: Calf sound: Peel: Port Erin	10,000
	Castletown bay: Bay Ny Carrickey	20,000
2878	Approaches to Milford Haven	25,000
3164	Barrow harbour and approaches	12,500
	Deep water berth and Ramsden dock entrance	5,000
3274	Milford Haven: St Ann's Head to Newton Noyes Pier	12,500

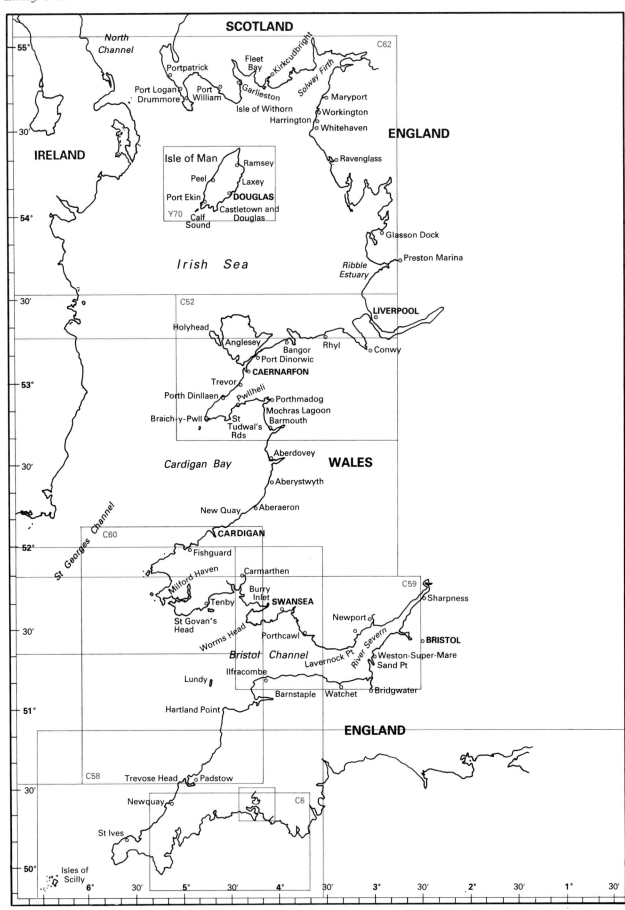

SCOTLAND

North Channel

55°

C62

Portpatrick

Fleet Bay

Kirkcudbright

Solway Firth

Port Logan
Drummore

Port William

Garlieston

Isle of Withorn

Maryport

Workington

Whitehaven

ENGLAND

30'

Harrington

IRELAND

Ravenglass

Isle of Man

Peel

Ramsey

Laxey

Port Ekin

DOUGLAS

Y70

Calf Sound

Castletown and Douglas

54°

Glasson Dock

Irish   Sea

Ribble Estuary

Preston Marina

30'

C52

LIVERPOOL

Holyhead

Anglesey

Bangor

Rhyl

Conwy

Port Dinorwic

53°

Trevor

CAERNARFON

Porth Dinllaen

Pwllheli

Porthmadog

Braich-y-Pwll

St Tudwal's Rds

Mochras Lagoon

Barmouth

30'

Aberdovey

Cardigan Bay

WALES

Aberystwyth

New Quay

Aberaeron

C60

CARDIGAN

St Georges Channel

52°

Fishguard

Carmarthen

C59

Milford Haven

Burry Inlet

Sharpness

Tenby

SWANSEA

Newport

River Severn

BRISTOL

St Govan's Head

Porthcawl

30'

Worms Head

Lavernock Pt

Weston-Super-Mare

Sand Pt

Bristol   Channel

Ilfracombe

Lundy

Barnstaple

Watchet

Bridgwater

51°

Hartland Point

ENGLAND

C58

Trevose Head

Padstow

30'

Newquay

C6

St Ives

50°

Isles of Scilly

6°   30'   5°   30'   4°   30'   3°   30'   2°   30'   1°   30'

British Admiralty Charts

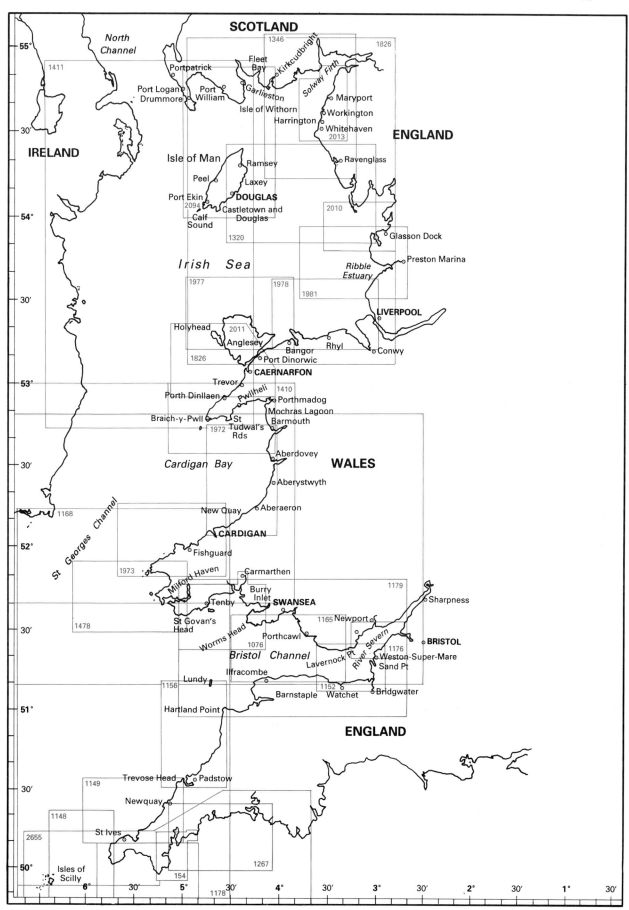

Imray Charts

Chart	Title	Scale
3275	Milford Haven: Milford dock to Picton Pt	12,500
	Pembroke Reach	5,000
	Continuation to River Cleddau	12,500
	Carew River; continuation of River Cleddau	50,000
3478	Manchester ship canal and upper Mersey	25,000
	Manchester docks: Runcorn and Western point docks: Ellesmere port and Stanlow oil docks: Partington basin	10,000
3490	Port of Liverpool	15,000

Imray charts

Chart	Title	Scale
C7	Falmouth to Trevose Head and Isles of Scilly	115,000
	Plans: Newquay Bay, Penzance Harbour, Mousehold, Newlyn Harbour, Porthleven, St Mary's Road, Portreath	
C16	Western Approaches to the British Isles	612,800
	Plans: Brest, Falmouth, Milford Haven, Crosshaven, Crookhaven	
C52	Cardigan Bay to Liverpool	140,700
	Plans: Caernarfon, Port Dinorwic, Holyhead, Menai Strait, Porthmadog, Abersoch, Mochras Lagoon, Pwllheli, Conwy, Porth Dinllaen, The Swellies, Barmouth	
C59	Bristol Channel – Worms Head and Bull Point to Sharpness	114,500
C60	Southwest Coasts of Wales	128,000
	Plans: Jack Sound, Milford Haven, Ramsey Sound, Tenby and Caldy Islands, Fishguard, Solav	
C61	St George's Channel – Wales to the East Coast of Ireland	270,000
	Plans: Portmadoc, Aberystwyth, Tremadoc Bay, Barmouth, Menai Strait, Aberdovey, Cardigan, New Quay, Dublin Bay, Wexford, Arklow, Wicklow, Dunmore East	
C62	Irish Sea	280,000
	Plans: Entrance to Carlingford Lough, Portavogie, Skerries Bay, Kilkeel Harbour, Malahide Inlet, Ardglass, Entrance to Strangford Lough	
C63	Firth of Clyde	150,000
	Plans: Ayr, Troon, Irvine, East Loch Tarbert, Campbeltown, Ardrishaig, Crinan, Gourock, Rothesay, Rhu, Helensburgh, Largs, Lamlash, Millport	
Y70	Isle of Man	85,150
	Plans: Douglas, Port Erin, Peel, Ramsey, Bay Ny Carricky and Castletown Bay	

II. BIBLIOGRAPHY

West Coast of England and Wales Pilot NP37, Hydrographer of the Navy

The Macmillan and Silk Cut Nautical Almanac, Macmillan

Cruising Association Handbook, Cruising Association

Bristol Channel Yachting Conference Handbook, Bristol Channel Yachting Conference

Cruising Anglesey, North West Venturers Yacht Club

Isle of Man Sailing Directions, Tidal Streams and Anchorages, Manx Sailing and Cruising Club

Solway Firth Sailing Directions and Anchorages, Solway SC, Kippford

Cruising Guide to Northwest England & Wales, George Griffiths, Imray

Index